D1116874

Medieval Ships and Shipping

Frontispiece: A lead pilgrim badge, found at the Thames Exchange in London, depicting St Thomas à Becket's return to England in a hulk (private collection – photo: Museum of London)

MEDIEVAL SHIPS
AND SHIPPING

—— GILLIAN HUTCHINSON ——

FAIRLEIGH DICKINSON UNIVERSITY PRESS

Rutherford • Madison • Teaneck

Associated University Presses
440 Forsgate Drive
Cranbury, NJ 08512

Library of Congress Cataloging-in-Publication Data

A CIP catalog record for this title is available from The Library of Congress

Hutchinson, Gillian, 1955–
    Medieval ships and shipping / Gillian Hutchinson.
      p.   cm.
    Includes bibliographical references (p.   ) and index.
    ISBN 0-8386-3628-4 (alk. paper)
    1. Ships, Medieval–Great Britain. 2. Shipbuilding–Great
Britain–History. 3. Shipping–Great Britain–History.
4. Excavations (Archaeology)–Europe, Northern. 5. Great Britain–
History–Medieval period, 1066–1485.   I. Title.
VM17.H88   1994
387.2'0941'0902–dc20   94-19229
                                                              CIP

ISBN 0–8386–3628–4

Printed in Great Britain

Contents

Acknowledgements

When Helen Clarke invited me to write a book for Leicester University Press neither of us imagined that it would take more than four years to write. I am grateful to Helen and to the publishers for not despairing of ever receiving the final manuscript while I enjoyed myself exploring a subject which extends in so many different directions. The National Maritime Museum has provided a great deal of support and allowed me three months study leave at the end of 1993 to bring the book to completion.

I have benefited enormously from the knowledge, skill and enthusiasm of many colleagues at the National Maritime Museum, some of whom I shall mention here. Ian Friel shared with me the results of his historical research and convinced me of the necessity to set finds in their broad cultural context rather than pursuing a narrow technological approach. Pieter van der Merwe read the entire text of the book in draft and made many corrections and valuable contributions, particularly from his study of southern European medieval ships. Alan Stimson similarly improved the chapter on navigation. The glossary is largely derived from the work of Eric Kentley and the index has been prepared by Elizabeth Wiggans.

Among the other people who have helped in various ways with the preparation of this book I am especially grateful to Marco Bonino, Martin Dean, Geoff Egan, Janet Lewis, Jerzy Litwin, Peter Marsden, Lawrence Mott, Andrew Russel, Robin Ward and David Watkins. Amanda Patton drew many of the illustrations, working almost miraculous transformations on my artless sketches.

Special thanks are due to my husband, Andrew Saunders, for his encouragement and constructive criticism. Our daughter, Anna, also helped, while growing much faster than the book and forming a rather curious idea of what it is that adults like to do at night.

List of figures

Introduction – medieval maritime Britain

Shipping was of vital importance to medieval Britain. Ships brought commodities from all over the known world and were the means of extending knowledge of the world itself. On board ships travelled invasion forces and pilgrims, epidemics, fashions and ideas. The fish brought to shore by boats working from nearly every inhabited harbour or beach formed an essential element of diet.

Land travel on the poor roads of the Middle Ages was arduous and loads were often better carried by water transport along the rivers and coast. Ports owed their very existence to shipping and their sites and fortunes could shift as a result of changes in ship design or because silting prevented ships from reaching them. Development of port facilities, waterfronts and wharfage was linked to that of trading vessels and coastal defences were built against attacks by hostile ships.

Yet despite all this, the practical reality of shipping, the ships and the structures and much of the human activity associated with them, has tended to be overlooked. Historians still write about invasions and archaeologists continue to refer to imported finds in purely abstract terms, with little thought for the creaking, stinking wooden vessels which carried them across heaving seas from one port to another.

The purpose of this book is to bring together information about material remains of shipping activity and to explain their significance by setting them in the context of medieval maritime Britain. Westerdahl (1992: 6) has coined the phrase 'the maritime cultural landscape' to signify 'the whole network of sailing routes, with ports and harbours along the coast, and its related constructions and remains of human activity, underwater as well as terrestrial'. Taken in its broadest sense, the maritime culture of medieval Britain can be detected in areas remote from the immediate coastal zone. Fresh sea-fish were distributed well inland, for example to Coventry, and preserved fish and imported goods reached all but the poorest and most inaccessible places. Shipping made it possible for wine to become a regular item of consumption for more and more of the population of a country which produced little wine itself. The import of wine increased from the time of the Conquest and continued to grow even when, at the beginning of the thirteenth century, the loss to the English crown of most of the territory of northern France meant that ships had to make the longer voyage through the Bay of Biscay to the English possessions in Gascony. Much of the agricultural production of Britain was locked into the export trade, most notably of wool, and monastic merchants' houses in rural settings were built with the profits of seaborne commerce. Trade was the formula for turning sheep into stone.

Material remains not only demonstrate the import of foreign items but they can also provide evidence for cultural diffusion by sea – the imitation of foreign techniques, practices and style. In the Norman period, for example, improvements in the shape and technique of wheel-thrown pots made at ports and large towns near the coast, such as Southampton and Winchester, were the result of trade contacts with Normandy. Meanwhile, further inland, handmade traditions continued (Dunning, 1959: 34).

The pace of new discovery of material remains of medieval shipping has been rapid. There is also a vast resource of historical and pictorial evidence to draw on. Ethnography and continuing practice can also enhance our understanding, particularly of subjects such as fishing, sailing and pilotage. With all these information sources there are of course problems of interpretation. What we have is not a perfect representation of the past. The archaeological record is the result of accidents of preservation and the opportunity to study complete ships, still less complete ports, must be extremely rare. Especially where shipping is concerned the archaeological record is episodic, the result of isolated events, providing glimpses of how things were at a particular time in a particular place. It is tempting to connect all the fragmentary data about ship construction into neat patterns, arranged into typologies and tied by lines of development. However, the information base is so very patchy that seamless narratives may need to be completely unravelled as soon as another discovery is made.

Interpretation of pictorial evidence has been discussed by Farrell (1979). Its reliability as a source depends on how well the artist understood his subject, the degree of realism attempted and the limitations of the medium. The format can impose distortions, as can be seen when images of ships were made to fit onto circular coins and seals. There is also the problem of scale. The medieval convention of exaggerating the size of human figures when they were shown with ships can give the thoroughly misleading impression that medieval ships were no bigger than modern yachts.

Friel (1983b) has provided a very useful survey of some of the types of documentary evidence for medieval ships. Documentary sources, while excellent for things which were subject to bureaucracy, such as the raising of fleets and the taxing of trade, can be disappointing for physical details. Medieval documents are very likely to tell you how much a ship's carpenter was paid but not what he did; to tell you the price of fish but not how it was caught.

Physical and documentary sources can provide some insights into both what shipping meant to people in medieval Britain and how it affected their lives. When, from the end of the twelfth century, towns had seals made for applying the stamp of civic pride and identity to their official documents, most inland towns chose to depict their walls while most ports had ships (Brindley, 1938). Some, like Bristol and Scarborough, had both. Great Yarmouth, meanwhile, chose the motif of three herrings for its coat of arms, perhaps in imitation of Lübeck. After Edward III's victory in the sea battle at Sluys in 1340 he had the gold coinage redesigned to show himself enthroned on a ship (Callender, 1912). The ports of medieval England had a high proportion of their churches dedicated to St Nicholas, the patron saint of seafarers, and pilgrim's badges remind us that a great number of people who were not employed in shipping had first-hand experience of sea voyages.

Among the thirteenth-century contents of pit 14 at Cuckoo Lane, Southampton, along with seeds of imported fruit and Malaga pottery, was the skull of a Barbary ape (Platt and Coleman-Smith, 1975: 293). The wealthy burgess who owned the house on the site probably kept the monkey as a pet, a strange and wonderful creature to excite the imagination about lands far across the sea.

Written sources are even more useful for revealing human feelings and behaviour which arose from the business of shipping in medieval Britain. The monk of Dunstable did not disguise his delight at the death in a shipwreck of Laurence of Ludlow, the greatest of contemporary wool merchants, who in the 1290s had been responsible for agreeing with Edward I an increase of 533 per cent in the export tax on wool. 'Because he sinned against the wool-mongers he was drowned in a ship laden with wool', the monk wrote (Power, 1941: 79, 112). The *Customs of the Sea* ruled that agreements made on the open sea were not valid, because 'at times men whom the sea makes sick go on board of ships, and if they had a thousand marks of silver they would promise it to anyone who would put them ashore' (Twiss, 1874: 445–7). The wreck of the White Ship in 1120, in which the heir to the English throne drowned along with about 300 other people, mostly nobles, was attributed to drunkenness and bravado. William of Malmsbury said that the sailors, who had had too much to drink, recklessly decided to overtake a ship which had set out already, 'since their own ship was of the best construction and newly equipped'. They failed to avoid a rock in the darkness. 'No ship ever brought so much misery to England' (Le Patourel, 1976: 87). Documents tell us about the rivalry between the men of Great Yarmouth and men of the Cinque Ports in home waters and between Englishmen and everyone else abroad. In the Bay of Bourgneuf, where ships came to load salt, nationals were separated to prevent quarrelling, the English and the Dutch especially (Bridbury, 1955: 81). Documents can also provide information about individual lives, such as that of St Godric of Finchale, born to a peasant family in late eleventh-century Lincolnshire. He started as a beachcomber, collecting and selling wreckage from the shore. Evidently he made sufficient profit from this, and he was insufficiently deterred by seeing so much debris from marine disasters, that he was able to set up as a merchant, trading by sea between England, Scotland, Denmark and Flanders. After a successful career he gave up his wealth and became a hermit (Power, 1941: 110).

The period under discussion in this book is a long one, beginning from about the time of the Norman Conquest and finishing at about 1500. In these centuries enormous changes took place in shipping and, because it played an essential role in medieval Britain, its study has exceptional potential. The sources of information are abundant and still largely unexplored. The possibilities for finding new evidence, particularly through underwater archaeology, and for forming new perceptions of what is already known are incalculable.

1 *Shipbuilding: the traditions of the northern seas*

By comparing the open, single-masted ships in use at the beginning of the medieval period with the multi-decked, fully rigged ships at the end, it is plain to see that far-reaching changes had taken place. Tracing the progress of those changes is not so easy, as it is confused by the diversity of regional shipbuilding traditions and variations in vessel design to suit particular purposes or conditions. Market forces and the imperatives of warfare meant that ships for trade and fighting were under constant development. Shipbuilding rivalled architecture as the most advanced technology of the Middle Ages. Change and development were made possible by the interaction of shipbuilding traditions from different parts of Europe and by the experiment and innovation undertaken by shipbuilders. It can be argued that there was a loss of diversity among the largest ships, so that by the end of the period the products of shipyards throughout Europe were more similar than ever before. They left behind them innumerable types of smaller vessels which were well adapted to the work they had to do and which underwent little change over centuries, some types surviving even into recent times.

The two opening chapters of this book introduce the technology of medieval shipbuilding, the methods of construction and the structure of hulls. Use of technical terms has been kept to a minimum and a glossary is provided towards the end of the book. The fitting and rigging of ships is treated separately in Chapter 3 and these three chapters together provide the technical background for the regional examples of ships presented in Chapter 4.

At the time of the Norman Conquest the boats and ships in use around the coasts of Britain were clinker-built, which is to say that their hulls were built up by lapping the bottom edge of each run of planking over the top of the one below and nailing them together through the area of overlap. Their hulls were similar in shape at each end, they were propelled by single square sails and oars and steered by side rudders. The scant evidence for Anglo-Saxon shipbuilding, primarily the Sutton Hoo ship (Bruce-Mitford, 1975: 345–435) and the Graveney boat (Fenwick, 1978), indicates vessel types similar to those used in Scandinavia and developed by the Vikings and their Norman descendants. Viking ships would have been familiar in those parts of Anglo-Saxon England which came under Scandinavian settlement.

The Norman invasion fleet of 1066 was capable of transporting large numbers of men and horses and its ships were the product of centuries of refinement. The structure of ships of the eleventh century exhibits a high degree of technical competence, as the wrecks excavated at Skuldelev in Roskilde Fjord, Denmark, demonstrate (Olsen and Crumlin-Pedersen, 1968; Olsen and Crumlin-Pedersen, 1978; Crumlin-Pedersen, 1991). These ships were deliberately sunk to make a defensive blockage of the principal navigable channel in the fjord. Of the five ships, two were cargo vessels, two were warships and the other may have been a fishing boat (figure 1.1). The warships were of lighter construction than the cargo ships and were long and narrow. Their length to beam ratio was as much as 7:1 as compared to the cargo vessels' 4:1, giving them a high speed capability under sail and oars. Tree ring studies have shown that the warship Skuldelev 2 was built in 1060–70 in Dublin (Bonde and Crumlin-Pedersen, 1990). The cargo vessels were quite different from each other. One was made of pine and may have been built in Norway. The Skuldelev finds show variety and specialisation within the clinker-building tradition. Shipbuilders had by the eleventh century acquired a thorough understanding of the scope and limitations of the materials, the properties of wood and the behaviour of fastenings, and of the performance of hulls in the water.

The clinker technique was used for building boats and ships throughout most of the Middle Ages in northern Europe. As long ago as 1914, Hagedorn, as a result of a study of ships depicted on seals, identified three different strands in medieval northern European shipbuilding and designated them 'keel', 'cog' and 'hulk'. All three employ the clinker technique but they represent different approaches to building the hull. They each had their origins as regional variations before the beginning of the period under study. They existed side by side throughout the period and came increasingly into contact with each other and with the quite distinct southern European shipbuilding tradition which used flush-laid, rather than clinker, planking.

Keel

The term 'keel' is used by ship archaeologists to denote ships, like those of the Anglo-Saxon and Scandinavian traditions referred to so far, which were built up from a keel, with planking running roughly horizontally between the stem and stern posts. As this was the normal method of building in medieval Britain the term may not have had much currency at the time. People would be more likely to refer simply to boats and ships, or use the names of specific types such as barges or farcosts which were variants within the keel construction tradition. In Anglo-Saxon literature 'ceol' was used as a poetic synonym for ship. Toll collectors in London in the eleventh century found it useful to be able to distinguish between ordinary ships, 'ceols', and vessels of another type referred to as 'hulcis'. In the later Middle Ages there were vessel types called keels on the Tyne, Humber and Severn and in Lincolnshire and London, and the application of the word to specific variants reinforces the idea that the keel tradition is more easily recognised in retrospect than it was at the time.

The sequence of construction of a keel is illustrated in figure 1.2. The first stage of assembly was to lay the keel, which was a baulk of timber cut from a tree-trunk. In Scandinavian finds the keel is almost invariably oak but elm also seems to have been favoured by English boatbuilders in the medieval as well as the post-medieval period. The keel was normally straight, without longitudinal vertical curvature (or 'rocker'). It could be made of two pieces scarfed together, though this was to be avoided ideally, as the scarf would be

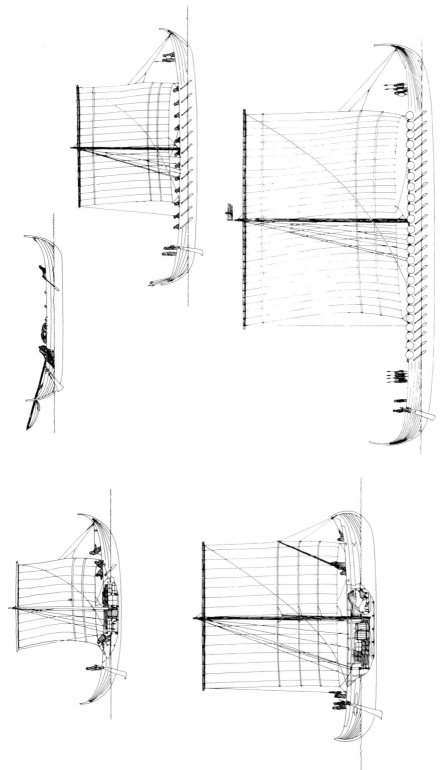

Figure 1.1 Reconstructions of the five eleventh-century vessels found at Skuldelev, Denmark (Viking Ship Museum, Roskilde).

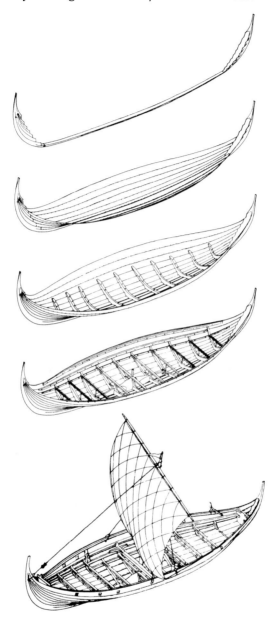

Figure 1.2　The sequence of construction of a keel-type vessel (Viking Ship Museum, Roskilde).

a potential area of weakness. The top of the keel was flat or dished from side to side. In profile the keel was T-shaped (though in some vessels the T was very squat) with the sides cut away to create a flange at the top. To the underside of this flange the lowest run of planking, the garboard strake, could be fastened. The keel could have parallel sides or it could be wider near the middle of the boat, or slightly forward of the middle, tapering towards the ends.

To the ends of the keel were scarfed the stem and stern posts. Timbers were chosen with grain following the long curve required for the finished components in order to provide strength. These were often in two pieces scarfed together: the stem post itself and an intermediate piece between the stem post and the keel. The stem and stern posts of Skuldelev 3, shown in figure 1.2, have false planking cut out of the solid wood to provide a secure transition between the posts and the hull planking. This technique required special skill and simpler posts were more common, as for example that of the Poole Foundry boat (figure 8.7).

Once this backbone was in place a start was made on planking the hull. Planks were made from radially split oak trunks or from tangentially split softwood trees (for the selection and conversion of timber for boatbuilding see McGrail, 1987: 23–43). A man can be seen preparing planking in the scene from the Bayeux Tapestry shown in figure 1.3. The first strake was fastened to the underside of the keel flange. A strake is a run of planking from one end of the vessel to the other, which might be made up of several planks scarfed together. The plank ends were tapered to a feather edge so that when they overlapped at the scarfs there was no increase in the thickness of the strake. Caulking (waterproofing material) was put between the strake edges and into the scarfs as they were assembled. This was made of animal hair or moss, generally mixed with tar. Samples of animal hair which have been analysed, from Dublin and London, show that it was frequently not sheep's wool but was often cow or even horse hair, probably the by-products of the tanning industry. A sample which did prove to be wool, from London, had been dyed and was probably textile waste (Musty, 1993: 33). At the Queen Street waterfront site at Newcastle, 73 small twisted rolls and flattened pads of fibre have been identified as caulking material from clinker-built vessels. Of the 25 samples examined for species analysis, 13 were of cattle hair and 10 of sheep's wool with two possible examples of goat hair (Walton, 1988: 78).

The edges of the strakes and the scarfs were fastened with iron clench nails. These nails had large round heads and were hammered from outboard to inboard through partly pre-bored holes. On the inboard face of the planking the shanks were hammered over and clenched against quadrilateral roves. The extreme ends of the strakes were feathered for fastening to the stem and stern posts with iron spike nails. The hull planking was built up as a shell, probably largely by eye as in more recent Scandinavian practice, without the use of formers. Levels and width gauges might be used to make the shape of the two sides of the hull as similar as possible but exact symmetry was rarely achieved.

When the bottom planks were in place the first transverse framing was inserted into the hull at regular intervals. These frame timbers, which crossed the bottom of the vessel including the keel, are called floors. They were cut from grown crooks, following the run of the grain. Their undersides were cut into steps or joggles so that they would be in contact with the planks as much as possible. They were fastened only to the planking and not to the keel by means of wooden pegs known as treenails. These were inserted from

Figure 1.3 Building the ships for the Norman Invasion of England (Bayeux Tapestry, eleventh century – with special authorisation of the Town of Bayeux).

outboard to inboard in augered holes. The treenails were knife-cut from timber, not from roundwood sticks. They usually had expanded heads outboard and were wedged on the inboard face of the framing so that they could not work loose in either direction.

After the floors were fastened, more side planking was added. Then the upper framing timbers, futtocks, were inserted. These were normally scarfed to the ends of the floors and secured to them by means of treenails running right through from the ouside of the planking. The rest of the construction varied more from vessel to vessel. Larger ones might have a second and higher tier of futtocks. The frames were often reinforced laterally by means of horizontal cross-beams, secured by knees. Longitudinal stiffness could be added by a keelson placed above the keel and by stringers which were strips of wood running fore-and-aft along the inboard face of the planking. Breasthooks at bow and stern could help to hold the ends of the vessel together. Fittings and decking were added according to the individual requirements of the vessel.

Clinker-building is today generally associated with small boats but in the medieval period very large vessels, both warships and merchant ships, were built in the keel technique. The English royal galleys of 1294 and the 'big ship' from the Bryggen at Bergen in Norway, built in the first half of the thirteenth century, were well over 30 metres in length.

Hulks

In the Anglo-Saxon period, the form of vessel discussed so far, with clinker planking on a backbone of keel, stem and stern post, was referred to as a 'ceol' or 'keel'. The term 'ceol' seems to have evoked images of the shape of the stem posts: 'high keel', 'steep keel'. Charters from London from the years 1000 and 1030 introduce the term 'hulc' to denote a type of ship which differs from the keel (Ellmers, 1972: 59). 'Hulc' in Anglo-Saxon meant 'hollow' or 'cavity'.

Ship archaeologists have applied the term 'hulk' to ships which share specific hull structural characteristics, rather than interpreting it as a general name for ships of a certain size or shape. The word continued to be used throughout the Middle Ages and it has been assumed that the ships termed 'hulk' in the fifteenth century had developed from those termed 'hulk' in the eleventh century. The characteristics of the hulk have been deduced entirely from iconographic evidence and the sole link between the verbal and the iconographic data for the whole of the period is the town seal of New Shoreham of 1295 (figure 1.4). The seal's inscription reads '*hoc hulci signo vocor os sic nomine digno* – By this sign of a hulk I am called Mouth which is a worthy name'. This statement, baffling at first sight, is a reference to New Shoreham's older name of Hulksmouth.

The New Shoreham seal depicts a vessel quite unlike the keel-type ships featuring on other contemporary town seals from the Cinque Ports, though it is very like the ship on the seal of Kingston-upon-Hull of about 1300 (Ewe, 1972: 144; Brindley, 1938: fig 33) and that of the Provostry of Southampton of about 1300 (Brindley, 1938: fig 15). The Hulksmouth ship has a thin

Figure 1.4 The late thirteenth-century town seal of 'Hulksmouth' or New Shoreham (National Maritime Museum).

crescent-shaped hull with planking running parallel to the lower and upper edge and finishing at the platforms for the castles, not at the stem and stern posts as is the case with the keel type. The position of the nail heads in relation to the edges of the strakes suggests that the hull was built in 'reverse clinker' technique – that is, with each strake fastened to the inside of the strake below, not to the outside as with normal clinker. This is shown more clearly in the picture of Henry I's ship, drawn before *c.*1140, shown in figure 1.5. In both images, the ends of the strakes appear to be 'gathered' at 'collars', or bands across the ends of the strake runs at bow and stern. In pictures pre-dating 1350 these collars are often shown surmounted by animal head carvings but they were gradually replaced by castles, as on the New Shoreham Seal, from the end of the thirteenth century.

Having established the basic characteristics of the hulk, earlier representations were sought out in order to follow the trail back to the origins of the type. Among these are the fonts of Winchester and Zedelghem, Belgium, which were made from Tournai marble, quarried and carved near the River

Figure 1.5 Henry I returning to England in a hulk (*Chronicle of John of Worcester, c.*1118–1140, Corpus Christi College, Oxford Ms 157, f.383).

Scheldt in about 1180. On the Winchester font (figure 1.6) most of the strakes end at a 'collar' at stem and stern and one of them ends at the sheer line (upper edge of the planking). This Tournai connection served to direct the search for the origins of the hulk to the Low Countries. Coins minted in Dorestad in 814–840 show vessels propelled by both oar and sail with 'banana'-shaped hull profiles. A boat found in 1930 at Utrecht, not far from Dorestad, has repeatedly been cited as the archaeological specimen of the early form of the hulk. The hull has a log-boat base with two strakes on each side joined to each other by a half-round wale. The small mast step near the forward end of the boat was most probably for a towing-mast rather than for sailing. A radiocarbon date of 790 ± 45 ad was obtained for the boat in 1960 and it was claimed that the arm of the river in which it lay was closed about 866. However, recent work has revised this dating and shown the boat to be rather later, with a probable date of sinking in the eleventh century (Vlek, 1987: 66). A very similar vessel was found in 1974 at Waterstraat, another site in Utrecht, and has also been dated to the eleventh century.

These boats from Utrecht are extended log-boats for use on rivers, not designed to be sailed, while the much earlier vessels depicted on the Carolingian coins are seagoing sailing ships. Clearly the Utrecht boat can no

Figure 1.6   A hulk on the Winchester Cathedral font, made in Belgium in about 1180 (National Maritime Museum).

longer be cited as an example of the early form of the hulk. Indeed Vlek rejects the idea that the Utrecht type has anything at all to do with the hulk. He concludes that 'this kind of vessel cannot have been the prototype, either in construction or in form, of the late medieval large seafaring hulk' (Vlek, 1987: 89).

The intense focus on the Low Countries may have diverted attention from the hulk's very strong French connections. The Dorestad coins referred to above are copies of those of Quentovic, a French seaport just south of Boulogne. Although the reference collection of pictures of medieval ships compiled at the National Maritime Museum contains only a very small and probably unrepresentative sample of the images created, it does appear that France has a considerably higher proportion of hulk pictures than other countries, followed at some distance by Britain. Several of the British images are of the return of Thomas à Becket from exile in France (e.g. frontispiece and figure 3.2) and are conceivably intended to represent French ships.

What are the constructional implications of the features of the hulk, the rounded hull, the run of the often reverse clinker planking to the sheerline? The most basic problems of wooden ship construction are how to bend and fashion straight planks to create a hull and how to fasten the ends of the planks in a secure and watertight way. If a clinker vessel is dismantled and its strakes are laid out flat it becomes clear that they are not straight strips.

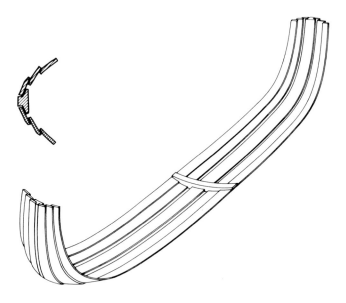

Figure 1.7   Conjectural diagram of the run of the lowest strakes in a hulk (National Maritime Museum).

With keels, the strakes taper to the post and, because of the fullness of the hull, tend to rise higher at the stems than in the mid-part of the hull. There is often a considerable amount of twisting necessary, particularly in the lowest strakes, as the hull narrows towards the posts. With the hulk form the need for twisting the lowest strakes is reduced. The ends of the vessel cannot be made as sharp as with keel construction. An explanation for the use of reverse clinker for building hulks is illustrated in figure 1.7. This is a hypothetical drawing of a hulk with reverse clinker planking. It can be seen that whereas the steps of the normal planking would resist the flow of the water, slowing down the vessel and inviting leaks through the plank seams, reversing the plank steps helps solve these problems. It is puzzling then that after 1300 the instances of representations of reverse clinker are heavily outnumbered by those of normal clinker-building. This may perhaps have been related to an increase in size which made the friction of the plank laps less significant.

To make a strong hull, the strake runs need to end on a rigid component. The 'collars' depicted were probably breast-hooks of some sort but until a hulk is discovered and excavated this aspect of the construction must remain a mystery. It has been suggested that the ropes sometimes depicted coiled round the 'necks' of hulks were for binding the ends together. This would have been structurally weak and it is far more likely that they represent mooring lines or anchor cables.

Until the middle of the fourteenth century, most pictures of hulks show hulls which were similar in shape and in the run of the planking at both bow and stern. Some are shown with narrow stems and wider sterns and there are a few 'hulk hybrids' in which the strakes end at the sheerline in hulk fashion at one end and at the post in keel fashion at the other. This can be seen on the thirteenth-century second seal of Southampton (Ewe, 1972: 191). Most pictures of hybrids which combine a hulk stern with a post stem seem to predate 1300. Representations of asymmetrical hull forms with hulk stems and post sterns became more common as the fourteenth century progressed and it is likely that the adoption of median rudders was a major influence. The transition seems to have taken place within a brief period of time and by 1350 all hulks are pictured with stern rudders rather than side rudders.

Cogs

The other main strand of the northern European medieval shipbuilding tradition is that of the cog. The cog was mentioned in documents as the ship of the Frisians as early as the ninth century. Roman period vessels like the second-century ship excavated at Bruges may have contributed to its ancestry. The numerous pictorial representations show a vessel with high sides, and comparatively straight stem and stern posts. The early development of the cog has been discussed by Crumlin-Pedersen (1979: 17–18), Ellmers (1979; 1985b) and Reinders (1985: 9–12). By the eleventh century, the cog was well established on both sides of what is now the Danish peninsula.

Cogs were known in Britain by the early 1200s and probably before: King John hired five Frisian cogs for his expedition to Ireland in 1210 (Brooks, 1929a: 29). The thirteenth-century seal of Ipswich (figure 1.8) also shows one, suggesting that such ships had close connections with the port and may have been built locally. The graffito of a cog shown in figure 1.9, from St Hilda's Church, Hartlepool, may date to about 1300. It was deeply incised on a slab of sandstone 0.76 by 0.38 metres and found in the vicinity of the former chapel dedicated to St Nicholas, the patron saint of sailors (Naish, 1940: 304–5). The ship has straight stem and stern posts and a level sheer. The mast is stepped forward of amidships and there is a high stern castle and simpler forecastle staging. The stone was photographed in 1937, a few years after it was found. It had then already started to crumble and now the picture is virtually obliterated.

References to cogs are very numerous in fourteenth-century English documents, by far outnumbering hulks, galleys and carracks, which were already present in significant numbers (Runyan, 1991: 201). The earliest extant lading contract from northern Europe is for a voyage undertaken by the Cog of Lyme in 1322 (Greenhill, 1980). Cogs, including Edward III's flagship, played an important part in the battle of Sluys in 1340.

No examples of cogs have yet been excavated in Britain but several finds, from Germany, Scandinavia and the Netherlands, provide information about the construction of this vessel type. When in 1956 Paul Heinsius published a study of cogs, *Das Schiff der hansischen Frühzeit*, the only archaeological data available to supplement the documentary and pictorial sources was that of finds from Kalmar in Sweden (Åkerlund, 1951), which have since been shown to be on the periphery of the cog-building tradition. It was not until

Figure 1.8 The cog-like vessel on the town seal of Ipswich of AD 1200 (National Maritime Museum).

1962, with the discovery of the Bremen cog in the River Weser in Germany, that the constructional features of the cog were revealed (Fliedner, 1964; Lahn, 1992). The ship appears to have been lost while it was still being built and was perhaps swept away from the berth where it was being fitted out in about 1380. Tree-ring studies have shown that the oak for the planking and cross-beams was felled in the Weser Hills to the south, in 1378. The crooks for the knees were from more local sources in the forests around Bremen (Lahn, 1992: 19). The superstructure had not been fully installed, the ship had not been ballasted and the only artefacts associated with the ship were a selection of shipwrights' tools, a half-finished anchor stock, a barrel of tar and a shoe. The excavated remains of the Bremen cog are remarkably complete and show that the ship was 24 metres long, eight metres in the beam and over four metres high. A long programme of conservation and research has elucidated the building sequence and provided enough information for the construction of an accurate replica (figure 3.7).

Figure 1.9 Graffito of a cog in St Hilda's Church, Hartlepool (National Maritime Museum).

The keel was made up of three parts scarfed together. The central part was 8.3 metres long, with a maximum width of 0.47 metres. The two end pieces, 3.73 metres and 4.78 metres long, were each made out of a trunk of timber with a branch coming out at an angle so that the change of angle between the ends of the keel and the stem and stern posts was worked out of solid timber. The stem and stern each consisted of an inner and outer post. The inner posts were scarfed to the inner side of the keel knee but the outer posts were not mounted until the planking was in place.

Figure 1.10 The framing of the Bremen cog, including a cross-beam and longitudinal deck beams (Deutches Schiffahrtsmuseum).

The forward section of the keel was not completely level but was raised slightly. The sides of the keel and the lower parts of the stems were rabbeted for the hull planking. The first four strakes to each side of the keel were flush-laid. That is to say, they were laid edge to edge and were not fastened to each other in the midships area. At the ends of the ship the planks go through a transition from flush-laid to clinker and this required very specialised joinery including the stepping-out of the plank edges. The ship had 12 strakes per side, each made up of three or four planks. The plank seams were coated with caulking compound before assembly. When the third strake was in place, further caulking was applied and inserted on the inside and held in place by oak strips fastened on by iron clamps or staples. The first four floors were inserted and held in place with small nails while the treenail holes were bored and the treenails hammered in. The fourth strake turned the bilge, then the remaining floor timbers, ending below the fifth strake, were put in place.

The keelson, which had an integral mast-step, was treenailed to the floors but not to the keel. Planking continued and, after strake eight, half of the futtocks and five heavy cross-beams were inserted (figure 1.10). The cross-beams were cut from oak trunks seven metres in length. They rested on futtocks which had tenons projecting from their tops. Strake nine had cut-outs to fit over the cross-beams. When strake ten was in place further framing was inserted and inner planking was fitted, which gave longitudinal strength. This was cut from less good and preused stock. The twelfth strake ended on the framing rather than running right to the posts and the channel wale for attachment of the lower end of the shrouds lay against it outboard. The washboard planks above strake 12 were not clenched. A framework of top timbers was left protruding in the area of the stern castle. The castles, decking, windlass and capstan will be mentioned in Chapter 3.

The outer stem reinforcement was held on by iron bolts. It gave protection to the strake ends and the fore-stay was fastened to it. The outer stern post was much lighter than the outer stem post. It had gudgeons for the rudder already mounted on it, showing that the cog was sufficiently complete to have been launched. Further construction could be carried out afloat.

The most significant features of the hull of the Bremen cog are the use of sawn, rather than radially split, planking and the construction of the bottom with flush-laid planking and its transition to clinker. Also notable are the upward-sloping keel and the elaborate jointing of the stem and stern posts. The use of caulking battens held on by distinctive clamps or staples seems to be diagnostic of the cog and the planking nails were not clenched on roves but hammered over so that their tips entered the planking again. Through-beams are known also from vessels in the keel tradition, such as the 'big ship' from Bergen, but they seem to have been essential to the cog. These structural features add detail to the general visual impression of hull shape obtained by studying the pictorial evidence. They also allow fragmentary finds which show evidence of similar features to be classified as cogs; though it is not necessarily the case that all cogs would have shared all these features. It is not known how far back in time these features can be traced, nor over what geographical area. It is by no means certain that cogs built in Britain or Ireland would have exhibited precisely the same constructional traits as those built in the Hanse homelands.

The lines of the Bremen cog (figure 1.11) go some way to counter the common misconception that cogs were unseaworthy boxes. The hull has a fine entry, with a narrow bow to cut through the water and a deep forefoot to maintain directional stability. The stern has a fine run, allowing the water to flow past the rudder with the minimum of turbulence. The angular turn of the bilge helps to resist heeling and leeway.

The earliest ship find yet identified as a cog is that which sank at Kollerup, on the northern coast of Denmark, in the early thirteenth century, shown in figure 1.12 (Jeppesen, 1979; Crumlin-Pedersen, 1979: 29–32). This did not have sawn planking but was instead constructed from very wide oak planks probably made by splitting a tree-trunk in half and using axes to cut a plank from each half (Crumlin-Pedersen, 1989: 32). Six strakes either side of the keel were flush-laid, with a transition to clinker planking at the ends of half of them.

Numerous other boat and ship finds have been identified as cogs on the grounds of having the lowest part of the hull constructed of flush-laid planks and by the presence of re-entrant nails and caulking clamps. Among these is

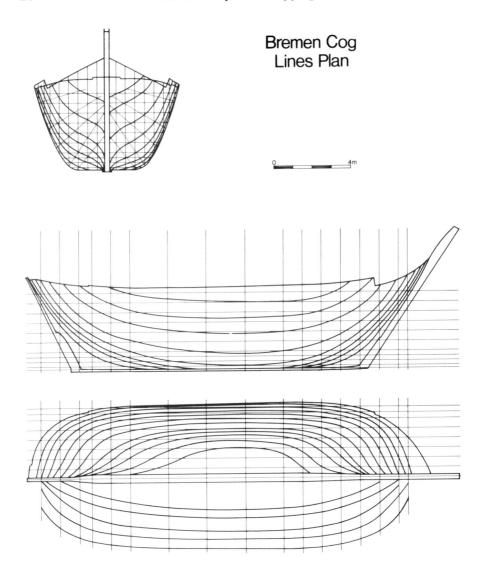

Figure 1.11 The lines of the Bremen cog (after Lahn, 1992).

the late fourteenth-century wreck at Vejby, Denmark (Crumlin-Pedersen, 1976). Many cogs have been excavated in the Netherlands, including the late thirteenth-century wreck at Rutten shown in figure 4.6 (Oosting, 1987), as well as several other thirteenth- and fourteenth-century vessels found in the polders (Reinders, 1979).

The cog seems to have ceased to be important as a large ship type soon after 1400. Some Netherlands and German inland vessels perhaps continued the tradition on a much reduced scale into later centuries.

Figure 1.12   The Kollerup cog under excavation (Viking Ship Museum, Roskilde).

Shipbuilding tools

In *The King's Mirror*, written in Norway in about 1250, a father instructs his son 'When at sea, bring with you nails of a size to suit your ship, axe, gouge and auger, and all other tools needed in shipbuilding' (Christensen, 1982: 329). More can be learnt about the tools which were used for building boats and ships from pictorial sources and from studying toolmarks on timbers. Examination of the grain of excavated vessel components provides information about the selection and conversion of timber. For making strakes, tree-trunks were selected for their straight grain, which is normally visible in the bark, and were split into radial segments with wedges and mallets. The rough planks were then trimmed with a broad axe or side axe, as shown on the Bayeux Tapestry (figure 1.3). Figure 1.13 shows a similar T-shaped axe excavated from an eleventh-century context at Milk Street, London. Axes and shaves were used for cutting the edges of strakes to shape. Framing members could also be cut entirely with axes from specially selected crooks of timber and at the beginning of the period shipbuilders did not use the saw at all. Saws were in use by the thirteenth century for making the planks for cogs. Sawing enabled poorer quality timber to be used, since the saw could cut through twisted grain and knots. Much of the fourteenth-century Bremen cog's planking had been patched to cover defects even though building had not finished at the time when the vessel was wrecked (Crumlin-Pedersen, 1989: 32). In the building of keels, sawing was used for

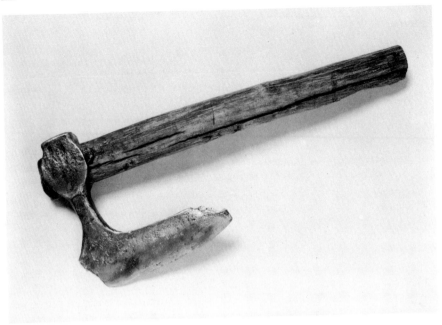

Figure 1.13   An eleventh-century T-shaped axe found in London (photo: Museum of London).

parts of the ship other than the hull planking at least as early as the end of the thirteenth century and sawyers were employed in the 1294 English royal galley-building programme. Toolmarks on the probably fifteenth-century assemblage of boatbuilding timbers found at the Poole Foundry site show that stems were sawn out of tree-trunks. For planking, however, English shipwrights seem to have used split, not sawn, oak boards throughout the medieval period. The *Grace Dieu*, built in the early fifteenth century, has saw marks on the sides of some of the frames but the grain of the planking shows that it was still split radially.

Knives were used for cutting treenails and for fine-trimming of other components. Augers were used to make treenail holes and a breast auger is shown being used for this purpose on the Bayeux Tapestry (figure 1.3). Clench nails also needed pre-bored holes, as they could split the planking if they were driven in blind. Larger nails, especially when of extreme dimensions, such as those for the fifteenth-century *Grace Dieu* which had square-sectioned shanks 2cm across, certainly needed them. Treenails were driven in with mallets and had wedges knocked into their inboard ends before they were trimmed off flush with the inboard face of the hull. Clench nails were hammered in and then, while they were held in position, pre-punched roves were forced onto them. An axe hammer or a dolley, a tool like a hammer with a hole in the middle, may have been used for this. Then the end of the nail was hammered flat to clench against the rove and the end was cut off.

Building sites

The financial accounts for the galleys ordered to be built by Edward II in 1294 and for the *Grace Dieu*, built between 1416 and 1420, provide valuable information about the organisation and processes of shipbuilding. The king ordered 26 towns to share in the building of 20 galleys and accounts for those built at Newcastle, York, Dunwich, Ipswich, London, Southampton and Lyme have been preserved (Whitwell and Johnson, 1926; Anderson, 1928; Tinniswood, 1949). The Southampton and Lyme accounts are just for galleys but in most cases the accounts include a barge with 30 to 40 oars and a boat as well. These centrally ordered exercises were on a larger scale than the local shipbuilding industries could accommodate and it was necessary to bring together teams of master-builders and workmen from different parts of the country and even from abroad.

The Southampton account gives a weekly break-down of costs, from start of build to launching, during 17 weeks in the winter of 1294 (Anderson, 1928: 222–33). This throws some light on shipbuilding practice as well as on the nature of the vessel being built. The workforce consisted of no fewer than four master-builders and ten each of the standard classes of craftsmen for clinker-building: plankers, clenchers (or hammermen) and holders. In addition, in the second week a master-builder of Bayonne was fetched from Portsmouth to supervise the design of the galley. Two men provided and inspected the timber and two boys were employed for site security. Blacksmiths were paid to make clench nails and other metalwork on site, from iron bought in an unworked state (over five tons of nails were used at Newcastle) but hasps, staples and hinges were bought from outside suppliers. At Southampton, wood sawyers were not hired until the eleventh week, by which time the hull was nearly complete, and carpenters not until after that, perhaps to help with the upper works.

The land for galley-building and houses for workshops and stores were rented. Before construction began, enclosures of hurdles and thorns were first created round the building sites. At London the fence had 120 posts and took six carpenters ten days to build. Also at London, 26 carpenters spent ten days building a store house with timbers and laths and thatched with reed. At York a smithy was built in the yard. It was of wattle and daub, roofed with turf and had a coal-fired hearth of broken tiles (Tinniswood, 1949: 280).

The first purchases were poles and planks for staging, then iron and timber for the first phase of building. At Southampton oak treenails were bought in the fifth week, showing that framing was being inserted. Planking and framing seem to have continued together until the twelfth week, when six elm beams were bought as well as spars and planks for making hatches and *pavesades*. Timber was bought by instalments, not all at once, and it was ordered not so much by dimensions, except for the planking which came in various lengths, as for the specific purpose it had to serve. Timbers were, for example, ordered for the keel, for 'kevels' (frames), for beams and for the rudder. This implies a search for timbers of appropriate shapes and sizes and perhaps some roughing-out off-site. At Newcastle timber was bought from over 50 different people and some of the timber was imported, obtained from merchants with connections with the Low Countries and the Baltic. The mast and yard, oars, ship's boat, anchors and hawsers were also bought in. The master and mates from the galley at Southampton went to Poole to buy a sail and bought a mast and yard, expensive items, from the Isle of Wight.

In the final stages substances for coating the hull were bought, along with pots in which they were prepared. At Southampton, rosin and grease were introduced in the fifteenth week, followed by tallow, pitch and lard in the sixteenth. Payments were made for painting the galleys and the Newcastle account gives the most information about their decorative treatment. The galley built there was whitewashed with lime inside the hold. The outside of the hull was sized with egg white and oil and more than a dozen pigments were used, as well as 18 pounds of varnish. Tinfoil was put over some of the nailheads before painting (Whitwell and Johnson, 1926: 157). The Southampton account records the purchase of *clavis de tin* in the tenth week, by which time they would have been above the galley's waterline, and *clavi stannati* (tinned nails) are also mentioned in the York account. Some of the nailheads from the planking on the Dublin waterfront were covered in a blue metal oxide and a yellowish-white substance coating the outboard surface of the possible galley planking from the Dublin waterfront was analysed and found to be composed of pine resin and calcium carbonate (McGrail, 1993a: 137). While the Southampton galley was being painted, 20 men were paid wages for six days to make a ditch to haul the galley to the sea.

Henry V's great ship *Grace Dieu* was built, from 1416, in a specially made 'dok' surrounded by an enclosure of stakes. It is likely that the ship was built on a low-lying strip of land with a temporary wall on the seaward side of the dock. This would allow launching to take place at high tide after the wall had been removed (Friel, 1993: 5). After the launching, the shores, piles and stakes were sold off. William Soper, the Keeper of the King's Ships, who was responsible for the construction of the *Grace Dieu*, built a storehouse at Southampton in 1416. It was 126ft long, made of New Forest timber with a tiled roof. It had an adjoining smithery, which may have been where the nails for the great ship were manufactured. Carpenters and sawyers were paid more than clenchers who in turn were paid more than holders and labourers. West Country men had been forced to work on her and absconded back home during the winter of 1416.

There is a potential medieval shipbuilding site, as yet unexplored, at Smallhythe on the River Rother in Kent. Large vessels were built there in the fifteenth century, when it was a thriving port, but by about 1600 silting had reduced it to a hamlet. Clench nails have been retrieved from a rectangular depressed feature, approximately 40 metres by 7.5 metres, which may be the remains of a dock.

The only site associated with medieval boatbuilding which has so far been examined in Britain is in Poole, in Dorset. Excavations on the Foundry site on the Poole waterfront in 1987 revealed a store of boatbuilding timber which had been neatly laid out on the medieval beach, not far from the parish church, in around 1400. The excavation may not have uncovered the total area of the boat yard site but the assemblage recovered consisted of 61 timbers. Of these, 11 had previously been used in boats. Most of the rest were unworked timbers, with their bark removed, clearly selected on grounds

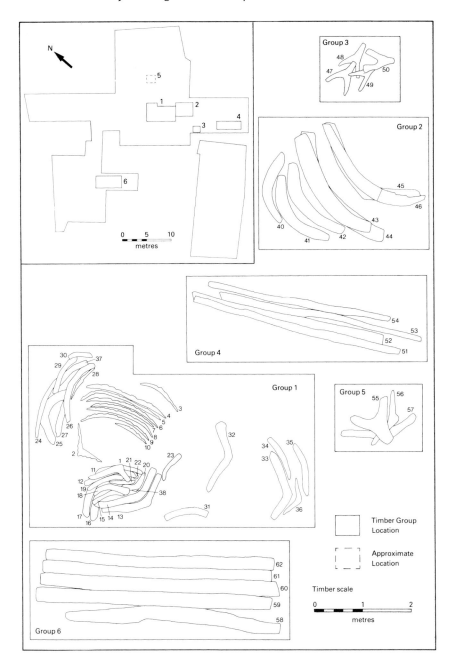

Figure 1.14 The medieval boatbuilder's timber store at Poole, Dorset (Poole Museums).

of shape and thickness. Some other timbers were in a semi-prepared state, cut to shape but not finished off (Hutchinson, 1994).

The timbers had been arranged in six separate groups, according to their shape and function (figure 1.14). Group 1 consisted of floors and futtocks with unworked timbers of similar sizes and shapes. Group 2 consisted of a used stem post made of two pieces, together with six roughed-out stems. Group 3 contained four Y-shaped timbers, probably intended as mast-crutches, in varying stages of preparation. Group 4 and Group 6 contained long baulks of timber probably for keels and keelsons. Group 5 contained three large timbers: one large forked shape, and two other grown crooks. All the timbers were of oak except for the baulks in Groups 4 and 6 which were of elm. The significant element missing from this assemblage is planking. A pot containing residues of pitch was recovered from the same horizon as the timbers.

All of the used timbers, with the exception of one futtock, could have come from two very similar boats. The rough-outs and unworked timbers were, with the exception of the timbers in Group 5, of similar scantlings. It seems likely that this boat yard produced a stock type of boat a little under eight metres long with a beam of about 2.5 metres, probably used for fishing (see reconstruction drawing, figure 8.7). The previously used timbers may well have been retained as a guide to achieving consistency of product. It is very unlikely that they were meant to serve as exact templates, nor that they were to be built into new boats, as in clinker construction the shape of the frames is dictated by the unique form of the planking of each hull. It is surprising that so much good boatbuilding timber was left unused on the beach.

2 Shipbuilding: interaction and innovation

The merging of northern hull types

Medieval ship pictures indicate that from about 1350 the clear divisions between the keel, hulk and cog ship-types were breaking down. In documents a greater number of specific vessel-types are mentioned, all except carracks presumably derived from one of the main clinker traditions, but large numbers of vessels were simply referred to as ships (naves). Northern European ships at this date were still single-masted and now had stern rudders and more developed castles. While the length to beam ratio of seagoing ships in each of the traditions was probably similar, there was increasing differentiation in the shape of the bow and stern. There may already have been some imitation of the hull shape, though not yet the method of construction, of the ships from southern Europe which northerners called carracks.

At this time, hulk hybrids, in which the strakes end on a post at one end of the ship and at the sheerline at the other, become common. The 1418–26 seal of Thomas Beaufort (figure 2.1a) shows a ship with a hulk stem and a keel stern. Ships with hulk planking at both ends also continue to be depicted. The seal of the Earl of Rutland, 1391–98, has hulk planking at both ends, with the stern wider than the stem. The ships shown on the fifteenth-century Admiralty seals of John Holand, Earl of Huntingdon, the first of 1421 and the second (figure 2.1b) of 1435–42, also have hulk planking at both ends.

Pictures are the prime source of information about the changes which were taking place but they leave many questions unanswered. It is relatively easy to identify ships built in the hulk tradition because the pictures often clearly show the run of the planking to the ends of the ship. However it is far less easy to distinguish cogs from keels because the method of planking the bottom is not depicted. The ships on the seals of Amsterdam of the early fifteenth century might be presumed to be cogs but the hull shape is very similar to that on the contemporary seal of Southampton, where the keel building tradition was flourishing and the *Grace Dieu* was then being built.

The wreck of the *Grace Dieu*, which began building in 1416, lies in the River Hamble in Hampshire, near Southampton (figure 2.2). It has been the subject of several archaeological excavations, and the work so far has been summarised by Friel (1993) and Clarke *et al.* (1993). This royal warship had a keel at least 38 metres long, and was built as the English answer to the carrack, such as those from Genoa used by the French. *Grace Dieu* was not built according to Mediterranean skeleton-building practice, which will be described below, but in an extension of the English keel clinker-building technique, using planking three layers thick. This unique triple-thickness

Figure 2.1   The Admiralty seals of: (a) Thomas Beaufort, 1418–26, and (b) John Holand, 1435–42 (National Maritime Museum).

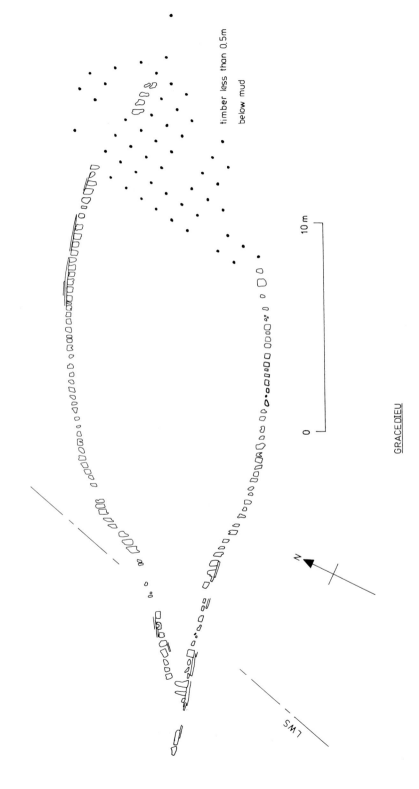

timber less than 0.5m

below mud

10 m

0

GRACE DIEU

N

LWS

Figure 2.2 Site plan of the wreck of the *Grace Dieu* (National Maritime Museum).

planking shows how the shipwrights responded to the construction challenges of scaling-up a clinker hull. They needed to increase the thickness of the ship's sides and to build in longitudinal strength to resist hogging.

Increasing the thickness of a clinker hull simply by using much thicker planks would reduce the flexibility of the planking to such an extent that it would not be possible to create the hull shape. It would also be extravagant of materials, as trees of much greater diameter would be needed to provide radial planks of sufficient thickness. The thickness of the strakes could, in theory, be doubled by laying two planks together (figure 2.3b). The consequences of this are that longer nails would be needed and the nails would also have to support far more weight. In a shell of planking the nails in the lower part of the hull have to support the entire weight of the planking above them, except to the extent that they are relieved by the framing. There would be a tendency for the nails to deform under this shearing force and so they would have to be made with larger shanks. The level to which it is watertight might well be a problem.

If even thicker planking were required and the shipwrights were to go one stage further and make strakes three planks thick, the problems would be compounded (figure 2.3c). The nails and treenails would be excessively long and the shearing pressures on the nails would be far worse. The planking would not be uniformly strong as it would vary from six planks in thickness at the strake overlaps to three planks thick in the mid-part of the strakes. So this is not how *Grace Dieu* was built and it is not what is meant by 'triple-thickness planking' in the context of this find. *Grace Dieu* was constructed in a modified form of double-thickness planking (figure 2.3d). There were two planks of full height and another plank, two-thirds the height of the other two, on the inside of the strake. This provided extra thickness and reduced the variation so that the hull was three planks thick in the mid-part of the strakes and five planks thick at the overlaps. Most importantly, the inner planks also served to relieve the nails by transmitting the downward pressure onto the tops of the planks of the strake below. Watertightness would also be improved since water would have further to penetrate and would not simply have to run along a straight seam. This method of increasing the thickness of the planking overcame many of the technical problems. Some still remained, however. It was difficult to avoid boring the treenail holes too close to the edge of the joggles. There was still a huge requirement for iron, as the shanks of the clench nails were 2cm square and 15cm long, spaced about 20cm apart along the strake overlaps, with an extra line of nails, spaced about 60cm apart, along the midline of the strakes. The supply of 17 tons of 'clench and roof' nails for the *Grace Dieu* and the smaller vessels built at the same time is recorded in the building accounts (Carpenter Turner, 1954).

It cannot have been easy to shape and assemble all the separate components. The planking seems to have been made up of pieces not more than six or seven feet (less than two metres) in length (Anderson, 1934: 165). So far it has not been determined whether each layer of planks was scarfed at the same place or whether the scarfs were staggered. Some clues as to how the shipwrights might have set about fastening the layers of a strake together and to the strake below can be seen in planks removed from the wreck

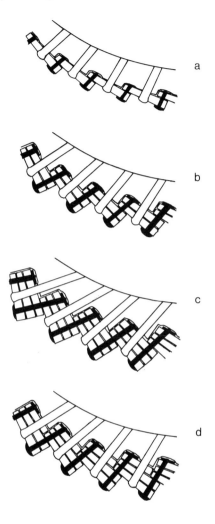

Figure 2.3 Clinker planking: (a) normal single thickness; (b) conjectural double thickness; (c) conjectural triple thickness; (d) *Grace Dieu* (National Maritime Museum).

(Clarke *et al.*, 1993: 25–33). Small nails in these planks indicate that while the composite strakes were being built up, the outer two layers of planking were tacked from both inboard and outboard. The only small nail on an inner plank occurs at a scarf. Tacking was necessary because the holes for the 20cm square shanks of the clench nails had to be prepared. Holes were quite frequently made in the wrong place or at the wrong angle and they had to be plugged with wooden pegs.

A ship which was wrecked at Aber Wrac'h on the north coast of Brittany in the first half of the fifteenth century (L'Hour and Veyrat, 1989) shares some characteristics with *Grace Dieu*. Particularly striking are the deep rove impressions on the inside of the planking, the concavities on the frames to

accommodate the roves and the use of moss and sphagnum caulking. The
ship was large, with an original length estimated as 25 metres. The keel was
of beech, with the stem, framing and planking of oak. The building accounts
for the *Grace Dieu* record the purchase of more than a thousand beech trees,
though it is not known what they were used for (Friel, 1993: 4). The after
part of the Aber Wrac'h ship (figure 2.4) was not preserved. The hull
construction was of normal single-thickness clinker planking, with localised
strengthening at the places where the planking was pierced for the ends of
the through beams (figure 2.5). The strakes below and above the beams
(though not the ones mostly cut away by the beams) were reinforced by
small boards on the inside face, in the manner of the inner plank of the
Grace Dieu strakes. The weight of each beam was mainly supported by a
futtock and a stringer. The scarves between the keel and the stem and stern
posts were both missing from the wreck. The part of the stem post which
was present showed that the strake ends ran onto the stem post in the keel
rather than the hulk manner.

Pottery found on the wreck was of Breton manufacture; and six Castilian
and two Breton coins indicate that the ship probably sank in the first quarter
of the fifteenth century (L'Hour and Veyrat, 1989: 294). Tree-ring study,
although inconclusive for dating, indicated that the ship was perhaps built
near Bordeaux or on the north coast of Spain. There was a substantial
shipbuilding industry at Bayonne in the fourteenth and fifteenth centuries,
supplying English as well as local clients. While *Grace Dieu* was being built,
another great ship was built for Henry V at Bayonne. The accounts indicate
that it was of clinker construction.

Grace Dieu and the Aber Wrac'h wreck provide evidence for ships built in
the mature development of the keel tradition. The closest parallel to them is
the fifteenth-century wreck raised from the sea-bed off Gdańsk in 1975–6
(figure 2.6). The Baltic is an area in which the cog was prevalent and the
Gdańsk W5 wreck may provide an indication of the course ship construction
took when cogs were superseded. The town seals of Gdańsk and Elbląg for
this period show a change of ship type from the classic cog, with straight
stem and stern posts, to more rounded hull shapes.

Gdańsk W5 has similarities with *Grace Dieu* and the Aber Wrac'h wreck
in the general appearance and dimensions of the components, including the
rove impressions in the planking and the presence of through-beams. Moss
was used for waterproofing the plank scarves but animal hair was used in
the lands. This ship did not have the flush-laid bottom strakes of the cog
but the jointing of the keel to the stern post is a clear survival of the cog
tradition. The ship had an inner and outer stern post like the Bremen cog. It
was clinker-built throughout, from where the garboard was rabetted into
the 16.34 metre long oak keel, and did not have the cog feature of flush-laid
bottom planks. Unlike ships in the keel tradition, the garboard near the
bows was fastened to the keel with treenails, though in the stern it was
fastened with iron nails in the normal manner. In the midships part of the
hull, the strakes were of considerable width – 37cm on average (Litwin,
1980: 222).

Timber available for shipbuilding in western Europe was becoming scarce
in the fifteenth century and timber prices were consequently rising. Gdańsk

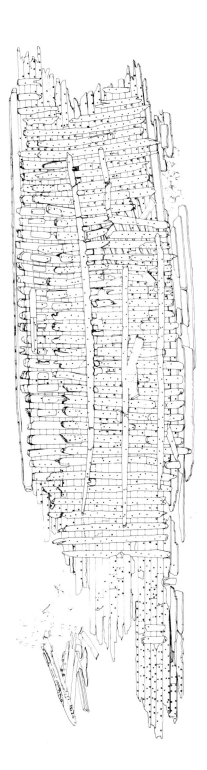

Figure 2.4 Plan of the Aber Wrac'h wreck (M. L'Hour).

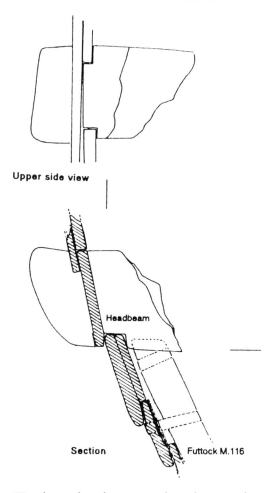

Figure 2.5 Aber Wrac'h wreck – diagram to show the strengthening of the hull planking where it is pierced by the through-beams (M. L'Hour).

developed a large shipbuilding export industry and by the end of the century was supplying English, Dutch and Italian buyers.

A votive model from the church of Ebersdorf near Dresden (Christensen, 1987: 69–70) appears to represent a cog in a similar state of evolution to that of Gdańsk W5. The hull is round and beamy, clinker-built from the keel, with a straight stern and curved stem post.

A ship found at Sandwich in Kent during pipe-laying operations in 1973 is potentially important for the study of later medieval clinker ship construction. The ship is tentatively dated to the fifteenth century on stratigraphic evidence and lies with its keel five metres below the current ground surface in the silted-up medieval town ditch (Trussler, 1974). Although some frames and planking, together with parts of the rudder, were removed at the time of discovery, much of the clinker-built hull, which may be as much as 33 metres long, remains in the ground.

Figure 2.6 The intact part of the Gdańsk W5 wreck after being raised from the sea-bed (photo: L. Nowicz).

The influence of southern ships

A detailed study of Mediterranean ships would be out of place in a book about shipping in medieval Britain but there are compelling reasons, apart from their intrinsic interest, why some account of them must be given here. Ships from the Mediterranean were operating in British waters and trading in British ports from the thirteenth century and the totally different approach to hull construction used in southern Europe was adopted in the north and began to replace clinker construction for the largest ships from the mid-fifteenth century.

The number of medieval ships so far excavated in southern Europe it not great, so regional and functional variations and chronological developments are still being explored. Pictorial evidence is much more abundant and Italian treatises on shipbuilding, largely concerned with galleys, survive from the fifteenth century. Here it is appropriate only to make some generalisations in order to show something of the technique which was to impact so very significantly on northern Europe.

Ships of southern Europe had been following an entirely separate course of development from those in the north. By the Middle Ages their planking was flush-laid and the planks were not joined to each other but just to the frames. This technique is known as 'carvel-building' and contrasts with clinker-building in which the planks are fastened to each other, edge to edge. The clinker method is termed 'shell-first' construction while its opposite is 'frame-first', where a complete skeleton of frames is erected, totally defining the form of the hull, before the planks are applied to it. However, just as northern clinker vessels only had to have some of their planking in place before frames were inserted, southern carvel vessels only had to have some of their framing in place before planking began.

In antiquity, Mediterranean vessels had been shell-built, not with overlapping strakes but with the planking of their hulls flush-laid and keyed together with tenons locked into mortises in the edges of the planks. This method persisted at least until the seventh century, as can be seen from the Yassi Ada ship (Bass and Doorninck, 1982), by which time frame-first construction had been introduced, as in the Saint Gervais II wreck (Jezegou, 1985). Frame-first construction in the eleventh century is demonstrated by the Serçe Liman vessel, which sank off Turkey in about 1025. Steffy (1991) has determined that when planking began, only two full frames and eight floor timbers were in place on the backbone of keel and stems, spanning only the central 2.7 metres of the approximately 14.36 metre long hull. The bottom strakes were nailed to these timbers, then framing and planking of the sides progressed together. Planking the difficult area at the turn of the bilge was left until some of the side planks were in place and was achieved with mostly short planks of irregular shape.

A well-preserved vessel dating to about 1300 was discovered in 1898 at Contarina in the Po delta, roughly 50 kilometres south of Venice (figures 2.7 and 2.8). It was 16.5 metres long on the keel, flat-bottomed and very nearly double-ended, tapering slightly more quickly aft than forward. The keel was fairly slender and shallow, with the floors and the keelson laid above it. To either side of the keel, just below the turn of the bilge, at the area of overlap between the floors and the futtocks, were longitudinal members of similar scantlings to that of the keel. Stringers were inserted at the corresponding positions on the inside of the hull so that the ends of the floors and futtocks were sandwiched between the bilge keels (or bilge wales) and the stringers. Higher up, where the futtocks overlapped with the top timbers, there was again a wale paired with a stringer. The keelson had mast-steps for lateen main and fore sails (Bonino, 1978). This disposition of keel, bilge keels and

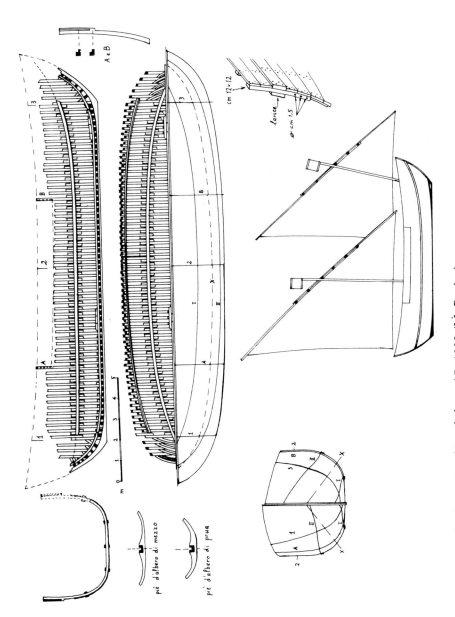

Figure 2.7 The Contarina ship of about AD 1300 (Ṁ. Bonino).

Figure 2.8 The excavation of the Contarina ship in 1898 (Museo Storico Navale, Venice).

wales would give the hull longitudinal strength and reinforce potential areas
of weakness in the framing. The bilge keels and wales may also be vestiges of
the hull design process as the shape of a hull could be defined by setting up
the keel and stems, establishing three key frames and running battens along
the sides of this framework from stem to stern.

Les Sorres X, a 10 metre long vessel found during the digging of the
Olympic Games rowing canal near Barcelona in 1990, is dated on pottery
evidence to the second half of the fourteenth century (Nieto, 1992). It shares
the constructional features of the Contarina 1 ship, except that the bilge keel
was reinforced by a double stringer on the inboard face of the hull. Similar
features can also be seen in the Lasize wreck, a Venetian galley which sank
in 1439 in Lake Garda (Scandurra, 1972: 209–10). The bottom of the hull
has been excavated and indicates that the overall length of this galley was
about 39.5 metres. The cross-section of the remains shows a deep projecting
keel bolted through the floor to the keelson. At the overlap of the floors and
futtocks there is a thicker strake or wale but this time, instead of projecting
outwards, it is inset into a notch on the underside of the framing. A stringer
lies directly above, sandwiching the floors and futtocks.

Detailed evidence for Catalan ship construction in the early fifteenth
century is provided by the votive model (figure 2.9) from a chapel in Mataro
in Catalonia, now in the Prins Hendrik Maritime Museum in Rotterdam
(Culver, 1929; van Nouhuys, 1931; Winter, 1956). The model is large, 1.23
metres overall, and it was clearly built by someone with a thorough
understanding of ship structure, undoubtedly a shipwright. The floors of the
Mataro model are notched to fit over the keel and are directly overlain by
the keelson which is secured to the keel by bolts in the spaces between the
floors. The step for the mainmast is integral with keelson, about half-way
along the ship's length. Futtocks abut the forward sides of the floors, running
from the keelson to the sheer. Four wales run along the framing. The lower
three extend from the stem post to the stern post but the top one, which
marks the sheerline of the forward part of the ship, is joined to the transom
of the stern. The through-beams at deck level rest on the next wale down.
There are 11 strakes per side. The third strake up from the keel was laid
immediately below the bottom wale. The garboard was laid next, prolonged
at each end by pieces which run well up on the stem and stern posts. The
second strake, which is very wide, was then applied in the space between the
other two (figure 2.9).

The early fifteenth-century Italian shipbuilding treatises set out the
principles involved in hull construction numerically and diagramatically. The
anonymous manuscript of the Venetian tradition, *Fabrica di Galere*
(Anderson, 1945), was probably first compiled in the early fifteenth century
but is known through a late fifteenth-century copy (figure 4.11). Rieth
(1991b) has pointed out that the manuscript reveals that the underlying
concept of hull construction had not changed from that demonstrated by the
seventh-century Saint Gervais II wreck, the eleventh-century Serçe Liman
wreck and the fourteenth-century Contarina 1 ship, as the manuscript still
deals with the dimensions and relationships of proportions of the principal
frames and the balancing frames at the two ends of the keel. The shipbuilder
needed to know how to calculate the reduction in size of the frames and the

Figure 2.9 The lower hull planking of the fifteenth-century Mataro model (Maritiem Museum 'Prins Hendrik', Rotterdam).

rise of the floors. This information was presented in diagrams based on segments of circles and on equilateral triangles. Lane (1934) and more recently Bellabarba (1993) have provided explanations of the 'rules' for designing hulls. The approach did change from the empiric to the mathematical, no doubt through an intermediate stage combining pre-planning and fine tuning, but the possibilities for modifying the shapes of hulls were not exploited until the post-medieval period.

A Genoese ship which sank in the early sixteenth century off the Mediterranean coast of France at Villefranche has been investigated under water since 1982 (Guerout *et al.*, 1989). The surviving hull structure is 35 metres long and the overall length was probably more than 40 metres. Because the wreck is lying at an angle on the sea-bed, parts of two levels of deck survive. Rieth has demonstrated that this large ship was built by the same technique of construction with the hull shape controlled by a few primary frames (Rieth, 1991a: 50). True skeleton technique, in which all the frames are designed, carved and positioned in advance of the planking

Figure 2.10 Fourteenth-century Mediterranean *cocche* from the Pizzigani chart (from Winter, 1956).

process, was developed after the period under study, notably in England in the late sixteenth century. It was not adopted in the Mediterranean until the end of the seventeenth century (Rieth, 1991b).

The earliest case where the separate shipbuilding traditions of the Mediterranean and northern shipping exerted an influence one on the other appears to have been the imitation by southern shipwrights of features of a northern ship type. A Florentine chronicler wrote that, in about 1304, men of Bayonne in cogs went plundering in the Mediterranean:

> And from that time on the Genoese, Venetians and Catalans have made a practice of navigating with cogs and have been leaving off use of the big ships to navigate more safely and because they are less expensive. This has been a great transformation in the shipping of our fleets. (Giovanni Villani, *Chronica*)

In fact the Genoese may have come to know this ship-type earlier because of their dealings in low-value bulk cargoes like alum and grain. In 1286 a *navis sive cocha* belonging to a Bayonne merchant in partnership with two Genoese brought alum to Flanders. In 1292 another *cocha* loaded with 285 tons of alum at Focea to go to Bruges. The first mention of a *cocha* in the Venetian documentation is from March 1312 (Balard, 1991: 119). Southern shipwrights did not adopt northern clinker-building, however, but instead created a flush-laid interpretation of the beamy and high-sided northern hull. Because of this, *coche* could be built much larger than cogs. They also adopted the square sail and the stern rudder, although *coche de duobus timonibus* – that is, with paired side rudders – also feature in the Genoese documentary sources until about 1375. The crucial characteristic identifying a *cocha* in the earlier part of the fourteenth century appears to have been the use of a square sail, with or without a supplementary lateen sail on a second mast (van der Merwe, 1983). From 1310 lateen ships were rapidly abandoned in favour of *coche* (Balard, 1991: 120) but the term *cocha* was itself being replaced at the end of the century by *navis*, as *coche* types came to be considered the norm. One- and two-masted *coche* are shown on the Pizzigani chart of 1367 (figure 2.10) (Guilleux la Roërie, 1957: 179–80). A particularly good late example is shown on a Hispano-Moresque bowl, made near Valencia in about 1430 (figure 2.11). To emphasise that ship

Figure 2.11   A *cocha* on a Hispano-Moresque bowl made in Valencia in about 1430 (Museum für Islamische Kunst, Staatliche Museen Preussische Kulturbesitz, Berlin).

development did not proceed at a uniform pace, it is worth noting that another such bowl of similar date carries what is probably the most famous early image of a full-rigged, three-masted sailing ship (figure 4.10).

From the 1340s the Genoese in particular were using *coche* in their trade with England and Flanders and it appears that in England these ships became known as carracks. This term makes its earliest appearance in a letter of Edward III in which he wrote of 'great ships of Genoa, commonly

Figure 2.12 Crusader carracks at Constantinople, from Froissart's *Chronicles*, about 1400 (photo: Bibliothèque Nationale, Paris MS Fr. 5594, f.217).

called *carakes*' (van der Merwe 1983: 126, citing Burnham). There is good documentary evidence up to 1396 that carracks were, in English sources, ships which the Genoese referred to as *coche* or sometimes *naves* (Burnham, 1974: 269–78). 'Carrack' seems to have been a northern vernacular term for large *coche* and had very little Mediterranean currency in the late medieval period. The fact that the word can be traced back to thirteenth-century Spain as a term for large (lateen) ships and that many Spaniards were involved in Genoese *coche* voyages to England may be significant here (van der Merwe, 1983: 125–6).

The rounded hull shape we now associate with carracks is shown in single-masted form in a French illustration of the siege of Constantinople, dating to about 1400 (figure 2.12). However, as Pizzigani's chart shows, the two-masted rig of square mainsail and lateen mizzen was then already current. It is from this that the new three-masted rig was developed, by the addition of a square-rigged foremast. Although this rig was to spread throughout Europe from the fifteenth century, its exact point and date of origin remains elusive. The earliest known illustration of a three-masted rig (figure 3.10) is in a Catalan document said to date to 1406 (Mott, 1991: 111) but in practice the development may have occurred almost simultaneously at various places along the route from Italy to the Channel at the opening of the fifteenth century.

The introduction of carvel-building to northern Europe

Throughout the medieval period it was well known that north and south Europe had different approaches to ship construction. Crusaders from the north came in contact with carvel-built (see page 36) ships in the Mediterranean and northern ships were trading beyond the Straits of Gibraltar at least from 1300. Merchant ships from the Mediterranean visited northern Europe regularly from the late thirteenth century and southern warships were hired to fight in the north. Clinker-building never was adopted in the Mediterranean but carvel-building became the standard method of constructing large ships in northern Europe by the end of the Middle Ages.

Carvel galleys had been built in northern France at the end of the thirteenth and in the fourteenth centuries. Philip the Fair's galley arsenal, *le clos des galées*, was founded at Rouen in 1293 and employed Genoese shipwrights to direct local craftsmen in building galleys of the Genoese type (Rieth, 1989). Italian specialists were also brought in to caulk the carvel planking and to make oars. But as Rieth has pointed out (1989: 74–5), although carvel-building was introduced at Rouen the method was not effectively transferred to French shipwrights since they did not apply it to any other ship forms.

Eight Genoese carracks were captured by the English in 1416 and 1417 and soon afterwards permission was sought to hire 'carpenters and caulkers of a foreign country' to repair the carracks, 'for in this country we shall find only a few people who know how to repair and amend them'. Payments were made to Venetians, Catalans and Portuguese for carrying out the work (Friel, 1983a: 131).

The term 'carvel' was applied in the fifteenth century to skeleton-built ships, specifically those from Portugal where in the early fifteenth century an apparently new family of ships, termed 'carvels' was developed (Paviot, 1991: 55). From the 1430s, carvels were being built in northern Europe, at first by southern master craftsmen and then by the local shipwrights who had learnt their skills. Between 1463 and 1466 a three-masted carvel was built for Sir John Howard at Dunwich in Suffolk (Friel, 1983a: 134) and it is quite possible that this was not the earliest to be built in England.

The carvel method was finally adopted in northern Europe because of its suitability for building very large ships. There are limitations to the size of clinker hulls. The larger the ship, the thicker the planking has to be to achieve rigidity and this puts a great deal of stress on the nails, potentially leading to problems with watertightness. Clinker construction of large ships was extravagant with iron, as a great number of long and thick clench nails had to be used. Carvel-building used fewer, less-massive nails, relying more on treenails. Clinker planking in the 'keel' tradition was made from radially split oak, requiring large trees, with straight grain free from knots. Cog builders had already economised by using sawn timber and carvel-building also used sawn planks, allowing the use of poorer quality timber stock. A

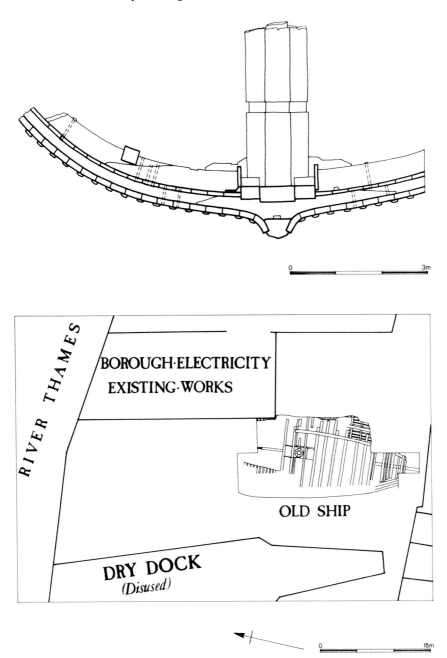

Figure 2.13 The ship found at Roff's Wharf, Woolwich in 1912 (after the contemporary drawing by W.E. Riley).

further great advantage of carvel-building was that it gave clear control of
the hull shape from the planning stage of the building operation, since the
shape of the principal framing members determined the eventual form of the
vessel. It is still not clear how shipwrights building large clinker ships,
without the guidance of pre-erected frames, made the shell of planking
conform to their intentions.

Clinker construction for even the largest ships lingered on into the final
decades of the fifteenth century. The ship found at Roff's Wharf, Woolwich,
in 1912 was originally built in the clinker technique (figure 2.13). Examination of its frames showed that it was rebuilt by taking off the planking,
dubbing off the frame joggles so that the outer faces were smooth and
considerably reduced in thickness, then nailing on flush planking (Salisbury,
1961). The remains of the ship have been postulated to be those of the
Sovereign, a royal ship of 800 tons built in 1488. Another royal ship, the
Regent, of 1,000 tons, was built in the previous year in carvel construction.
The *Sovereign* was rebuilt in 1509. A lack of faith in the watertightness of
carvel-built hulls is demonstrated by the presence of battens, fastened over
the plank seams on the outside of the hull of the Woolwich ship, to prevent
the caulking from falling out. This feature is also found on the early
sixteenth-century *Mary Rose* (Rule, 1982: 69). The Woolwich ship's
importance is that it stands at the transition from clinker to flush-laid
construction. It also demonstrates that exactly the same hull shape could be
built in both techniques.

3 Fitting, steering and rigging

Decks and superstructure

In the early part of the medieval period, ship's holds were covered by loose boards, termed 'hatches'. The date of introduction of fixed decking is unclear. The hatch nails itemised in the accounts for the galleys of Lyme and Newcastle, built in 1294–96, indicate that these vessels had fixed decking, perhaps in the castles. The main deck of the Bremen cog of about 1380 had been partly laid, made of oak boards more than 3cm thick. Although no traces of nailing were found it is assumed that, except for one board which has a finger hole, the deck boards were intended to be nailed down. The stern-castle deck was nailed down and caulked. The fore castle had a raised gangplank rather than a full fore-castle deck (Lahn, 1992: 117–26). On the early fifteenth-century Catalan Mataro model the main deck is laid with planks running fore and aft and has a pronounced camber. The single hatchway which gives access to the hold has high coamings to prevent water from running in, and is capped by a sloping hatch cover (Culver, 1929: 215). The stern-castle deck also has considerable camber but is laid with planks running diagonally from a central fore-and-aft beam. The decks, like the hull planking, are caulked with hemp fibre and payed with pitch.

Superstructure seems first to have been built on ships for defensive purposes and Chapter 9 will discuss the introduction and development of fighting platforms and castles. By the fourteenth century, castles were integral parts of the hull and in the Bremen cog the framing of the hull extended above the sheer to support the castles (Lahn, 1992: 90). Castles also provided accommodation for those on board. Provision of cabins is recorded as early as 1228, when a ship sent to Gascony was fitted with a chamber for the king's 'things' and in 1242 chambers were constructed with panelling in a ship for the king and queen's voyage to Gascony (Salzman, 1931: 230). From the fourteenth century the south-west ports set up a thriving trade transporting pilgrims to the shrine of St James in Compostella. They could carry as many as 200 passengers at a time (Oppenheim, 1968: 20). A poem about a voyage on a pilgrim ship, preserved in a fifteenth-century manuscript at Trinity College Cambridge, has the owner of the ship calling a carpenter to make cabins and little compartments here and there (Anderson and Anderson, 1926: 91–5).

Fittings and gear

Most ships carried either a windlass or a capstan and larger ships had both. A capstan has a vertical axis and is driven by men walking round the central drum. It is stronger and faster than a windlass, which has a horizontal axis and is worked by pulling on levers on the drum. The Bremen cog, of the late fourteenth century, was equipped with both a windlass and a capstan in the

Figure 3.1 The early fourteenth-century town seal of Winchelsea (National Maritime Museum).

stern, for raising the mast, yard and anchor. The windlass was 3.53 metres long and nearly 55cm in diameter and had four sets of handspike holes. Experiments with the replica of the cog in Kiel showed that with eight men working the windlass a load of 2.5 tonnes can be lifted by direct draught (Lahn, 1992: 127–9). The two metre high capstan is one of the most impressive structural members of the Bremen cog. It had holes for six capstan bars (Lahn, 1992: 160). At the Bryggen excavations in Bergen a huge windlass drum, 5.40 metres long and about 50cm in diameter, was found in close contact with the keelson and mast beams of the 'big ship' of the thirteenth century. The windlass has holes for three sets of handspikes and has half-round rubbing-strips treenailed to it (Christensen, 1985: 180–81). A windlass is itemised in the building accounts for the 1294 Southampton galley and the seal of Winchelsea (figure 3.1) shows a windlass in use for raising the anchor.

Windlasses could be used to remove water from the bilges by winding a loop of rope or chain with buckets attached which could be dropped to the ship's bottom, filled and lifted again. The buckets were known as *wyndynngbalies*, and the verb 'to bail' is derived from their use (Ward, 1991: 42). To direct the water over the side, the Bremen cog had a draining box with a capacity of about 86 litres on the port side beside the windlass, with a long spout leading to the side of the ship (Lahn, 1992: 163). Pumps were introduced in the late Middle Ages and the early fifteenth-century *Grace Dieu* had at least two (Friel, 1993: 6). The poem about the pilgrim voyage, mentioned above, tells of the passengers' discomfort at having to sleep near the pump: 'A man were as good to be dede as smell therof the stynk' (Anderson and Anderson, 1926: 93). The earliest ship's pump found in Britain is that belonging to the early sixteenth-century Iberian wreck in Studland Bay, Dorset. A walnut pump base and a leather flap were recovered. A pump tube containing a piston of flexible leather disks would have fitted over the foot so that on the downstroke water would pass around the leathers and be lifted on the upstroke (Ladle, 1993: 21). The Bremen cog was fitted with a ship's latrine in the overhanging part of the stern castle (Lahn, 1992: 165–6) and a 'draining board' which probably served as a urinal was installed in the enclosed side compartment (Lahn, 1992: 162). That such amenities were not universally used is demonstrated by the results of environmental sampling of deposits in the bilge of the fifteenth-century Aber Wrac'h wreck, which revealed the presence of human faeces (L'Hour and Veyrat, 1989: 297).

Anchors enable a ship to remain stationary in port or when awaiting favourable winds or tides and were dropped as a last resort to avoid being grounded by an onshore wind. They are frequently depicted in medieval pictures, from the Bayeux tapestry to the Hastings manuscript (figure 10.7). They are mostly of the two-armed type, like those in figures 10.7 and 3.4, though the large Genoese ships in figure 4.12 have four-armed grapnels. Building accounts for the *Grace Dieu* and the two smaller vessels constructed at the same time record receipt of 24 anchors. Six of these were described as 'great anchors' and had an average weight of just over one ton. The dimensions of one of these anchors was recorded in 1450 when it was transferred to a different ship. The anchor shaft was 17ft 2in (5.23 metres) long and the arms were 11ft 6in (3.51 metres) wide (Friel, 1993: 9–10). An anchor, more than two metres long, was found beside the keel of the wreck of the fifteenth-century Gdańsk W5 ship (figure 2.6). The fourteenth-century Vejby wreck, which had foundered on a beach, was found to have an anchor cable housed in a leather sleeve to prevent chafing, stretched taut beneath the stern (Crumlin-Pedersen, 1985: 73). As yet there is no evidence that chain was used between medieval anchors and their cables, as it was later, to decrease the angle of pull on the anchor and so increase its resistance to dragging. The fourteenth-century Catalan *Customs of the Sea* required that anchor tackle should be sufficient for a ship bigger than the one on which it was to be used (Twiss, 1874: 291) and that, in drying harbours, floats were to be put on the anchors so that other ships could avoid settling on them as the tide went out (Twiss, 1874: 23). Cork buoys are mentioned in numerous fifteenth-century ship inventories (Oppenheim, 1896). The 1420 inventory for the *Grace Dieu* lists three cork buoys and five wooden buoys called 'dobles' (Friel, 1993: 9).

Steering: side rudders and stern rudders

In northern Europe at the beginning of the medieval period ships were steered by means of a single side rudder, usually mounted on the starboard quarter. Boats sometimes used steering oars, which unlike side rudders had only a single pivot and were not fastened to the side of the hull. Contemporary southern European ships had paired side rudders. In the thirteenth century, northern pictorial evidence shows the gradual replacement of side rudders by stern rudders. By the second half of the thirteenth century almost all seagoing vessels had stern rudders. The side rudder on the town seal of Bristol as late as 1340 may be anachronistic. The carvings of hulks on the fonts of Winchester (figure 1.6) and Zedelghem, made near Tournai in about 1180, have been cited as the earliest evidence for the use of stern rudders (Brindley, 1927: 86). However, this is far from conclusive as the rudders definitely lap the side of the ships. The sterns of hulks were singularly unsuitable for fixing rudders as they have so much curvature. Cogs with their straight stern posts are, by contrast, well adapted for mounting stern rudders and it is likely that this is the ship-type for which they were first developed. Hanse town seals show that stern rudders were becoming standard equipment for cogs by 1250 and the ship on the thirteenth-century town seal of Ipswich (figure 1.8) has a very handsome example. The helmsman and the end of the tiller can just be seen at the forward side of the castle.

The transition from the use of side rudders to stern rudders has been regarded as a great technological step forward but the performance of the side rudder deserves more respect than it is generally given. The side rudder is balanced and exerts pressure on either side of its centre of effort. It is therefore more efficient, causing less drag and needing less effort to keep it at the required angle, than the stern post rudder which is unbalanced because it swings from its leading edge. Rudders mounted on the stern post were also less effective because of the turbulence caused by the ship's hull, whereas side rudders operated in clearer water. The adoption of stern rudders was a necessary adaptation to changes in ship design and increases in vessel size which provided greater carrying capacity at the expense of sailing performance. The side rudder works well on a ship which is itself in balance, with the centre of effort of the sail in the correct position in relation to the centre of lateral resistance of the hull and with trim achieved by the careful positioning of cargo and ballast (Andersen, 1986). As ships increased in size the fine tuning of balance became harder.

There is a limit to the height of ship on which a side rudder can be used. The whole length of the rudder has to be cut out of a single tree-trunk. The longest side rudders yet found are a thirteenth-century example from the Bryggen site in Bergen, Norway, which measures 6.70 metres (Christensen, pers. comm.) and another, coincidentally of the same length, from Rye Bay, East Sussex (Marsden, 1992: 126–7). Radiocarbon dating of the Rye rudder suggests a date of manufacture in the twelfth or thirteenth century. Size

Figure 3.2 A hulk from a *Life of St Thomas of Canterbury*, *c.*1230–40 (J. Paul Getty).

limitation is also imposed by the leverage forces operating on its attachment point. A side rudder is pivoted from a point part way down the ship's quarter. Because the side of the hull slopes in towards the keel, a boss or other protruberance needs to be fitted, at a frame position to reduce stress to the hull planking. In the Viking period the rudder was attached with a withy rope but the strain of the rudder is concentrated here and later on stronger attachment methods were adopted.

The early thirteenth-century ship in figure 3.2 has what appear to be linked iron loops, one on the ship, one on the rudder, to support the rudder while still allowing it to pivot. The two side rudders found separately on the Suffolk coast near Southwold (Hutchinson, 1986), which were probably made in the eleventh century, had traces of iron bars running through their pivoting points. The Southwold rudders were of similar overall shape but the variation in their dimensions shows that they were designed to fit different ships (figure 3.3). They are 3.91 metres and 4.36 metres long and their tiller positions indicate that they were from vessels with sheers roughly two metres and three metres above the waterline at the rudder position. They both have narrow blades with a slight extension at the heel which would have reduced turbulence by facilitating base ventilation; the air drawn down the afterside of the rudder would be released as a thin streak of bubbles.

The blades of side rudders became broader throughout their period of use, to exert more control over larger or less well balanced ships. Four of the probably thirteenth-century side rudders from the Bryggen excavations in

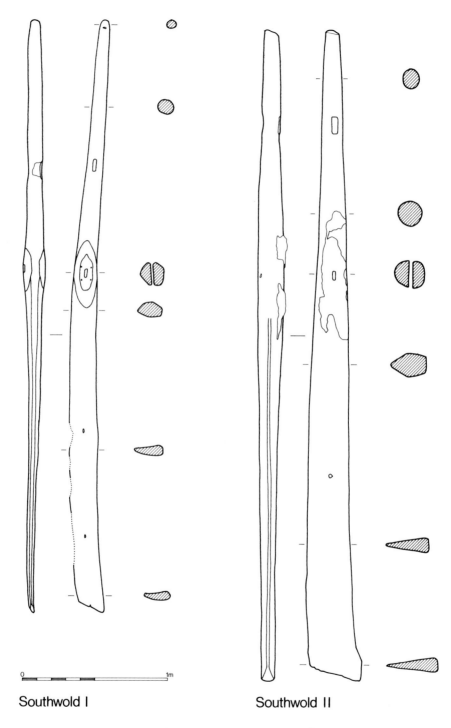

Southwold I   Southwold II

Figure 3.3 The two side rudders found at Southwold, Suffolk (National Maritime Museum).

Bergen were made in two parts, with a narrow extension attached to the afterside of the blade (Christensen, 1985: 152–6, 229). The 4.1 metre long Rebæek rudder, an undated find from Kolding Fjord in Denmark (Sølver, 1946), has traces of a similar feature. They may have been made this way because the size of the parent log was not sufficient to allow them to be made in one piece, or perhaps rudders were fine tuned to match the performance of the ship they had to steer. The side rudder trawled up from the sea-bed off Rye, East Sussex, mentioned above, has no holes either for the tiller or for attachment to the ship (Marsden, 1992: 126–7). It is possible, therefore, that it was not completed. Its blade is rather narrow and it may have been intended to have a supplementary piece joined to it.

Supporting a rudder on two or more pairs of fittings on a stern post is a strong arrangement which would minimise the potentially disastrous risk of losing or breaking the steering gear at sea. Fittings similar to a type of medieval door hinge were used, consisting of gudgeons and pintles. Pintles, cylindrical bars projecting down from iron straps, were attached to the leading edge of the rudder and fitted into the gudgeons, sockets within iron bands which were bent round into a U-shape and fastened to the stern post. Iron bands were also used for strapping together large rudder blades made of several slabs of wood. The rudder of the ship depicted on the *Luttrell Psalter* of about 1335–40, shown in figure 3.4, looks very much like a door, with elaborate ironwork. Rudder gudgeons have been found on the Bremen cog (Lahn, 1992: 110) and with the medieval vessel excavated at Vigsø in Denmark (Crumlin-Pedersen, 1979: 22–3). The lower part of a rudder was recovered from the possibly fifteenth-century ship found at Sandwich, Kent (Trussler, 1974: 168). The base of the rudder was shod with iron and shows that the stern post was raked at an angle of 117 degrees. A pintle and gudgeon were preserved 82cm above the baseline, with the positions of two others above it, at intervals of about a metre.

In addition to the side rudder already mentioned, a medieval stern rudder has been found in Rye Bay (Marsden, 1992: 127). The heartwood in this rudder has been radiocarbon dated to about 1315–1405 ad. The rudder was approximately 4.6 metres long, substantially complete, and has a fitting for the tiller at its head. The tiller on a stern rudder could be set so that it swung above the top of the stern post. Contemporary pictures also show ships with high stern posts equipped with curved tillers reaching around them.

Hulks, which did not have straight projecting stern posts, presented problems in fitting a stern centreline rudder. Several French fourteenth-century pictures show rudders like broad sweeps extending from the sterns of hulks. Figure 3.5 shows the junction between the blade and the tiller which protrudes from an aperture at the base of the stern castle. The pivot point of this type of rudder must have been on the tiller itself. In 1340 records of the Board of Customs in Holland referred to 'ships without hangroeder' (Arenhold, 1911: 298). 'Hangroeder' has been taken to mean 'side rudder' but it may refer to this type of hulk stern rudder instead. It appears that the area of connection between the long unsupported blade and the tiller would have been subject to great strain.

Round-sterned ships were adapted to have straight stern posts, with the area in the angle between the stern post and the keel filled by solid timber

Figure 3.4 Cog with a stern rudder from the *Luttrell Psalter*, c.1335–40 (BL Add 42130, f. 161v. By permission of the British Library).

Figure 3.5 Two-masted hulk from a fourteenth-century French manuscript (photo: Bibliothèque Nationale, Paris. Ms Fr. 101, f.349).

termed the 'deadwood'. This had a beneficial effect on a ship's performance as it reduced turbulence in the flow of water to the rudder. The fifteenth-century Mataro model has an almost vertical stern post with a large area of deadwood leading up to it. The rudder is clearly differentiated into a narrow stock and wider blade, with the bottom of the leading edge protected by the skeg projecting from the after end of the keel (figure 4.9). The tiller extends almost as far forward as the mainmast to provide as much mechanical advantage as possible when turning the rudder. The problem of how to manage the weight of an unbalanced rudder was not solved until the whip-staff was invented in the sixteenth century.

Rigging and sails

The only complete medieval mast yet found is a probably fourteenth-century example from Bryggen, Bergen. It is 7.50 metres in length with a diameter, which does not vary a great deal, of about 12.5cm, suggesting that it is from a boat not much more than 11 metres long (Christensen, 1985: 132, 138). Near its top the mast has a shoulder to prevent the standing rigging from slipping down. Just below this is the hole for the halyard, the rope which was used to raise the yard. A bone bar was set across the lower part of the halyard hole, to help the rope to run smoothly and to reduce wear on the mast, which was made of softwood.

The mast of the *Grace Dieu* was said to be 200 feet (nearly 61 metres) high and seven feet (2.13 metres) in diameter at the deck (Friel, 1993: 17). The great size of the mast means that it must have been of composite construction. The mast of the Woolwich ship, which may have been the *Sovereign* of 1488, shows how composite masts could be made. It consisted of a spindle of pine surrounded by baulks of oak bound together with iron bands (figure 2.13). The diameter was 1.32 metres (Salisbury, 1961: 85). 'Wooldings' or rope bindings around masts begin to appear on pictures of large ships in the fourteenth century.

In vessels which did not have fixed decking amidships the mast could be lowered and supported on a mast crutch. Mast crutches, sometimes referred to as 'mykes', are Y-shaped, cut from forks of timber. Two large mast crutches have been found in contexts dating to around 1200 on the Dublin waterfront (McGrail, 1993a: 104, 109). They could have held masts of 75cm and 85cm. Smaller mast crutches have been found at Newcastle (O'Brien *et al.*, 1988: 104–6) and at the Poole Foundry site (Hutchinson, 1994: 29, 33).

Yards, the wooden spars onto which the sails were laced, are not surprisingly elusive in the archaeological record. Broken or redundant ones could be put to other uses or burnt as firewood and those on shipwrecks would most probably be washed away. The same applies to bowsprits, which seem to have been introduced in the thirteenth century to provide an attachment point for a line led forward from the windward edge of the sail. They supplemented but did not replace 'luffs' which were poles used to brace the 'tack', the windward bottom corner, of the sail. The yard was held against the mast by a parrel, a U-shaped piece of wood with a hole towards each end for the bindings to the yard. The dimensions of the inside of the curve of the parrel can give some indication of the size of the mast. Two parrels, predating 1200, excavated on the Dublin waterfront, were from ships with masts less than 50cm in diameter (McGrail, 1993a: 77). Rope parrels with wooden beads threaded on them to act as rollers to reduce friction as the yard was raised were in use by the beginning of the fourteenth century. One is depicted in a French manuscript of 1307 (Villain-Gandossi, 1979: 217). By the fifteenth century parrels with several rows of beads, spaced by strips of wood termed 'parrel ribs', appear in pictures of large ships. Parrel assemblies of this type have been recovered from the stores of the *Mary Rose*, which sank in 1545 (Rule, 1982: 140–41, 145).

The 'standing' or fixed rigging of a sailing ship consisted of stays, which supported the mast longitudinally, and shrouds, which supported it laterally. The forestay, running between the bow and the top of the mast, prevented it from tipping back. One or more backstays from the masthead to the stern counteracted much of the force of the wind in the sail. The halyard, used to haul up the yard and sail, could also be led aft and made fast as an additional backstay. Holes for the shrouds are sometimes found on the excavated remains of the upper parts of the sides of boats and ships. The Bremen cog had a wale treenailed to the outside of the planking with 14 holes drilled through it for rigging. Remains of rope were found in all of them (Lahn, 1992: 109). From at least as early as the fifteenth century, shrouds could be set up on chains, as accounts and inventories for English royal ships show (Friel, 1993: 9). As a result, the parts of the side of a ship where the shrouds were attached came to be termed the 'chains', 'chain wale' and 'channelling'. Wooden blocks called 'deadeyes' were used for tensioning the shrouds. The 'running' rigging is that used to hoist and control the sails. The principal elements of the rigging are marked in figure 3.6 on a photograph of a bench-end from the Chapel of St Nicholas, King's Lynn. The carving was probably carried out during the rebuilding of the Chapel which was completed in 1419.

Viking Age ships in Scandinavia used woollen sails and rope made from lime bast and walrus hide. It is possible that hemp rope and canvas sailcloth were in use in Britain from the beginning of the medieval period but there were some reversions to earlier practices for specific purposes or for local craft. For example, the galley *La Phelipe* built at Lynn in 1336 had walrus hide cords for the parrel (Tinniswood, 1949: 308) and woollen sails were used in Kent in the late fifteenth century (Fenwick, 1978: 251).

From the thirteenth century or earlier, shipbuilding timber and hemp and flax for cordage and sails were imported to supplement indigenous supplies. The rope industry at Bridport was active from before 1200 and in the fourteenth and fifteenth centuries Bridport supplied the ships of Plymouth and Southampton (Lane-Poole, 1956). Much of the flax brought from Ireland and landed at Bristol may have been destined for the Bridport rope and sail industry. Some cordage also came from the Baltic. In 1226 there was a market at Lothingland near Great Yarmouth selling nets and rope (Salzman, 1931: 136). Cordage has been recovered from thirteenth-century contexts at Newcastle, including a thick three-ply cord of vegetable fibre and a thick, eight-strand plait of hair (Walton, 1988: 80–81). The hair rope has strands of different pigments and compares with braided ropes found at Bergen, worked from black and white goat-hair yarn.

It is known that Brittany canvas was brought back with cargoes of salt from the Bay of Bourgneuf (Bridbury, 1955: 82); but evidence for sails in medieval Britain so far comes only from documentary and pictorial sources. Shipbuilding accounts sometimes specify the quantities of canvas bought for a sail but uncertainty about the size of the 'ell', used to measure the cloth, and the possibility that the cloth was used in double thickness create problems in interpretation (Anderson, 1976: 48–50). When sailing in strong winds vessels have to reduce their sail area to maintain stability. In the earlier part of the medieval period this was done by reefing: taking a tuck in the sail using short cords or ties, called 'reef points', sewn into it. This literally shortens the sail to reduce its area and also allows the yard to be lowered down the mast, so that the wind exerts less leverage or heeling force on the vessel. Reef points are shown on seals from the twelfth century (Brindley, 1912: 130). In the mid-fourteenth century a new approach to changing the sail area was adopted for large ships. Instead of reducing the area of a large sail when the wind became too strong, ships carried extra strips of sail, called 'bonnets' which could be laced to the foot of the sail in light wind conditions.

Figure 3.6 The rigging of the ship on the King's Lynn bench end, *c.*1415–20 (National Maritime Museum).

1. main topmast
2. topcastle
3. lift (uptie)
4. parrel
5. brace (yard rope)
6. mizzen topcastle
7. mizzen mast
8. mizzen yard
9. lateen sail

10. backstays
11. shrouds with ratlines
12. stern castle
13. rudder
14. gadds
15. standard staff
16. mainmast
17. lift (uptie)
18. main yard

19. brace (yard rope)
20. forestay
21. bowsprit
22. fore castle
23. hawse hole
24. stem post
25. wale
26. through-beam end

Sailing and rig

Square sails are so-called not just on account of their shape but because they are rigged so that, when the wind is not acting on the sails, the yard and sail hang at right angles (or square on) to the long axis of the vessel. The sails are symmetrical about the vertical axis and either side can become the leading edge depending on the vessel's heading in relation to the wind. By contrast, fore-and-aft sails – for example, modern yacht sails and the lateen sails of medieval Mediterranean ships – are set along the length of the vessel. They have one leading edge and a trailing edge and are usually asymmetrical. In sailing, the plane of a square sail and its yard are turned to make best use of the wind. It is a misconception that the sails of medieval ships acted simply like windbags and were only useful for propelling ships downwind. By leading one edge of the sail forward to the stem post and sheeting the other aft, the sail could behave in the same way as a fore-and-aft sail. When the wind meets a sail at an angle, it is forced to change its direction. A deflected air flow forms around the curved surfaces of the sail, with a different speed and pressure on its two sides. The pressure on the windward side increases while the pressure on the leeward side decreases, so that the sail is being both pushed and sucked along at the same time. The suction, or forward, side of the sail is in fact much more effective than the pressure side and it yields the greater part of the driving force. It is this which makes it possible for a sailing vessel to make progress to windward by 'tacking' or zig-zagging towards the wind. Sea trials with replicas of Viking ships have shown that they can sail a course at approximately 55 degrees from the wind direction. Leeway, the effect of the wind and swell pushing the vessel sideways, means that the course made good is about 60 degrees from the wind. At this angle the vessel has to sail twice the actual distance as the crow flies (Andersen, 1986). Oared warships and small merchant vessels could use oars as auxiliary power to make progress against head winds. The use of oars will be discussed further in Chapter 9.

Sailing experiments with replicas of excavated vessels are providing much useful new data about the performance and the practical aspects of handling medieval ships (Crumlin-Pedersen and Vinner, 1986). Figure 3.7 shows the replica of the Bremen cog built in Kiel in 1990, during trials of a low-aspect ratio sail with one bonnet laced on.

Cogs generally had their masts stepped further forward than other ship types. The early thirteenth-century Kollerup cog (Andersen, 1983) is the most extreme example, with the mast about one-third of the ship's length from the stem (figure 3.8). The hull of a vessel has a theoretical pivot point, called the centre of lateral resistance, which is in the middle of the submerged mass of the hull and so normally located about half way along the keel. The force of the wind on the sails is transmitted to the hull primarily through the mast. The effect of having the mast stepped forward of the centre of lateral resistance is that wind pressure on the sail will make the ship tend to turn away from the wind. The rudder has to be turned at a considerable angle to correct this tendency, which is termed 'lee-helm'. It can also make it difficult to tack; that is, to change course by turning the head of the vessel through the eye of the wind. If the mast is stepped aft of the centre of lateral

Figure 3.7 The Kiel replica of the Bremen cog undergoing sea trials (photo: Jochen Sachse).

resistance, wind on the sail will make the ship tend to turn its bows towards the wind unless it is constantly corrected by the rudder. This is known as 'weather-helm'. Excessive lee-helm or weather-helm can both lead to the dangerous situation of being 'taken aback', with the wind blowing against the wrong side of the sail and driving the ship stern-first downwind.

Large ships became equipped with two masts in the mid-fourteenth century. Some had a mizzen mast stepped near the stern; others had a

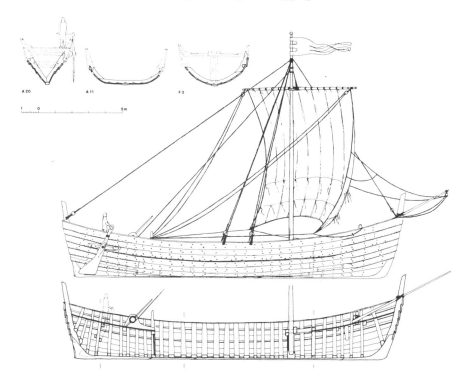

Figure 3.8 Reconstruction drawing of the Kollerup cog (P.K. Andersen).

foremast. The Pizzigani chart of 1367 shows a *cocha* or early carrack with a square-rigged mainsail and a lateen-rigged mizzen (figure 2.10). The earliest two-masted ship in the English royal fleet was a carrack, probably Genoese, acquired in about 1410. By 1420 the Crown had 13 two-masters, many of them foreign-built carracks but including at least five English-built ships (Friel, 1983a: 132). The single-masted rig is the most efficient way of producing propulsive power, as sails always interfere with the wind-flow on each other, but there were important advantages in dividing the sail plan. Increases in the size and weight of the single mast, yard and sail required more and stronger rigging to hold up the mast, control the yard and adjust the sail, also placing great strain on the central part of the keel. Far more importantly, the addition of extra masts aided steering. When a ship turns, it pivots about its centre of lateral resistance, a point roughly half-way along its keel. A sail set on a mast stepped at one end or the other of the keel will exert a strong turning force when the wind blows against it. Most two-masted ships appear to have had a square mainsail and a fore-and-aft lateen mizzen at the stern, the typical carrack rig at the beginning of the fifteenth century. Others, including a high proportion of hulk types, had the square mainsail with a little square foresail. Pictorial evidence suggests that the foresail was used on hulks rather than cogs.

Figure 3.9 shows the effect of the addition of fore and mizzen sails during

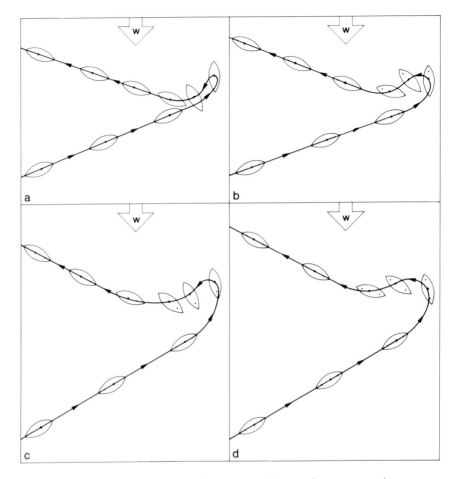

Figure 3.9 Diagram to show the effect of the addition of masts on tacking
performance: (a) single-masted vessel; (b) vessel with mainmast and mizzen; (c) vessel
with mainmast and foremast; (d) three-masted ship (National Maritime Museum).

the manoeuvre of tacking, when a ship is beating its way to windward.
When tacking a single-masted, square-rigged ship (figure 3.9a) the rudder is
put hard over to bring the head of the ship into the wind. The sail is then
backed, to bring the head round onto the new tack. This has the effect of
driving the ship astern until it has turned sufficiently for the sail to be swung
quickly around and set on the other side of the ship. This is the dangerous
stage of the operation. If the tack is executed smoothly the sail fills with
wind and the ship gathers speed on the other tack. If it is not, the ship can
be swept helplessly down wind, at best losing a lot of ground and at worst
foundering on a lee shore.

The addition of a foresail (figure 3.9b) does little to increase the speed of
the ship but it does make tacking more reliable. By backing the foresail the
head of the ship can be turned quickly and the foresail can maintain the
ship's heading while the mainsail is swung around. Adding a lateen mizzen

Figure 3.10 Sketch of a three-masted ship on a Catalan manuscript of 1406 (Archivo Municipal Barcelona. Photo: L.V. Mott).

to the square mainsail (figure 3.9c) improves the windward performance of a ship and allows it to sail a little closer to the wind. On the approach to the tack the turning force of the mizzen can thrust the head of the ship through the wind but it does not help during the crucial manoeuvre of swinging the mainsail round. Rigging a ship with all three masts (figure 3.9d) optimises windward ability and provides the potential for efficient tacking.

The depiction of a three-masted ship shown in figure 3.10 is the earliest identified so far. This sketch comes from a Catalan manuscript dated 1406 (Mott, 1994). The new rig was adopted all over Europe by the middle decades of the fifteenth century. A three-masted ship is depicted on a Norwegian calendar stick for 1457 (figure 4.4). It has been suggested that examination of the *Peter* of La Rochelle in Gdańsk in 1462 led to the rapid adoption of three-masted carvel ships in the eastern Baltic (van der Merwe, 1983: 121). Further development followed rapidly. The foresail and the lateen mizzen were made larger. The mizzen in particular increased to such a size that it could provide considerable propulsive force when sailing to windward. Two new sails were introduced between about 1450 and 1470, the spritsail and the main-topsail. The spritsail was a square sail set from a yard supported by the bowsprit. Although it was small it could exert significant leverage and might have helped to balance the enlarged mizzen sail. The topsail was set at the head of the mainmast and operated in the relatively undisturbed air flows high above the ship. It provided extra driving power and helped to lift the bows, counteracting the depressing effect of the spritsail (McGowan, 1981: 13–14). Inventories of Henry VII confirm that these sails were in use in 1485 and that large ships already had a fore-topsail and a fourth mast, behind the mizzen (Oppenheim, 1896).

By combining the carvel-built hull with the three- (or more) masted rig, a ship-type had been created which was not, unlike all those before it, a regional product. It represented a fusion of technology and, with local variations of detail, was built and used all over Europe.

4 *British horizons, foreign ships*

Shipping is essentially international and throughout the Middle Ages ships of many different regions and shipbuilding traditions rubbed up against each other in harbours all over Europe. The interchange intensified as the volume of trade and the length of trading voyages increased. The following survey sketches in the context of maritime contact between Britain and the other regions of Europe, the flow of trade and the impact of war. Against this background the seagoing ships belonging to the various regions are described. The map (figure 4.1) shows places mentioned in the text.

Ireland

There were large fleets of ships in Ireland before the Norman invasion in 1169–70, notably those of the Ostmen, the Hiberno-Norse of Dublin and Wexford. In the eleventh century there was trade between Dublin and the ports of Bristol and Chester. This included the export of English slaves to Ireland. By the first half of the twelfth century there was substantial seaborne trade between England and Ireland. Ireland also imported wine from Poitou and Bordeaux in exchange for hides and pelts.

Henry II granted Dublin 'to his men of Bristol' in 1171–72, probably in recognition that the economies of Bristol and Dublin were mutually important already. In 1174 the King granted Dublin freedom from toll, passage and custom throughout the King's realms and this was a considerable stimulus to trade. These privileges were later extended to other Irish ports. Customs records for the period 1171 to 1250 show a predominance of food exports, especially cereals. Wheat and oats, beans, cheese and bacon are listed.

Excavations along the medieval waterfront in Dublin, between 1962 and 1981, revealed a large number of timbers from boats and ships of the tenth to thirteenth centuries (McGrail, 1993a). Although it is not possible to reconstruct any one of these vessels in detail, it is clear that they were built in the keel tradition and their features are closely paralleled in contemporary Scandinavian boats and ships. Three individual vessels can be recognised from the groups of hull planking: TG10, a late eleventh-century boat; TG9 with TG6, a late twelfth-century large ship (figure 4.2); and TG3, a thirteenth-century large ship (McGrail, 1993a: 93). Tree ring studies have shown that the components which have been sampled match the Dublin master chronology. McGrail (1993a: 87) takes the view that the majority of the timbers were from boats and ships dismantled and reused close to the site where they were built. Some were unfinished, lacking fastening holes, and this supports the argument that there was a building yard close by. The size of vessel represented in the archaeological record increases over time. This may be partly accounted for by the fact that the vessels are from different sites, the later ones from Wood Quay and the earlier ones mostly from

Medieval ships and shipping

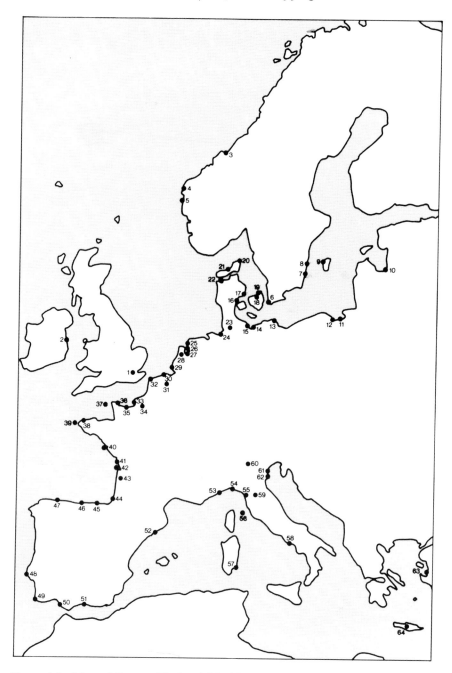

Figure 4.1 Map of Europe (National Maritime Museum).

Figure 4.1 Key

1. London	23. Hamburg	45. Bilbao
2. Dublin	24. Bremen	46. Santander
3. Trondheim	25. Staveren	47. San Sebastian
4. Korssund	26. Rutten	48. Lisbon
5. Bergen	27. Harderwijk	49. Cape St Vincent
6. Skanor	28. Amsterdam	50. Cadiz
7. Kalmar	29. Vlaardingen	51. Malaga
8. Oskarshamn	30. Sluys	52. Barcelona
9. Visby	31. Tournai	53. Villefranche
10. Riga	32. Calais	54. Genoa
11. Elbląg	33. Harfleur	55. Pisa
12. Gdańsk	34. Rouen	56. Elba
13. Stralsund	35. Caen	57. Cavoli
14. Wismar	36. Barfleur	58. Amalfi
15. Lübeck	37. Guernsey	59. Florence
16. Kolding	38. Aber Wrac'h	60. Lake Garda
17. Kyholm	39. Ushant	61. Venice
18. Skuldelev	40. Bourgneuf Bay	62. Contarina
19. Vejby	41. La Rochelle	63. Foçea
20. The Skaw	42. Oléron	64. Crete
21. Kollerup	43. Bordeaux	
22. Limfjord	44. Bayonne	

Fishamble Street. These waterfront areas may have had different functions and different mooring facilities. The largest timbers, from the late twelfth or early thirteenth century, may have belonged to ships in the region of 25 metres long (McGrail, 1993a: 16).

Between 1171 and 1250 contemporary documentary sources distinguish two types of vessel in Dublin: namely, 'navis' (ships) and galleys. Galleys were built at Dublin for the English kings in the thirteenth century. In 1306 it was stated that no fully laden 'great ship' could reach the port of Dublin; they had to be partly unloaded at Dalkey. Irish ships from Dublin, Waterford, Drogheda and Limerick, arriving in foreign ports from the early fourteenth century, were recorded as 'cog', 'navis', 'nef' or simply ship. There are records of cogs being built in Ireland in the fourteenth century. In later medieval documents Irish merchants are recorded as owning hulks, barges, *balingers* and *pickards* (de Courcy Ireland, 1989a; 1989b).

By the end of the fifteenth century, Ireland was thoroughly integrated into European trade. The most active ports were Waterford, Ross, Drogheda, Galway, Limerick, Dublin, Youghal, Cork, Kinsale, Carrickfergus, Arklow and Wexford. They traded with Seville and Lisbon, the Galician ports, Bordeaux, Brittany, Normandy, Bruges, Antwerp, Hamburg, Lübeck, Gdańsk, Reykjavik, Chester, Liverpool, Wales, Cornwall, Bristol, Bridgwater and western Scotland. More Irish ships than English were involved in trade with Chester and Bristol (Childs, 1982). Irish exports included fish, hides and leather, woolfells, woollen cloth and cloaks, yarn, tallow, linen yarn, timber, grain, livestock and re-exported French and Iberian wine. Imports included wine, honey, iron, manufactured items such as knives and weapons, tin, nails, spices, silk clothing, soap, hops, salt, and (a new and increasing

Figure 4.2 Remains of a large late twelfth-century ship from the Dublin waterfront (National Maritime Museum).

import) coal. During the fifteenth century, flotillas of Wexford-built cotts carried fish to Bridgwater and imported coal from Wales. Each cott carried from eight to ten tons of coal (O'Neill, 1987).

Norway

The traffic between the North Sea ports and Norway was established before the Conquest. According to tradition, Bergen was founded about 1070 and it rapidly became one of the largest medieval ports of northern Europe. Artefacts traded from England have been found in the earliest layers. In the twelfth century Norway had active seaborne contact with Britain and Germany. King Sverri made a speech in Bergen in 1186 comparing the merits of German and English traders. The Germans brought wine in such quantities 'that it was no dearer than ale' and took away butter and dried fish. By contrast, traders from England, Orkney, Shetland, the Faroes and Iceland brought useful products: wheat, honey, flour, cloth, linen, flax, wax and cauldrons. After the fire which destroyed much of Bergen in 1198, English pottery gains predominance in the archaeological record, taking over from continental imports (Herteig, 1959: 182–4). In the thirteenth century, England supplied grain to Norway in return for dried fish, whale oil and falcons, hawks and furs. The Hanse was also supplying grain to Norway and there was a triangular trade: grain was shipped from Lübeck to Bergen, cod from Bergen to Boston in Lincolnshire, and cloth from Boston to Lübeck. Nedkvitne (1977 and 1985) has written extensively about medieval trade between Norway and England.

In the rebuilding and extension of the wharf which followed a fire at Bergen in 1248, ships' timbers were reused as building materials. They provide important evidence for the type of large trading vessel used in early thirteenth-century Norway. Christensen (1985) has demonstrated that many of the timbers came from one very large ship which was perhaps quite new when it was broken up. The timbers show little wear or use and fire damage to a deckbeam and other components suggests that the vessel may have been a casualty of the 1248 blaze. The use of pine and some similarities with other finds, such as the thirteenth-century Norwegian Sjøvøllen boat (Christensen, 1968), suggest that it was built in Norway. The principal component found was the keelson (figure 4.3). It is 12.5 metres long, made of two pieces scarfed together, and it has notches on its underside for 27 floor timbers spaced about 50cm apart. Parts of 19 cross-beams from just above the keelson were also recovered. The cross-beams sat closely above the floor timbers with the keelson in between, to give a very strong bottom to the hull. The keel would have given the bottom a sharp profile, unlike a cog. One deck cross-beam with rabbets for deck-boards was recovered and also the drum of the massive windlass, 5.40 metres long with a diameter of about 50 cms, for raising the mast, yard and anchor. Fragments of at least two other ships of comparable size were found at the Bryggen, represented by cross-beams with protruding heads.

Christensen estimates the minimum total length of the vessel to have been around 30 metres, with a maximum beam of between nine and ten metres

Figure 4.3   The keelson of the 'big ship' from Bryggen, Bergen (Bryggens Museum).

and depth in hold of about three to five metres. This would provide a
minimum cargo space of 165 cubic metres (Christensen, 1985: 182;
Christensen, 1989: 18–19). The larger trading ship from Skuldelev had
about 30 cubic metres of cargo space in the hold and this may serve to
illustrate the increase in trade between the eleventh and the thirteenth
centuries. It also goes to show that cogs were not the only large cargo
carriers trading to the north. Ships built in the Scandinavian keel tradition
could be of equal or larger capacity.

The Isle of Man and the Western and Northern Isles of Scotland were part
of the kingdom of Norway. In 1266 Norway rented Man and the Western
Isles to the Scots but the Northern Isles continued to owe allegiance to
Norway until the fifteenth century (Mitchison, 1970: 33, 76). The
shipbuilding tradition of north Britain was Nordic and timber for building
ships was imported from Norway.

At the end of the thirteenth century Norway surrendered control over
shipping to the Hanse. The Bergen trade fell largely into the hands of Lübeck
grain merchants. Customs accounts, which use 'buss' as the usual term for a
Norwegian cargo vessel, show that trade with England continued.

A Norwegian wooden calendar staff for 1457 (figure 4.4) has pictures of
four different large ships incised on it. The clearest of them is very likely to
be the earliest precisely dated three-masted ship representation known from
northern Europe. Leibgott (1973) has postulated that the calendar may have
belonged to a seafaring merchant.

Figure 4.4 One of the four ships carved on a Norwegian calendar staff for 1457 (Copenhagen, National Museum).

The Hanse, the Danish peninsula and the Baltic

From the early thirteenth century the trade of northern Europe was dominated by the Hanse. Hamburg and Lübeck controlled the ends of the overland transit route across the base of the Danish peninsula and in the early thirteenth century these towns formed an alliance with other trading towns of northern Germany and the North and Baltic Sea coasts. This became known as the Hanse or Hanseatic League and its function was to co-ordinate the commercial initiatives and protect the interests of its members. By organising in this way, the Hanseatic towns were able to defeat outside competition. For example, at the beginning of the thirteenth century Denmark had looked set to predominate in Baltic trade but the rise of the Hanse effectively put a stop to that (Unger, 1980: 162) and Hanseatic trade in the Baltic expanded strongly between 1250 and 1300.

The overland route from the North Sea to the Baltic, by way of Hamburg and Lübeck, was of crucial importance in the twelfth and thirteenth centuries, as trading ships seldom risked the dangerous passage around the Skaw at the north of Denmark. In the Viking period, ships had avoided the Skaw by sailing through the sheltered waters of the Limfjord which cuts through the Danish promontory near its tip. However, in the twelfth century, while ships were increasing in size, the Limfjord was silting up and it eventually ceased to function as a through channel (Crumlin-Pedersen, 1972: 190).

The Baltic area exported grain, iron, copper, silver and lead, timber, tar and pitch, furs, hemp, flax, wax and fish. In return it obtained wool and cloth, manufactured goods, wine and salt. French salt was needed to supplement local supplies for the extremely important Baltic herring trade. By 1262 tolls were levied on salt from the Bay of Bourgneuf at the transhipment point at Hamburg. The 1292 shipping law of Hamburg concerns journeys to La Rochelle for wine and salt. By the end of the thirteenth century, English, Flemish and Frisian ships were shut out of the Baltic. From 1294 Norway, defeated by a Hanse blockade, conceded the right to carry all trade from ports south of Bergen. By 1300 the Hanse had reached a peak of prosperity and control over northern trade.

The cog was the principal type of ship in use in the region. As early as 1197 German cogs went to rescue Christian prisoners from Beirut (Scammell, 1981: 77). This, incidentally, puts Villani's statement that cogs made their first appearance in the Mediterranean in 1304 into perspective (see page 41). Town seals dating to the first half of the thirteenth century from Elbląg, Staveren and Wismar and from the second half of the century those of Harderwijk, Stralsund and Gdańsk, show ships with high sides, straight stem and stern posts, stern rudders and no castles (Ewe, 1972). Castles make their first appearance on the town seals from 1300 onwards.

Several cog-finds dating to the thirteenth century have been found around Denmark and in the Baltic. The cog found at Kollerup on the northwest coast of Jutland (page 59) may have been attempting to make its way into the Limfjord when it was wrecked (Crumlin-Pedersen, 1979: 27–31; Møller, 1980). The Kollerup cog is narrow (about six metres) in relation to its length (about 22 metres) and its mast is stepped very far forward (figures 1.14 and

3.8). The cargo space was about eight metres long with partitions fore and aft. The finds include a tally-stick and pottery. A cog found on the east coast of Sweden at Bossholmen near Oskarshamn has been dated by dendrochronology to the late thirteenth century (Cederlund, 1990; Adams, 1990). Its find-spot lies on the sailing route between Denmark and Estonia (Cederlund, 1989).

In the early fourteenth century there was vigorous trade between the Hanse and England. Hanse ships imported mixed cargoes, including timber from Gdańsk and some Rhenish wine, and exported cloth from Boston and other ports. English kings gave the Hanse privileges in exchange for loans (Scammell, 1981: 67).

Early in the fourteenth century, ships began to use the sea route around the Skaw into the Baltic (the 'Umlandfahrt') to avoid the delay and expense of transhipment at Hamburg. This caused the decline of the overland route and of Lübeck. From the mid-1300s the Germans were trading to Poitou and Gascony. By the late fourteenth century German merchants handled Polish surplus grain through Baltic ports, shipping wheat and – even more important – rye, as well as timber and herrings to urban centres of western Europe, especially in Flanders. To have a full load of back cargo they loaded salt (high volume but low value) at the Bay of Bourgneuf and cloth (high value but low volume) in Flanders. The Hanse Bay Fleet was inaugurated in the 1370s to import large quantities of Bourgneuf salt into the Baltic.

The cog of Bremen, already described (figures 1.13 and 3.7), sank in about 1380. At about the same time another cog was wrecked at Vejby, Denmark (figures 4.5 and 5.6). Coin evidence indicates that the Vejby cog was built in around 1350 in the Elbląg region and sank soon after 1377. Contents of the wreck suggest that it was voyaging from western Europe (see Chapter 5). This cog was originally between 16 and 18 metres long, with a beam of five to six metres. The bottom was flush-laid, with clinker sides above. The strakes were of sawn oak. Only the bottom of the ship, consisting of the outer planking, the floor timbers, the ceiling planking and the keelson, had survived (Crumlin-Pedersen, 1976; Crumlin-Pedersen, 1979: 24–9; Crumlin-Pedersen, 1985: 71–3).

By 1388 there was an English factory in Gdańsk, set up by English merchants whose aim was to secure in the Baltic privileges similar to those enjoyed by the Hanse in England. Meanwhile Hanse trade with western Europe was growing. In 1405 three Hanse ships sailed to Bruges with nearly 500,000 furs. In the fifteenth century, cloth made up 90 per cent of all German exports from England, 6,000 to 12,000 pieces a year (Scammell, 1981: 50–52). The salt trade with France was very important in the fifteenth century and in 1449 a major international incident occured when English privateers captured the Bay Fleet. This consisted of 60 Hanse ships and 50 from the Low Countries (Postan, 1933: 127–30). The fleet was intercepted between Guernsey and Portland and taken to the Isle of Wight (Hattendorf *et al.*, 1993: 30–31). The Low Countries ships and their contents were released but the privateers kept the Hanse property. The Hanse retaliated by confiscating English merchandise from the factory in Gdańsk. A truce was declared but English privateers captured the Bay Fleet again in 1458. Even this did not cause lasting disruption to trade, however, and in 1471 Edward

Figure 4.5 The Vejby cog on a raft, after being raised from the sea-bed (National Maritime Museum).

IV was restored to the throne with Hanseatic support and in 1474 a treaty signed with the Hanse led to confirmation of their rights in the steelyards at London, Boston and King's Lynn (Scammell, 1981: 49–67).

The wreck of the fifteenth-century trading ship Gdańsk W5, described in Chapter 2 and Chapter 5, provides some evidence for the measures that Hanse shipowners had to take to protect their vessels from piratical attack. Stone shot was recovered as well as cross-bow bolts, probably from the weapons of the crew, found between the frames (Smolarek, 1979: 62).

Low Countries

The development of the cloth industry in Flanders in the twelfth century created a surge in demand for English wool and prompted the rapid growth of sheep farming. The Flemings handled the shipping of much of the wool themselves, through a body of merchants known as the Flemish Hanse of London (Power, 1941: 53). Around 1200 Flanders was one of the most densely populated parts of Europe and relied heavily on imports for industrial raw materials and also for food. England and even Ireland, as well as north France and east Germany, supplied grain. The import of Flemish textiles into England rose slowly through the twelfth and thirteenth centuries and became significant before 1300. From 1269 trade between England and Flanders was intermittant, interrupted in the pursuit of foreign policy objectives. Cloth production was not Flanders' only source of prosperity, however, as by 1300 it had became an international money market and produce exchange. It dealt in wine from the Rhineland and Bordeaux, Biscay salt, Spanish iron, Baltic and oriental goods.

Some of the commerce of the Hanse flowed through the Netherlands. Goods from the eastlands completed their journey to Flanders along Dutch waterways to escape the hazards of the passage around the Skaw; those from the Rhine towns travelled down similar routes towards England. The north Netherlands became an essential part of the Hanseatic commercial empire, although the Dutch towns were excluded from formal membership (Scammell, 1981: 373–5). Town seals of the Low Countries from the thirteenth and early fourteenth centuries, including those of Staveren, Harderwijk, Damme and Vlaardingen, show cogs just like those of the Hanse Baltic towns.

Excavations in the Dutch polders during land reclamation have revealed the remains of several cogs. One found at Rutten (figure 4.6) in the Noordoostpolder, dated by pottery evidence to the late thirteenth century, has a bottom larger than that of the Bremen cog (Oosting, 1987). More than 30 medieval boats and ships have been found in the Ijsselmeer polders (Reinders, 1979; Reinders, 1985). Over half of them can be classified as cogs because of their structural features, including the plank keel, the stem and stern hooks, the planking of the hull and the caulking and fastening methods. The transverse and longitudinal stiffening varies according to the size of the vessels and the positioning of the mast may have been determined by their rigging and functional requirements.

During the fourteenth century the Low Countries increased their trade

Figure 4.6 The Rutten cog under excavation in the Noordoostpolder (photo: Centre for Ship Archaeology, Dronten, Netherlands).

with the Baltic and reduced that with France. War with France at the beginning of the century meant that Flanders came to depend on Baltic grain. The fourteenth century saw a decline in the Flemish cloth industry and English merchants moved into that market. At the same time Dutch towns developed a textile industry producing heavier, cheaper cloth better suited to the market and climate in the Baltic. Dutch merchants voyaged round the Skaw to the Scanian market rather than dealing with Hanseatic middlemen. In the later fourteenth century the Dutch were rivalling the Hanse carrying trade, with salt among their principal cargoes. In 1384 Dutch towns, which did not belong to the Hanse, were excluded from the Scanian market which caused them to deal directly with other Baltic ports.

The presence of English merchants in the Baltic in the fourteenth century had diverted Hanse attention from the more serious encroachment by the Dutch, who had effectively destroyed the Hanse monopoly of Europe's commerce with the Baltic by 1500. By 1498 Dutch-owned ships carried 50 per cent of the value of Gdańsk imports. In the 1440s the Dutch had started trading French and Portuguese salt into the Baltic, not just importing it for their own fisheries. As we have seen, nearly half of the Bay Fleet which was captured in 1449 was made up of ships from the Low Countries.

France

France is the country with which Britain had the most maritime contact during the Middle Ages. Even before the Conquest, tolls and imports show that there was a high level of cross-Channel trade with France as well as with the Rhineland. As a result of the Norman invasion there was constant traffic between the Norman landholders who had estates both in England and in France. Le Patourel (1976: 164) estimates that William the Conqueror made the Channel crossing about 17 times in the 21 years between his coronation and his death. At the beginning of the thirteenth century the Angevin kings of England held more than half of the land of present-day France. After the loss of Normandy in 1204 (and with it Anjou, Maine, Touraine and Poitou) and Brittany two years later, Bordeaux and Gascony, which were vitally important to England as a source of wine, remained subject to the English crown until 1453.

Northern France had by the eleventh century adopted Norman Viking shipbuilding techniques. It is possible that hulk-building was established earlier and that hulks continued to be developed as seagoing ships as well as inland craft. Thirteenth-century stained glass in Chartres and Nôtre Dame cathedrals depicts fishing vessels with characteristic hulk planking and a 1317 illustration of wine arriving at the port of Paris (figure 5.3) shows the barrels being transported in small hulks. There is very little evidence for the shipbuilding practices of the western and southern French coasts. It is possible that they were unaffected by Viking influence and continued Gallo-Roman traditions. Henry II's acquisition of Aquitaine in 1152 meant that there was a regular traffic of English-built ships to the south-west of France. The Association of Bayonne merchants controlled Biscay from the early thirteenth century despite a private war with the seamen of the ports of Normandy. It is unclear what their ships were like. However, for the last few years a watch has been kept on a wreck of about 1300 in the harbour of St Peter Port, Guernsey, which is suffering gradual erosion as a result of large vessels passing above it. The wreck has yet to be fully investigated but is about 30 metres long and has yielded large quantities of Saintonge pottery from the Bordeaux area of France (see page 99). This site has exciting potential for the study of medieval shipping and the Bordeaux wine trade.

Throughout the thirteenth and early fourteenth centuries the trade between Bordeaux and England remained the virtual monopoly of the Bayonnese, with Southampton and Bristol as the chief English centres of the Gascon wine trade. At its height, England imported more than 20,000 tuns of wine each year from Gascony, or about a quarter of the region's total export. The Hundred Years War between England and France, which began in 1336–37, had an immediate effect on the Gascon trade, reducing exports of wine to less than a quarter of previous levels (James, 1971: 15). It appears that the volume of trade picked up after the first few years of the war. In the 1350s and 1360s Gascony was still a major market for the expanding English cloth industry. Because Gascony produced wine to the neglect of other agricultural products some foodstuffs had to be imported. In the 1370s English ships took food to Bordeaux and Bayonne and in 1372 Froissart recorded the arrival of 200 British and Irish ships. Ships sailed in convoy, that is to say, they were sailed in organised groups under escort of armed ships (Waters, 1957: 1–3) and this lasted until 1500 in the case of the salt fleets from Bourgneuf Bay.

Despite the Hundred Years War, trade between Britain and France continued, often handled by neutral middlemen. For example, in 1367 stone for Rochester Castle was brought from Caen and in 1414 Nottingham alabaster was being exported for the Abbot of Fécamp (Salzman, 1923: 87, 97). The loss of Gascony to the French king in 1453 created problems with safe conducts for English ships and much of the handling trade went to foreign merchants.

After the loss of Normandy and Brittany, the ports of Rouen and La Rochelle were developed as bases for the French royal fleet. The *clos des galées* was established at Rouen in 1293 for the construction, repair and storage of war galleys which were intended to control the Channel and the route to Gascony (Rieth, 1989). The galleys were carvel-built of Genoese design but clinker-built Norman barges and galleys up to 30 metres long with oars and a square sail were also constructed there. It was of considerable importance during the Hundred Years War, until destroyed by fire in 1419 (Sumption, 1990: 156–7). The French also boosted their seapower by hiring contract fleets of Italian galleys and carracks.

Medieval depictions of French ships show a considerable variety of hull shapes (see, for example, Villain-Gandossi, 1978; 1979). A large number of them have hulk features and there are very few cogs. The only medieval clinker-built ship to have been excavated in France has been dated by coins on board to the first half of the fifteenth century. The wreck was found in 1985 at the Aber Wrac'h river mouth on the north coast of Brittany (figure 4.7). The tree ring curves obtained from the ship's oak planking best match those from south-west France or the north coast of Spain (L'Hour and Veyrat, 1989). Ten metres of the beech keel remained, with a detached oak stem preserved to a length of 2.5 metres. Parts of 24 oak clinker strakes, 23cm wide and 3cm thick, were preserved on the port side. The vessel had heavy frames, 15cm to 25cm wide, closely spaced. The depth of the frames at keel level is 25cm, decreasing to 15cm. There were at least 52 frames on each side as well as the six cant timbers piled up in the lower part of the wreck. About half of the second futtocks were fitted before the lower ones so

Figure 4.7 The Aber Wrac'h wreck (M. L'Hour – photo: Frederic Osada).

that their upper ends were correctly positioned to support the cross-beams. On the outside of the hull the cross-beam heads were protected by cone-shaped pieces of wood, made of elm and alder, fitted in front of the beam with their tips pointing towards the stem. Part of the mast-step support was preserved. Ceiling planking was treenailed through the frames to the outer planking, up to the turn of the bilge. The thicker ceiling planks were in effect stringers, joggled over the frames, and thicker stringers were located higher up in the hull.

The excavators estimate that the overall length of the ship was about 25 metres with a maximum beam of eight metres. They have suggested a link with the documented wreck of an English-owned ship which sank when entering the Aber Wrac'h river in 1435 (L'Hour and Veyrat, 1989: 298).

Atlantic Iberia

By the end of the eleventh century and the beginning of the twelfth century, Normans were using Iberian north-western ports during their involvement in the Crusades. Chronicle evidence suggests that at the same time Saracen raids from Seville and other southern ports were ravaging the Galician shore. The first Archbishop of Compostela sent to Italian cities for shipwrights. In 1115 two galleys were built by Genoese craftsmen for the defence of Galicia and another was built in 1120 under the direction of a Pisan (Filgueiras, 1991). So by the mid-twelfth century, when Lisbon was captured from the Moors, seagoing ships of northern Spain and Portugal belonged to two different

Figure 4.8   Thirteenth-century town seal of San Sebastian (National Maritime Museum).

foreign traditions: northern European keels and Italian carvel-built galleys. Indigenous vessel types may only have survived in inland waters.

Early in the reign of Henry III (1216–72), England imported iron, hides and wine from northern Spain. During the thirteenth century Castilian kings achieved the reconquest of Andalusia and Murcia from the Moors and increased the range of Spain's export commodities to include Merino wool, fruits, olive oil, kermes dye, salt, sweet wines and mercury. These were shipped from Santander, Bilbao and San Sebastian (Childs, 1978). The oldest town seal of Santander, which predates 1228, depicts a ship of the northern keel-type, and the thirteenth-century seal of San Sebastian (figure 4.8) bears a remarkable similarity, both in image and in inscription, to the contemporary seals of the Cinque Ports, especially Pevensey, Winchelsea and Sandwich (figures 3.1 and 9.4). Documentary sources suggest that Southampton and London were the principal English ports visited by Spanish ships, on their way to Flanders. In 1263 Henry III granted protection to Spanish merchants visiting Southampton. It may have been the organisation of the Cinque Ports, along with their corporate identity, that the merchants of the Castilian ports were keen to emulate, since by the end of the thirteenth century they themselves had formed an association.

During the Hundred Years War, Castilians were among the privateers attacking English ships. In 1350 a Castilian trading fleet was attacked by an English fleet as it sailed out from the harbour at Sluys in Flanders. The Spaniards lost 14 ships. This battle, which became known as 'Les Espagnols sur Mer' is described in a contemporary chronicle. Unfortunately this gives us no information about the appearance of the Spanish ships other than that they were larger than the English ones.

From the thirteenth century England also had close trading connections with Portugal, which was a source of olive oil, kermes dye, wine, fruit and salt. By the 1300s Portuguese ships were voyaging both to the Canaries and to the English Channel.

In Portugal by the early fifteenth century an apparently new family of ships, termed 'carvels', was developed. This may have been motivated by the voyages of exploration down the Atlantic coast of Africa which by about 1420 had led to the discovery of Madeira and the Azores and by 1460 had reached as far south as Sierra Leone. Portuguese shipwrights built carvels in northern Europe from the 1430s (Paviot, 1991).

The earliest ship of southern European carvel construction so far found in British waters is the Studland Bay wreck. This ship, which sank near Poole in Dorset soon after 1520, has been identified as of Iberian origin. The ceramics found on the wreck were made in Malaga and Seville. The ballast contained stones which occur on the Atlantic coast of Iberia. The hull shape, fastenings and arrangement of the framing resemble that of several other Iberian 'discovery period' ships and the later sixteenth-century Basque wreck at Red Bay in Labrador (Hutchinson, 1991; Grenier, 1988).

Mediterranean Spain

By the early fourteenth century the Crown of Aragon, which included Catalonia, had become the foremost power in the Mediterranean, ruling all the islands as far east as Sicily, half of Italy and part of Greece. Its overseas trade, dominated from the beginning by Barcelona, encompassed an Atlantic trading route. From the fourteenth century, tin and wool were imported from England and textiles and fish from Flanders, in exchange for eastern spices and other southern produce. In the 1350s Aragon allied with the Venetians against Genoa and virtually destroyed the Genoese fleet. War with Genoa continued until the late fifteenth century. In 1378 the municipal authorities rebuilt the shipyard in Barcelona and it became the great shipbuilding centre of the western Mediterranean in the later Middle Ages (Bisson, 1991: 170).

The earliest closely-dated depiction of a three-masted ship has recently been discovered in the archives in Barcelona by Lawrence Mott (figure 3.10). It is a small ink drawing accompanying text dated 10 May 1409 in the *Llibre de les Ordinaciones de l'Administrador de les Places*, Folio 67R.

Figure 4.9 The Mataro ship model (Maritime Museum 'Prins Hendrik').

The votive ship model from Mataro (figure 2.9 and 4.9) of a substantial Catalan trading ship of the early fifteenth century has been described in Chapter 2. The 1.3 metre long model appears to have been two-masted originally, with mainmast and mizzen. A third mast was added at a later date, inserted through a hole crudely made in the foredeck (van Nouhuys, 1931: 343). Although recognising that this is not an exact scale model, de Groot (1984) has analysed the stability and carrying capacity of a ship 16, 18, 20 and 22 times its size. He calculated that a ship of this form would have to carry ballast equivalent to 20 per cent of its total displacement. On

Figure 4.10 A three-masted ship on a Hispano-Moresque bowl of about 1425 (Courtesy of the board of Trustees of the V&A).

this basis a Mataro-type ship 22 metres in overall length with a beam of 11 metres would have a total unladen weight of 246 tons and a maximum carrying capacity of 154 tons.

A wreck found off Cavoli, Sardinia, is that of a large Aragonese ship which sank in about 1450, probably during a voyage from Valencia to Sicily. The wreck is scattered and poorly preserved, with the oak planking surviving rather better than the pine frames. The ship was carrying at least 20 guns, apparently stored as ballast in the hold, and personal weapons as well as a mixed cargo including ceramics (Martin-Bueno, 1992; Martin-Bueno, 1993).

It is interesting that one of the earliest representations of a three-masted ship, that on a bowl now in the Victoria and Albert Museum and dated on stylistic grounds to about 1425 (figure 4.10), was probably manufactured in Malaga and was produced by Muslims living in medieval Europe. The ship is depicted with the arms of Portugal on the mainsail and can be assumed to belong to the southern European carvel-building tradition. Since Muslim

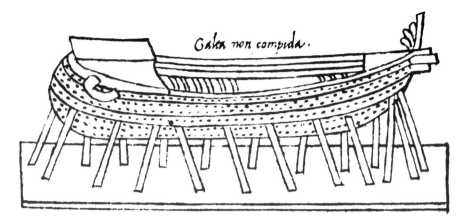

Gаlта non compıdа.

Figure 4.11 A galley from the fifteenth-century shipbuilding treatise, *Fabrica di Galere* (Biblioteca Nazionale, Florence).

ships are not known to have sailed into British waters they will not be discussed in this book but the interaction of shipbuilding traditions on all coasts of the Mediterranean is one which deserves close study elsewhere.

Italy

In the thirteenth century the cloth industry of Italy relied on imported wool, especially that from England and Scotland. The wool was shipped across the Channel and then taken overland to Italy until the sea route via Biscay and the Straits of Gibraltar became an established alternative towards the end of the century. Disruptions to trans-continental trade routes caused by Franco-Flemish wars probably created an incentive for Italian merchants to adopt the sea route. The first voyage of Genoese ships to Bruges and Southampton took place in 1277–78. The Venetians followed this lead in the early fourteenth century. By 1300 Genoa and Venice were both at a peak of commercial prosperity and were also at war with each other throughout the fourteenth century (Scammell, 1981: 110–11, 165).

In exchange for the wool exported from England and cloth from northern Europe, the Venetians brought luxury goods from the Mediterranean and from sources in the east, traded through Constantinople and the Black Sea. Because they dealt in high-value, low-volume cargoes much of their trade was carried in galleys (figure 4.11), of which they developed a specifically merchant type with a cargo capacity of about 150 tons (Lane, 1934: 1–34). The merchant galleys were effective sailing craft and the use of their oars was largely restricted to entering and leaving harbour. Sailing in a strict, state-controlled and seasonal convoy system, heavily manned and defended by paid mariners, their high operating costs were justified by the value of their cargoes and their extremely predictable voyage times.

The Genoese controlled the alum mines at Foçea in what is now Turkey. Alum was used in the cloth industry for fixing dyes and was increasingly in demand in England as its cloth industry grew in the fourteenth century. Because alum was a bulky and relatively low-value cargo, it was transported in high-capacity sailing ships. As we have seen, the Genoese built *coche* in imitation of the northern cogs and were sending loads of alum in these vessels to Southampton by the mid-fourteenth century. (Their knowledge of the port was no doubt useful when they helped the French to sack it in 1338.) Although the Genoese had been the originators of the galley trade to the Channel, the *cocha* type proved so successful for their bulk goods that it had completely taken over on this route by the 1340s.

In 1378 Mediterranean merchants were allowed to use Southampton as the Staple for wool exports, instead of Calais, provided they did not land wool anywhere in the Staple market of western Europe (Power, 1941: 101). At the end of the fourteenth century Venetian ships would sail, loaded with silks, from Venice to Cadiz and Lisbon, where they would take on fruit and dyes, then on to Flanders where they collected German furs. They spent the winter in England and returned to Venice in the spring. The handling of malmsey caused contention between Venice and England. Malmsey was very popular in the fifteenth century and Venetian imports of Cretan malmsey are recorded in the accounts of the convent of Durham (Scammell, 1981: 105–6).

Both Venice and Genoa, which specialised in building bulk carriers for their alum and grain trades, had by the mid-fourteenth century developed ships which in England at least were beginning to be known as carracks. The Southampton Port Books for 1430 record the arrival of Venetian and Florentine galleys, Genoese carracks and Catalan ships. Because of the difficult approaches of the Thames, Genoese ships used Southampton and Sandwich in preference to London. Walsingham's *Historia Anglia* (quoted in Salzman, 1931: 78) records that in 1383 a Genoese 'carrick' was driven by a storm into Sandwich harbour:

> It was of astonishing size, full of treasures, which might easily have supplied the needs of all the country; but the London merchants, so it is said, having in their houses much stale merchandise of fruit, spices of various kinds, oil and so forth, lest these be thrown away on the arrival of fresh goods, made an agreement with the Genoeses [*sic*] to leave the port and sail to Flanders.

Early in the fifteenth century seven or eight Genoese carracks were working the English Channel each year. In 1445 nine ships sailed for Southampton and Flanders with cotton and alum. In 1455 the Genoese lost the alum mines of Foçea to the Turks. This, together with serious competition from Iberian shipping, caused a sharp decline in their seaborne commerce with the north. By the end of the century Genoese ships had become very large indeed (figure 4.12) but only one or two a year sailed to the Channel and they concentrated their trade on Flanders.

In the second half of the fifteenth century there was a notable increase in the English shipping industry. English ships carried 80 per cent of the wool trade to the Mediterranean and Italians the other 20 per cent (Power, 1941: 55). From the late 1470s, English royal ships were chartered out to merchants and privately owned ships were also soon carrying cloth to Italy (Scammell, 1981: 460). Henry VII was keen to establish British dominance in

Figure 4.12 Genoese ships in 1480 (Museo Navale di Genova-Pegli).

the carriage of French wines as well. This trade was mostly handled by Breton and Spanish shippers but in 1485 the king ordered that wines of Gascony and Guienne were to imported only in ships of England, Ireland or Wales (James, 1971: 49). In this he was unsuccessful and the coasts of Britain continued to be frequented by large numbers of foreign ships.

5 Carrying trade

Most medieval ships were built to carry cargoes on trading voyages. Specialised warships were very rare until the end of the period and most ships used in war, for fighting and as troop transports, were merchant ships requisitioned or chartered from their owners. The cargoes that merchant ships carried, the routes they sailed and the arrangements for loading and unloading them all had consequences for ship design.

Much is known about medieval trade because it was subject to a high degree of government intervention, for raising revenue and pursuing foreign policy objectives. Extensive documentary records survive and this is just as well, since archaeological evidence alone would give a very distorted view of the nature and relative quantities and importance of commodities traded. The majority of them – wine, salt, grain and other foodstuffs, wool and cloth – were organic and these goods leave few traces on the land sites which were the destination of their travels. However, those which failed to reach their destinations are rather more likely to be preserved on shipwreck sites. Durable commodities, such as pottery and items of metalwork, did not make up whole cargoes and it is not always easy to determine whether they were imported as objects of trade or were personal belongings or gifts. Building stone is the only commodity where the source of imports and the volume of the trade can be reliably established from the surviving material evidence.

The customs accounts of England, unparalleled elsewhere in Europe except for Italy, are an invaluable source for the study of trade from the late thirteenth century onwards (see Clarke, 1983). Customs were first introduced on a regular basis in 1275 and applied to the export of wool, woolfells and hides by both native and alien merchants. In 1303 additional taxes were introduced on imports as well, to be paid only by alien merchants. The customs system is explained by Gras (1918). There are long lists of dues on merchandise – ranging from bears to peppercorns – in the records of many seaports, for example Norwich, King's Lynn, Hull and Southampton. Other documentary sources for trade (and for disruption to trade) include laws, tolls, aulnage accounts for cloth, charter parties between merchants and shipmasters, royal arrests of shipping for use in time of war, complaints by shipowners and merchants whose property had been pirated or otherwise appropriated, royal butlers' accounts of goods purchased, chronicles and letters and trading treaties. There are also records of taxes levied on shipping such as port dues and anchorage charges.

The documentary sources are not without their pitfalls. They are much better for the later periods and may give the misleading impression that the relative scarcity of records for the earlier period indicates a commensurate lack of activity. They are also heavily Anglo-centric, making it difficult to give a balanced picture of the trade of the whole of Britain. An unquantifiable amount of trade also evaded record, though Carus-Wilson and Coleman (1963, 22–3) take the view that potential profits would not have justified the hazards and problems involved in smuggling.

Commodities

Wool was the principal export of England and Scotland from before the Conquest. During the twelfth century, sheep farming grew rapidly, partly as a result of the founding of new monastic houses, chiefly Cistercian, which specialised in it. For a great part of the Middle Ages, England was the largest and most important source of fine wool, supplying a good part of the Italian cloth industry and nearly the whole of the industry of the Low Countries (Power, 1941: 16). In the mid-fourteenth century England was exporting about 30,000 sacks of wool per year, plus 12,000 broadcloths and an unknown quantity of other cloths (Pelham, 1948a: 240). When England developed its cloth industry during the fourteenth century it had the advantage of being the only country in which the cloth export trade did not depend on imported raw materials. Other exports included grain in years of surplus, tin and lead. Manufactured pewter goods had become quite an important commodity by the end of the Middle Ages (Homer, 1991: 73). England was a net exporter of salt until the mid-fourteenth century, by which time new methods of preserving herrings had increased demand. Stone – such as Purbeck marble – and coal were exported in smaller quantities.

Wine was the largest component of England's import trade. In the early fourteenth century England's imports of Gascon wine are believed to have exceeded 20,000 tuns a year (James, 1971: 10). Commodities for the cloth industry, including dyes and mordants, were also major imports, as was salt from the fourteenth century. Forestry products, including timber and tar, building stone, iron and copper, spices and foodstuffs and fabrics and furs accounted for most of the rest.

Packaging

The way in which cargoes were packaged for transport by sea and their stowage in ships has been largely overlooked. It was certainly a technically developed area, whatever the jumble of casks, bales, sacks and loose metalware or pottery shown in the fourteenth-century illustration, figure 5.1, would suggest to the contrary.

Wine was transported in casks, most commonly in tuns, though smaller capacity casks were also used especially for high-value wines and brandy. The tun, or the space it occupied, was the standard unit for measuring the carrying capacity of a ship. It is not a simple matter to pin down the exact size of a tun as units of measurement varied from place to place and showed a marked tendency to grow larger throughout the Middle Ages. This was, to a large measure, in response to taxation. Taxes were usually levied on the gross unit (e.g. the tun of wine, roll of cloth, chalder of coal) so by increasing the size of the gross unit, the tax per sub-unit (gallon of wine, yard of cloth etc.) was proportionately less (Salzman, 1923: 18, 240).

In 1423 it was enacted by statute that the wine tun should contain 252 gallons. The gallon itself was not defined but can be expected to have been no larger than the Tudor standard of about 3.78 litres. On this basis the

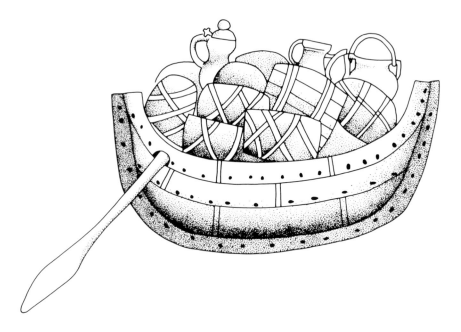

Figure 5.1 A 'ship full of all kinds of merchandise', redrawn from BL Sloane Ms 3983, f.13r, second quarter of the fourteenth century (National Maritime Museum).

capacity of a fifteenth-century wine tun would have been about 954 litres (Zupko, 1977: 29–30). Gascon tuns seem to have contained from 750 to 900 litres (Renouard, 1953, cited in James, 1971: xvi). A late twelfth-century cask (figure 5.2), reused to line a pit at Goldsmith Street in Exeter, has an approximate capacity of 815 litres (Allan, 1984: 313). Its height is reconstructed to 1.42 metres and its maximum diameter to about 0.94 metres. By comparison, a mid-eighteenth-century tun of 252 gallons (by then equivalent to 1145 litres), preserved at the Coopers' Company in London, is 1.52 metres high, with a maximum diameter of 1.17 metres.

The Exeter cask was made of oak staves bound together by hoops made of split roundwood rods of coppiced hazel. The ends of each hoop were seized by fine strands of split hazel or elder. Similar casks are depicted in figure 5.3. Hazel hoops and oak staves and ends from four different sizes of cask have been recovered from the early sixteenth-century Studland Bay wreck (Ladle, 1993: 16).

Empty tuns from the wine sold by the Gascons at Boston fair were a hereditary perquisite (James, 1971: 73) but the *Customs of the Sea* refer to merchants hiring casks for their trading voyages, with empty casks needing to be returned within an agreed period (Twiss, 1874: 293). The shipowner had to calculate whether it would be more profitable to carry the casks whole and not have room for other cargo or to break them down into staves, making room for more cargo, but incurring the expense of having them rebuilt (Twiss, 1874: 531–3). The fifteenth-century Gdańsk W5 wreck

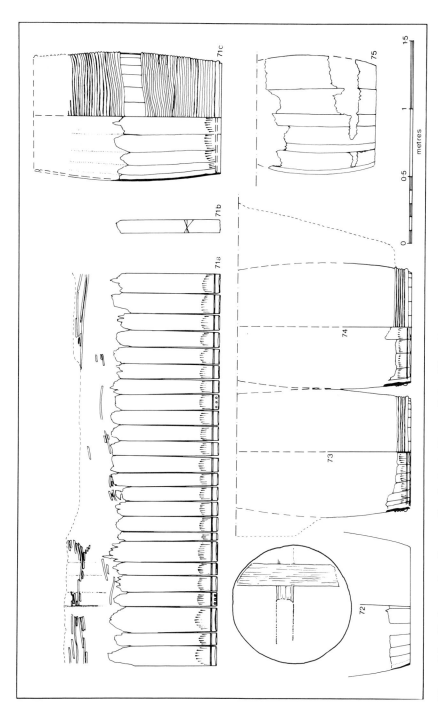

Figure 5.2 Casks used to line medieval pits in Exeter (John Allan, Exeter City Museums).

Figure 5.3 Casks of wine in hulk-like lighters at the port of Paris (photo: Bibliothèque Nationale, Paris. Ms Fr. 2091-2, f.125).

contained more than 200 small planks for making barrel staves, manufactured in the Baltic region for export (Litwin, 1985: 46).

The ancient right of prise entitled the king of England to one tun of wine from ships laden with between ten and 19 tuns; and two tuns (one from before and one from abaft the mast) from ships carrying 20 or more tuns. From 1302 foreign merchants were required to pay customs instead and this was set at a rate whereby importers of more than 60 tuns would have been better off paying prisage (James, 1971: 4). This reflects the increasing size of merchant ships. In the mid-thirteenth century ships of 100 tuns were rare in the Anglo-Gascon wine trade but by the early fourteenth century although 81 per cent were less than 150 tuns, 16 per cent were between 150 and 200 tuns, 3 per cent were over 200 tuns and the largest reached 300 tuns.

Medieval tunnage measurements of ships cannot be used to give more than a rough guide to their dimensions. Tunnage literally meant the number of tuns that a ship could carry. It did not refer to the weight of the cargo or the displacement of the ship (Lane, 1964). The tun may have been a little larger at the end of the period than at the beginning and, more importantly, the internal layout of a ship might affect its carrying capacity. It was not until the sixteenth century that empiric tunnage was converted into the formula, known as 'Baker's old rule', of (keel × beam × depth) ÷ 100 = tons burden (Friel, 1984: 135).

Casks were principally used for carrying liquids or wet products, including herrings, but their strength and rigidity also made them useful for other commodities. The cargo of a ship pirated on a voyage from Southampton to Seaton in 1446 included a pipe (a cask half the size of a tun) of white soap (Platt, 1973: 162). More than 100 casks have been excavated from the Gdańsk W5 shipwreck, containing pitch, birch tar, wood ash (used to dissolve dyes), resin and wax (Smolarek, 1979: 62). Casks on board ships were laid on their sides with their ends facing towards the ends of the ship. They were secured with wooden supports to ensure that they did not break loose. So far the only medieval archaeological site where these supports have been identified is the Gdańsk W5 wreck (see below).

The freight measurements of bulk cargos were related to tunnage. The standard measure for grain and salt was the quarter, with four quarters occupying a space in a ship's hold equivalent to that of a tun (Salzman, 1931: 50). Grain and salt were transported in sacks and perhaps also loose. Figure 5.4 shows grain being landed loose in a lighter and then being measured into sacks. Bridbury (1955: 83–5) says that salt was also shipped loose from the Bay of Bourgneuf, though his description of 'Hanse ships. . . weighed down by the loose grey salt piled high above their gunwales' can be dismissed as fanciful. Good stowage and ship-handling practice required nothing to be carried on deck except the ship's equipment and the victuals (Twiss, 1874: 245–7). During the fifteenth century ships in the Hanse Bay Fleet could be as large as 800 tons.

In 1351 a large quantity of grain was shipped from Yorkshire to London. Some of it was ground into flour at Hull and packed into 30 casks which were carried to Grimsby in two boats, then loaded into one of the four ships hired for the voyage to London. Laths were bought for dunnage as well as 'mattes large and small', planking, and litter for stowage. A total of 950 quarters of grain were measured into sacks and carried to the ships (Salzman, 1931: 216). Sacks were also used for other foodstuffs such as onions and beans.

Wool was sold by the sack, each weighing 26 stones (164 kg). The weight of the standard package was therefore less than for grain or salt but, because of the low density of wool, it may have taken up more space. A 'poke' held the equivalent of half a sack and a larger package called a sarplar held the same as 2½ sacks (Carus-Wilson and Coleman, 1963: 22). The 1447–48 customs accounts list both wool and cloth by the sack (Power, 1941: 37) but the 1414 list of lighterage charges at Southampton (Platt, 1973: 83) show that rolls of cloth were transported by the bale. A bale was a package wrapped in a covering, perhaps of canvas, and trussed with bands or cord (figure 5.5). A bale was a half-load for a mule or pack-horse and in Italy, the source of much of the Southampton imports, a bale weighed 80–85 kg (Mallett, 1967: 178). The 1414 Southampton schedule of lighterage charges show that alum (a mordant for fixing dye), woad and other dyestuffs were shipped in bales.

Figure 5.4 Unloading and measuring grain at a Mediterranean port (Vatican Museum).

Figure 5.5 Cargo handling at the quays (French, early sixteenth century. Photo: Bibliothèque Nationale, Paris. Ms Fr 2810, f. 86v).

Furs and hides were also transported in bales, as were spices, including pepper, anise, ginger and cumin. In the late fifteenth century a London merchant bought 12 bales of pepper for a prodigious total price of more than £200. He was understandably unhappy when one of the bales became 24 pounds lighter as it dried out and he found that the pepper it contained was musty (Salzman, 1931: 180).

Fruit, brought to England in ships from Italy and Iberia, would have required careful packing. On the Venetian galleys currants and molasses were not to be stored in the hold but should be between decks instead (Salzman, 1931: 231). Oranges were even more susceptible to spoiling because of the motion of the ship. Fig seeds have been excavated from the wreck of the Iberian ship which sank at Studland Bay, Dorset, in the early sixteenth century (Hutchinson, 1991: 174). They were associated with scraps of loosely woven material which may have been fragments of frails, which were rush baskets for holding figs, raisins and other dried fruit.

Coal mined in the vicinity of Newcastle was packed loose into barges called keels. From early times each keel held 20 chalders, the standard measure of coal weighing between 18 and 20 hundredweight or slightly less than a ton. Because export duty on coal was set at 2d per keel-load, it became the practice to build keels of 22- or 23-chalder burden. This was forbidden in 1385 and by Act of Parliament of 1421 the actual capacity in chalders of each keel had to be marked upon it. After that the size of the chalder increased rapidly (Salzman, 1923: 18). The keels took the coal to a point below Newcastle bridge where it was re-loaded into seagoing vessels (Pelham, 1948a: 258). The average capacity of the vessels which carried coal from Newcastle to the Low Countries in 1377–78 was a little less than 50 chalder but the shipping activity must have been great because 7,338 chalder of coal were exported in that year (Salzman, 1923: 19).

Metals were transported in blocks and bars, stowed low in the hold. Comparison of the merchants' cargo list and the English customs accounts for the Florentine galleys which left Southampton in 1444 show that 62 pieces of lead went unnoticed by the officials, probably because they were among the ballast (Mallett, 1967: 139–40). The size of the pieces of lead and tin is not recorded. The port books show that worked tin and lead was carried in baskets, crates and barrels.

Stone was carried in blocks. The cost of stone lay mainly in transport, with the carriage cost perhaps twice the price of the stone at the quarry, but it was no more expensive to import stone from Caen to London than to carry it coastwise from Beer in Devon; and the traffic was considerable. The Tower of London alone used 75 shiploads of Caen stone in 1278 (Salzman, 1952: 135–6).

Pottery and glassware, such as the fine tablewares brought in Venetian galleys, were at the other end of the scale of fragility. It is not clear how they were packaged for transport by sea. It does seem that pottery was generally only a small part of a cargo and was perhaps a commodity which could be packed in among other goods. Large quantities of Saintonge pottery was included with cargoes of wine from south-west France. The best evidence for trade by sea of the products of a British medieval pottery centre is provided by the distribution of finds of thirteenth- and fourteenth-century Scarborough ware. Some of these high-quality glazed and decorated vessels are found inland but many more were taken by sea to Newcastle, Perth and Aberdeen as well as to Norway and the Northern Isles (McCarthy and Brooks, 1988: 94–6). *Wadmal*, a coarse cloth used as packing material around fragile goods, was produced in both Norway and Iceland from double-coated sheep. A piece of cloth excavated at the waterfront at King's Lynn has been identified as *wadmal* (Clarke, 1984: 136) and other examples have been found in London and Newcastle (Walton, 1988: 81–2).

Single commodity cargoes were probably quite rare. The ships which loaded with salt at the Bay of Bourgneuf might also have taken on wine, canvas and linen, fruit, sugar and oil (Bridbury, 1955: 127). Alum and dyestuffs were generally carried as part of mixed cargoes, which might include wine and salt from France or, for example, green ginger and cotton from the Mediterranean.

The *Nicholas* was a ship belonging to a London merchant which was attacked by some Flemish pirates while anchored near Sandwich in 1318. The pirates killed most of the crew, stole the ship's contents and sank the ship. The three merchants whose goods were on board submitted the following valuation of the ship and its cargo (Cal. Close Rolls, 1313–1318: 594). This is a claim for compensation, so it is possible that exaggeration has crept in:

The ship and gear	£166.13s.4d.
178 tuns and 9 pipes of wine	£1,095
10 quarters of wheaten flour	£10
6 quintals of whalebone	£104
1 tun and 2 barrels of nut oil	£11
1 pipe of vinegar	£3
saffron and pepper	£43
armour	£13
money	£40
silver cups, beds, robes, chests and other goods of the master, mariners and merchants	£20
Total	£1,505.13s.4d

When the goods of more than one merchant were carried in the same ship they could not be stowed separately as the heaviest goods of each of them had to be stowed low in the hold. Merchant's marks had to be put on the packages before loading so that they could be identified. Such marks have been found on casks from the Gdańsk W5 wreck (Litwin, 1985: 47). The *Customs of the Sea* acknowledged the dangers posed by vermin, ruling that: 'If goods shall be damaged by rats on board a ship, and there be no cat in the ship, the managing owner of the ship is bound to make compensation', unless the cat died during the voyage (Twiss, 1874: 99). The master of a *cocha* bringing a bale of wool from Southampton to Genoa in 1384 was obliged to pay compensation for its being damaged by water and rats. He denied the charge and said in his defence that '*in eius nave habeat musipulos prout debebat*' (in his ship he had mousetraps, just as he ought to have) (Liagre de Sturler, 1969: 610).

Ballast, additional to that stowed permanently to provide stability and trim, was taken onto ships to compensate for the offloading of heavy cargo. Ballast mounds consisting of stone from all over Europe must have formed on the foreshores of British ports. Especially during the fifteenth century Kingston-upon-Hull imported large quantities of stockfish, a light commodity, and Hull's streets are said to have been paved with the Icelandic stone brought in with it (Buckland and Sadler, 1990: 118). Metamorphic and igneous rocks of Scandinavian origin have been recognised in medieval structures in King's Lynn (Clarke and Carter, 1977: 440) and no doubt reached the port as ships' ballast.

Voyages

Ships on trading voyages faced dangers from hostile vessels and from foul weather. A convoy system was instituted as a result of the war between England and France from 1324, in order to supply Bordeaux with victuals and bring wine back to England (James, 1971: 126). The convoys concentrated the trading activity to two sailings per year, one in late autumn for the vintage wines and another in early spring for the more mature reek wines which were strained off in January and February. Protection at sea involved a double or even triple complement of men, including archers, aboard each ship (James, 1971: 71). The fleets under convoy were often large even during periods of active warfare: between May 1339 and July 1340 some 235 English-owned ships brought cargoes back to England (James, 1971: 129). Ships did still try to sail alone before the rest of the fleet, to gain commercial advantage by being the first to bring home the vintage wine, until Richard II enforced the convoy system in the 1370s (James, 1971: 75).

Commercial pressure meant that trading voyages were undertaken all year round, not just in the summer months. Winter sailing was of course especially hazardous. Off the coasts of north-west Europe today gales of force 7 and above are eight times more frequent in winter than in summer and rough seas may be expected on average every fourth day in winter, compared with every twelfth day in summer (McGrail, 1987: 260). As well as the risks to the safety of a ship caught in storms, rough weather causes increased wear and tear on a ship and its gear and the crew operate less efficiently when numb with cold. There are many documented winter voyages, some of which ended in shipwreck (Platt, 1973: 126; Rose, 1982: 35, 48, 51). In the late fourteenth century it was important for English merchants to import wine from Bordeaux as early in the season as possible. In 1384 the wine fleet left Southampton in September and returned there in the following January and February (Platt, 1973: 70, 74, 129). Despite frequent official prohibitions of sailing between November and April, as for example by the Hanse governing council in 1403 (Scammell, 1981: 54), the practice continued. In the fifteenth century, London received more than a quarter of its annual supply of salt between November and the beginning of March (Bridbury, 1955: 112). The increase in the size of ships does not seem to have relieved the problem; instead it made each loss a greater disaster. As late as 1532 legislation was enacted against winter sailing for Bordeaux wine because of the mounting toll of losses (Waters, 1967: 11).

James (1971: 119–24) has studied the routes that the wine ships took between England and Gascony. The voyages were made hazardous by the rocky coasts and prevailing south-westerly onshore winds. Ships had to be prepared to wait a long time for favourable winds, so voyage lengths varied considerably. The Solent was often the first stage in voyages from the east coast and from London. Ships would assemble there to make the passage together. From the Isle of Wight they would either cross to Brittany then round the French coast; or follow the English coast along to Cornwall and then head to Brittany. St Mathieu was frequently a port of call for victualling. The Breton coast was an important half-way house in the transit of the wine, providing havens against storms but also harbouring pirates who could be equally dangerous. The purser's accounts survive for the voyage of the *Margret Cely* to Bordeaux in 1486–88. In 1486 the ship embarked meat and bread at the start of the voyage at London, took on more bread, salt, salted and fresh fish and beer at Plymouth and further bread supplies at La Rochelle, at Ile de Rhe and at Blaye. At Bordeaux they replenished supplies of mutton, beef, bread, beverage and ship's stores.

The Channel Islands remained part of the Angevin Empire after the loss of Normandy to the French crown and so St Peter Port in particular became an important asylum for English and Bayonnese vessels (Williams, 1948: 271). The considerable quantity of Saintonge pottery revealed by erosion on the large medieval wreck at St Peter Port has enabled the loss of the ship to be dated to 1290–1310 (R. Burns, pers. comm.). From the thirteenth century, Saintonge in south-west France was one of the primary production centres for supplying luxury pottery to Britain and northern Europe. This was linked with the English acquisition of Gascony and the development of the wine trade (Barton, 1963; Hurst *et al.*, 1986: 76). The Guernsey ship was presumably outward bound from Gascony. Future excavation of the site may reveal more about how pottery was packed for transport by sea and about the rest of the cargo, which can be expected to have consisted mainly of casks of wine.

The Aber Wrac'h ship, which was wrecked off Brittany in the early fifteenth century, was carrying at least 25 to 30 tonnes of ballast. Analysis of this has shown that it was of such a mixture that it cannot be said to have been loaded in any one region; rather, it demonstrates the diversity of the contents of the ballast mounds in the ports of medieval Europe (L'Hour and Veyrat, 1989: 293). Among this, 1200 fragments of animal bones were recovered, from sheep, goats, deer, cattle, fowl and a small quantity of pig. It appears that some animals, particularly sheep, were carried whole and perhaps alive. This meat may all have been intended to be eaten by the ship's company but some may have been cargo. Gascony needed victuals because it grew vines to the neglect of anything else and meat, fish and grain needed to be imported. Analysis of the sediments overlying the ballast led to the identification of human faeces including remains of walnuts, hazelnuts, chestnuts, grape and apple pips, plum stones and rye seeds. This suggests an exceptionally varied and nutritious diet, with ingredients from southern Europe. According to the Catalan *Customs of the Sea*, mariners were to have meat on three days a week, porridge on the others and bread with cheese, onions or fish every evening. With this they were to have either wine or prunes or figs (Twiss, 1874: 211–13). Merchants, who voyaged with their goods, took along their own victuals as well as a servant, bed and chest (Twiss, 1874: 107).

Two coins from the Elbląg region placed in the mast step of the cog wrecked on the Danish coast at Vejby indicate where it was built. The presence of a cooking pot of Baltic origin suggests that the ship was fitted out there. The finds on the wreck site support the interpretation that the ship was on its homeward voyage at the time of loss in about 1380 (Crumlin-Pedersen, 1985: 72–3). It appears that it failed to make the entrance to the narrow Oresund between Denmark and Sweden and foundered in shallow water at the foot of high clay cliffs. A part of the anchor cable, housed in a leather sleeve, lay beneath the stern, showing that the main anchor had been dropped in an attempt to save the vessel. Eighteen tons of ballast stones, originating from somewhere along the Atlantic seaboard, were excavated from the site. A concentration of metal finds lay around the stern, including coins, pewter plates and tripod pitchers (figure 5.6). One hundred and nine English gold coins of Edward III were recovered, ranging in date between

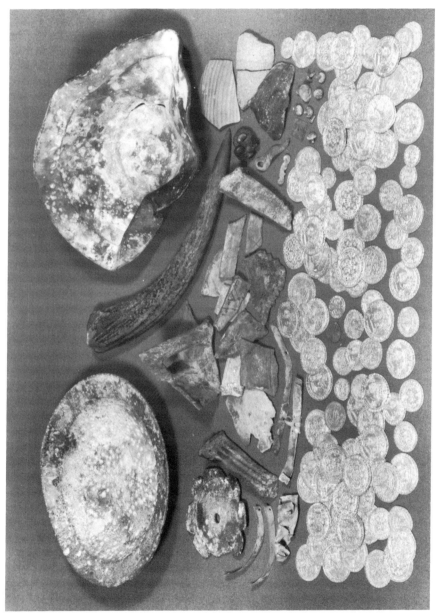

Figure 5.6 Finds from the wreck site of the Vejby cog (photo: Ole Crumlin-Pedersen).

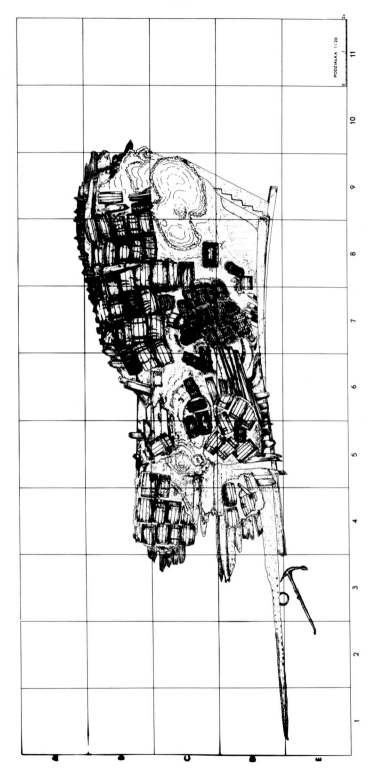

Figure 5.7 Site plan of the Gdańsk W5 wreck site (Jerzy Litwin).

Figure 5.8   Bundles of iron bars from the Gdańsk W5 wreck (photo: L. Nowicz).

1351 and 1377, and minted in London and Calais. There was also a gold coin from Lübeck and a small Flemish 'mite'. The first ever English gold coins had been minted less than half a century before and England was at pains to attract and retain bullion. The export of coin and gold and silver was constantly forbidden and merchants were required to export merchandise instead. It was not until 1400 that merchants importing goods into England were allowed to take half of the proceeds in coin, provided that they spent the other half on English goods and obtained a licence from the king (Salzman, 1931: 19–20). The Vejby wreck is a witness to the difficulty of enforcing such regulations.

The Gdańsk W5 ship appears to have sunk soon after leaving port, loaded with a cargo of forestry and mining products. The wreck lay on the sea-bed tipped onto its starboard side (figure 5.7). After the upper layers of cargo were removed, a well defined and deliberate stowage plan revealed itself (Litwin, 1985: 46–7). Oak planks were laid on the bottom of the hold. Casks of iron ore and bundles of iron bars rested on them, with all the free spaces between the casks packed with wedges to prevent movement of the cargo. The very heavy iron bars, fastened into bundles with cord and copper alloy bands (figure 5.8) were stowed towards the stern of the ship. The 52 bundles recovered contained an average of 80 bars each and there were also some others found loose. The bars are about 80cm long with a rectangular cross-section, tapering towards one end. Copper, transported in the form of large disc-shaped ingots (figure 5.9), was stowed in the midships area. There were 213 ingots raised. Above this were laid casks containing pitch, birch tar, wood ash, resin and wax. The tar was transported in 69 and 99 litre

Figure 5.9 One of the copper ingots retrieved from the Gdańsk W5 wreck (photo: L. Nowicz).

casks and the smaller ones were cylindrical rather than the typical 'barrel' shape.

The activities and the shore-based facilities involved in loading and unloading cargoes were substantial and to these let us now turn.

6 Ports

Virtually all the towns of medieval Britain were served by water transport along rivers but the term 'port' is used here to distinguish those settlements whose economy depended on the operation of ships. At the beginning of the period few of the major ports were sited on the coast. They tended to be as far up estuaries or rivers as they could be while still allowing sufficient deep water for ships to manoeuvre, unimpeded by obstructions such as bridges. Ports sited away from the coast could be near the centres of their areas of catchment and distribution, rather than on the fringes. They had access to the sea but shelter from it and also protection from the depredations of hostile shipping.

The phenomenal urban expansion which took place in the eleventh to thirteenth centuries resulted in the growth of existing towns and the foundation of new ones, including Newcastle, Hull, Boston and King's Lynn (Clarke, 1979: 158). This can largely be attributed to the expansion of overseas trade. Some of the more inland towns established earlier found their trade was taken away from them by ports closer to the coast. Ships were increasing in size and needing greater depths of water, while rivers were suffering silting and becoming shallower. From the twelfth century, for example, there were difficulties bringing ships up the Exe as far as Exeter, even before the construction of weirs, and the city was served by the out-port of Topsham, six kilometres away (Allan, 1984: 20). Richborough's traffic had been taken over by Stonar in the Anglo-Saxon period and that port was in turn superseded by Sandwich (Hill, 1981: 14). Bristol's future was secured by a far-sighted and vastly expensive scheme to alter the course of the River Frome. Beginning in 1239, the citizens paid £5,000 to canalise the Frome and construct a new quay (Sherborne, 1965: 5). Another thirteenth-century civil engineering project diverted the Great Ouse from Wisbech to King's Lynn and initiated the development of an important trading town (Clarke and Carter, 1977). Silting and the increase in ship sizes were important determinants of the success of ports throughout the Middle Ages. At Bridport in Dorset the river was continually blocked by bars of sand and pebbles and attempts to improve the harbour in 1385–96 failed (Williams, 1948: 279). By the fifteenth century the approaches to Dublin were so dangerous that ships above 100 tuns could not enter but discharged at the southern end of Dublin Bay, off Dalkey (de Courcy Ireland, 1989b: 24). Even London was affected: large Italian ships preferred to discharge at Sandwich than face the difficult tides and shallows of the Thames estuary.

Fluctuations in the fortunes of medieval ports had other causes too. The confederation of south-eastern towns known as the Cinque Ports eventually extended from Brightlingsea in Essex to Seaford in Sussex in the thirteenth century. After the English crown lost possession of much of northern France at the beginning of the thirteenth century, the ports of the south-west grew in importance and the Cinque Ports began their decline. The ports of the east coast suffered during the fourteenth century as the wool trade was increasingly concentrated in London and the trade of the North Sea was progressively dominated by Hanse merchants. Plague, particularly devastating in towns, was a set-back to urbanism all over Europe from the mid-fourteenth century. Yet ports seem to have shown great resilience in their recovery from other disasters, natural and man-made, such as the gales of 1377 which washed away the harbour at Lyme in Dorset (Williams, 1948: 279) and the French raids on south coast ports in the fourteenth and early fifteenth centuries.

Waterfronts

Shore-based handling facilities were developed for unloading, processing and storing ships' cargoes. The activities involved in cargo-handling varied according to the size of the ships and the facilities available at the port. Before the twelfth century, cargo seems to have been carried to and from vessels drawn up on the foreshore. Ellmers (1985a) has discussed the problem of detecting archaeological evidence for the loading and unloading of ships using a horse and cart, standing in the water. This might include consolidation of the foreshore and scattered remains of dropped cargo. The growth of urbanism in the twelfth century was accompanied by the construction of waterfront revetments and wharfs in many ports, allowing cargoes to be transferred directly between ships and dry land.

Sequences of quayside structures have been investigated in London. They show a continuing process of reclamation of riverside land behind a series of waterfront revetments. Warehouses and residential streets were built on the deposits of rubbish and other landfill, even before it had time to settle. The development of the London riverfront appears to have radiated out from three late Saxon centres: Queenhithe, Billingsgate with New Fresh Wharf, and the pre-Conquest foreign settlement at Dowgate, close to the site of the later Hanseatic Steelyard (Schofield, 1981: 24). At New Fresh Wharf in the Anglo-Saxon period a hard surface, consisting of a rubble bank laced by oak timbers, was laid on the foreshore. This was followed by a higher and more extensive timber and clay embankment in the late tenth century. In the late eleventh century a timber-revetted waterfront was constructed on the site, the earliest example known in Britain. It was quickly succeeded by two further revetments, each lying between one and two metres closer to the river than its precedecessor, with the area in between filled with dumped material (Miller, 1977; Hobley, 1981: 3–7). Documentary evidence suggests that New Fresh Wharf was the busiest sector of the medieval waterfront, already well developed by the twelfth century.

On the foreshore at the Seal House site, just above London Bridge, the first waterfront revetment was built soon after 1140, followed by a second after about 1170 and a third after 1210. A series of waterfront buildings was associated with the third structure, including a house with two ground-floor rooms and a large shed with a drain emptying over the quayside. A ragstone wall was built on the riverward face of the third revetment (Hobley and Schofield, 1977: 37–9). Excavations on several other London waterfront sites, notably Trig Lane (Milne and Milne, 1982) and the Customs House

Figure 6.1 Map of Britain (National Maritime Museum).

Figure 6.1 Key

1. Western Isles	31. Rochester	61. Scilly
2. Shetland	32. Queenborough	62. Padstow
3. Orkney	33. Reculver	63. Barnstaple
4. Aberdeen	34. Sandwich	64. Ilfracombe
5. Arbroath	35. Dover	65. Minehead
6. Perth	36. Hythe	66. Bristol
7. Edinburgh	37. Rye and Winchelsea	67. Gloucester
8. Berwick	38. Hastings	68. Chepstow
9. Newcastle	39. Pevensey	69. Cardiff
10. Hartlepool	40. Seaford	70. Carmarthen
11. Whitby	41. New Shoreham	71. Tenby
12. Scarborough	42. Bosham	72. Cardigan
13. Bridlington	43. Portsmouth	73. Carnarfon
14. York	44. Isle of Wight	74. Beaumaris
15. Hull	45. Hamble and Southampton	75. Chester
16. Lincoln	46. Beaulieu	76. Oak Mere
17. Boston	47. Poole	77. Liverpool
18. King's Lynn	48. Weymouth	78. Walney
19. Cromer	49. Portland	79. Giggleswick
20. Whittlesey	50. Abbotsbury	80. Kentmere
21. Norwich	51. Bridport	81. Isle of Man
22. Great Yarmouth	52. Lyme	82. Threave
23. Lowestoft	53. Exeter	83. Carrickfergus
24. Dunwich	54. Dartmouth	84. Drogheda
25. Ipswich	55. Plymouth	85. Dublin
26. Caldecotte	56. Looe	86. Wexford
27. Harwich	57. Fowey	87. Waterford
28. Southend	58. Falmouth	88. Cork
29. London	59. Porthallow and Porthoustock	89. Limerick
30. Woolwich	60. Penzance	

(Tatton-Brown, 1974 and 1975), have confirmed the general sequence. In the twelfth and early thirteenth centuries the structures which were being built along much of the waterfront incorporated a large proportion of reused timber, including ships' timbers, while in the later thirteenth century the timber was specially cut for the purpose. A complex array of carpentry techniques was employed (Milne, 1982), bearing very little resemblance to those used for shipbuilding. In the fourteenth century, stone riverfront walls became common and docks were constructed. From the eleventh to the sixteenth century reclamation advanced the bank of the Thames by between 50 and a 100 metres by a series of rubbish-backed revetments, with deposits in excess of ten metres deep (Hobley, 1981: 7).

Waterfront structures were being built not only in London but in ports throughout northern Europe from the twelfth century. In Britain they have been revealed in excavations in Newcastle (O'Brien *et al.*, 1988; O'Brien, 1991); Hartlepool (Young, 1987; Daniels, 1991); Hull (Ayres, 1981); York (Hall, 1991); Lincoln (Jones and Jones, 1981); King's Lynn (Clarke and Carter, 1977; Clarke, 1979; 1981); Kingston (Potter, 1991); Portsmouth (Moorhouse, 1971: 204; Fox, 1981); Poole (Horsey, 1991; Watkins, 1994); Plymouth (Barber, 1971; Barber and Gaskell-Brown, 1981); and Bristol (Ponsford, 1981; 1985; Jones, 1991). The excavation at Canynges House at Redcliffe, Bristol, shows the rapid and extensive reclamation which took

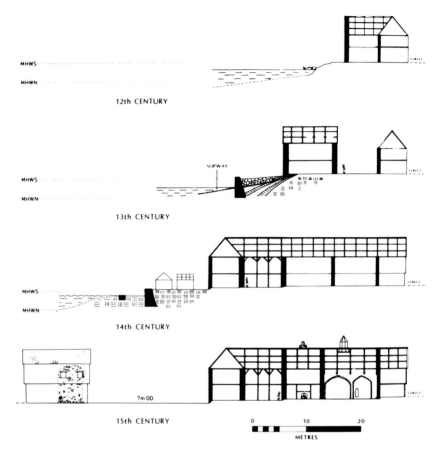

MHWS

MHWN

12th CENTURY

MHWS

MHWN

SLIPWAY

13th CENTURY

MHWS

MHWN

14th CENTURY

7m OD

15th CENTURY

0   10   20

METRES

Figure 6.2 Development of the medieval riverbank at Canynges House, Bristol (Bristol City Museum).

place at a waterside property from the twelfth to the fifteenth century (figure 6.2). There is a very large tidal range at Bristol and the complexity of the waterfront development was increased because quays were constructed which could be used at different states of the tide.

Timbers from boats and ships have been found reused in waterfront structures in several ports, although no assemblage from a single site in Britain is as large or as informative as those from Dublin (McGrail, 1993a) and Bergen (Christensen, 1985) which have been described in Chapter 4. In London, a late thirteenth- or early fourteenth-century revetment at the Custom House site included slabs of still-fastened boat planking. The bottom of the boat, which was relatively flat, was used in large sections while the curving sides had to be broken into smaller pieces to serve their new purpose (Marsden, 1979: 86–7). At Kingston the first waterfront development, provisionally dated to 1300, included a 11.5 metre long revetment largely made up of reused boat planking (figure 6.3) Two other large sections of boat planking were found at the Kingston Horsefair site, one of them as

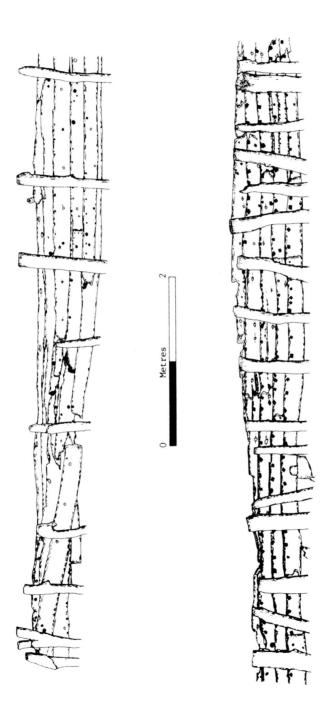

Figure 6.3   Planking from a clinker vessel reused in a revetment at Kingston (Museum of London).

much as 13 metres long by nearly a metre wide. The Kingston boats show evidence of extensive repair and were broken up when they were in an unseaworthy condition (Potter, 1991: 143; Goodburn, 1991: 108–11).

At York, boat strakes were found in the thirteenth- and fourteenth-century waterfronts at both Hungate and Coppergate and those at Hungate were up to 3.66 metres long (Richardson, 1959: 67–9; Youngs *et al.*, 1983). At Lincoln, the thirteenth-century wharf at Dickinson's Mill was made partly out of a reused boat hull (Jones and Jones, 1981: 138). A late thirteenth-century revetment at the Penner Wharf site in Bristol incorporated small pieces of boat planking. At Newcastle, where the mast crutches mentioned in Chapter 3 were found, small fragments of boat planking and treenails were recovered from thirteenth-century waterfront contexts. Plank fragments and a possible frame fragment were found in an early thirteenth-century waterfront structure at Southgate Area A in Hartlepool (Daniels, 1991: 45).

It is seldom possible to reconstruct the original shape and size of the vessels whose components are found reused in waterfronts. Even when the remains are not broken into very small pieces, as they were at Bristol, the preserved elements of the vessels are those which were deliberately selected for their lack of features. The preferred material was flat planking of fairly constant width. Framing is rarely found, though part of the keel was included with the planking reused in the thirteenth-century revetment at Fenning's Wharf, adjacent to London Bridge. Indications of the size of a vessel are provided by the thickness and width of the planks and the dimensions of the fastenings. The spacing of the treenail holes along the strakes may show how robustly the vessel was built. (For the analysis of fragmentary planking see Hutchinson, 1984 and the attribute list for clinker planking published by McGrail, 1993a: 169–71.)

Docks

The earliest dock yet located is that constructed in about 1213 in Southgate Area A in Hartlepool. It was more than 20 metres long and had stone side walls. One of these was lined with timbering, including the boat planking referred to above, as a protective fender between the docked vessels and the stonework (Young, 1987; Daniels, 1991).

In London, excavation beside Baynard's Castle revealed a dock basin of the fourteenth and fifteenth centuries (figure 6.4). The dock was a rectangular basin surrounded by stone walls, with the castle on its east side and a large gravelled area for unloading on the west side. Oak rubbing posts lined the dock to protect the boats from being damaged by the rough stonework. On the west side these posts had been renewed several times before the dock was filled in at the end of the fifteenth century. An oak mooring post was found just outside the dock entrance, while towards the dock head were two posts which perhaps once supported an unloading platform that had projected over the basin. Fronting the unloading area on the inshore side was a stone building with an arcade along the ground floor (Marsden, 1981: 14–16). Another dock, built at about the same time as that at Baynard's Castle, has also been excavated in London at the Sun and

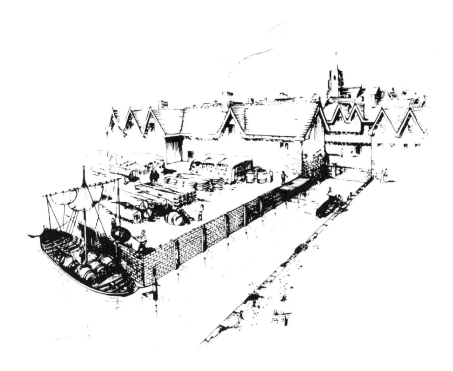

Figure 6.4 Reconstruction of the fifteenth-century dock at Baynards Castle, London (Museum of London).

Topping's Wharf site on the south bank of the Thames. There is documentary evidence that this dock was in existence by 1323. It formed the entry to a gated landing place known as the Watergate (Sheldon, 1974). Fourteenth-century docks have also been located at Bristol Bridge and Canynges House (Jones, 1991: 23).

The dock found in excavations at Oyster Street, Portsmouth, was a gully or inlet with banks supported by timber and wattle fencing. A wooden quay extended along the shingle shoreline from either side of the dock, which fell out of use in the fifteenth century (Hurst, 1970: 176–7; Moorhouse, 1971: 204).

A financial account is preserved for the building of a dry dock for the King's shops at Portsmouth in 1496 (Hattendorf *et al.*, 1993: 116–18). Timber, iron, stone and clay were used. The dock was lined with timber and had inner and outer gates at its head.

Loading and unloading

The construction of quays allowed ships to moor for loading and unloading cargo. Large ships anchored off and smaller vessels, called lighters, made the intermediate journeys to the quays. The royal butler's accounts of the reigns of Edward I to Edward III in the thirteenth and fourteenth centuries record charges for unloading wine casks at quays and by means of boats from ships anchored off, as at the Pool of London (James, 1971: 139). Lighters were used for unloading carracks, moored to piles out in Southampton Water (Cobb, 1961: xxxiv).

The *Laws of Oléron*, the earliest surviving maritime code, was probably compiled in the twelfth century and gained currency throughout Atlantic and northern Europe. Much of it is concerned with the responsibilities of shipmasters and one section says that when a ship arrives in port, the master must show the merchants the ropes that he will use to hoist the cargo. If he does not, he has to pay full compensation to the merchants for any losses caused by the ropes breaking (Twiss, 1874: 16–17).

Cranes may have been introduced to waterfronts from the second half of the twelfth century. For the rebuilding of Canterbury Cathedral in 1175, special cranes were invented for discharging the boatloads of Caen stone (Salzman, 1923: 104–5). Ellmers (1989) has traced the origins of harbour cranes to three different models, each of which was previously used for other purposes. The first type, the hoisting spar, or 'wippe', was a mast with a yard which could lift goods and swing them round (figure 6.5). The Bergen town law of 1250 refers to cranes of this type (Ellmers, 1989: 48). The second type, the windlass, had been used for raising goods to the upper floors of merchants' houses. This type of windlass was operated not by turning the drum by means of handspikes but remotely, by turning a large wheel linked to the windlass drum by a chain or rope loop. The windlass could be mounted on a support with the wheel below, with a turning jib. The third type was the crane with a treadwheel. Cranes like these had been used for building churches and were adopted in Netherlands harbours in the first half of the thirteenth century or perhaps before.

In London there were cranes on public and private wharves in the fourteenth and fifteenth centuries (Schofield, 1981: 31). At Southampton Quay there was a crane from the early fifteenth century (Cobb, 1961: xxxvi). Very occasionally at Southampton, tuns of wine were recorded as being exempt from cranage charges because they were 'raised by hand'. Unlike tuns of wine, bales and sacks were charged wharfage rather than cranage, indicating that these were unloaded manually or with the ship's own lifting gear. The crane garth at York, the place where all waterborne cargoes owned by non-citizens had to be landed, weighed, checked and charged toll, is first mentioned in a document of 1417.

The Southampton steward's accounts for the end of the fifteenth century record that the town hired out equipment called 'styves' (from the Italian *stivare*, to stow) for unloading the Italian galleys at a rate of £5 per galley with extra charges for breakages. The accounts for the making of new styves in 1493 show that elm, oak, ash and elder timber was used and that the apparatus included derricks, pulleys and windlasses. Venetian galley carpenters helped with the work (Ruddock, 1942).

Figure 6.5 Reconstruction of a hoisting spar used for cargo handling in Bergen (Universitetet i Bergen Historisk Museum).

Warehouses and merchants' quarters

In the larger ports, separate areas of the waterfront were used for handling different commodities. In London, for example, Queenhithe was the place where grain was landed. In 1300 there were eight master measurers of grain there, each with three assistants. They measured the grain into cylindrical vessels called bushels, levelled at the brim. Eight of these were equivalent to one quarter of grain (Salzman, 1931: 56). Individual ports had their own measures and weighing equipment. In an attempt to impose uniformity in weights and measures, weighing beams were distributed from the Exchequer. In 1352, £40 was spent on making 12 new beams for ports (Salzman, 1931: 59). The name given to the Hanseatic headquarters, the 'Steelyard', refers to the weighing equipment which was to ensure fair dealing. The Custom House quay at London was the control point for the wool trade perhaps from the time that the Great Custom was imposed on wool in 1275. In the late thirteenth or early fourteenth century a large braced structure at least 2.2

Figure 6.6 The twelfth-century wine vault on Castle Quay, Southampton
(Southampton City Heritage Services).

metres high was built on the foreshore, incorporating the hull planking
mentioned above. There was also a large timber jetty running north–south,
most probably the main jetty for the Wool Quay (Tatton-Brown, 1974).

Specially built granaries and warehouses would have been needed at the
accredited hythes for goods awaiting distribution or transhipment.
Warehouse ranges with open arcading have been located at Billingsgate
and the Custom House. Merchants also had private warehouses. In London
the wine trade was concentrated at the Vintry, where there were large houses
with vaults for wine storage. They had access to the wharf on one side and a
shop frontage on the other. There is documentary evidence for at least ten
vaults there in 1376 (Schofield, 1981: 25). Several medieval stores survive at
Southampton, including the late twelfth-century vaulted wine cellar which
still stands on the former Castle Quay (figure 6.6). The vault is 5.7 metres
wide, 17.05 metres long and 4.0 metres high and now lacks all of its ribs
and most of its corbels. At King's Lynn, in the thirteenth and fourteenth
centuries, documents and standing buildings suggest that merchants' houses
were often built as 'divided properties' with their living accommodation on
the landward side of the street while their warehouses and quays were
between the street and the river. The fifteenth-century warehouse at

Hampton Court in King's Lynn was built parallel to the river with an open arcade of eight bays as its west wall, so opening directly onto the river (Clarke, 1979: 162–3).

Foreign merchants often stayed several months in port and rented cellars and houses. At Southampton the oarsmen of the galleys had their own quarters and a memorial stone from their burial ground has been found at North Stoneham (Williams, 1948: 277). Hanse merchants had establishments in Britain at London, King's Lynn, Boston and Hull. In London their Steelyard complex, on the site of the present Cannon Street station, included a council chamber, a wine tavern, houses for merchants and rows of warehouses running to a quay on which there was a crane. At the south-west corner of the site stood the Hanse Master's house, which is known from engravings to have resembled that which still stands at King's Lynn (Schofield, 1981: 30). The King's Lynn Steelyard, a fifteenth-century brick and timber structure, is the only surviving building of the Hanse in Britain (Clarke, 1979: 163).

Functional zoning

The proximity of substantial merchants' houses to the quays suggests that medieval waterfronts were not predominantly the low-status areas they tended to become in later centuries, when they were largely taken over by noxious industries such as tanning, brewing and dying. In medieval Bristol weavers, dyers and fullers were concentrated away from the merchants' quarters, south of the River Avon in Redcliffe and Temple. More needs to be known about functional zoning within ports and the localisation of trades along the waterfront. For example, it is not yet clear to what extent fishing quays and fishmongers' houses were separated from cargo-handling areas. Shipbuilding needed open space near the foreshore. In London documentary evidence for the quays between the Tower and the Custom House from 1319 until about the mid-fifteenth century shows that the most commonly recorded trade of the owners or occupiers was that of shipwright (Tatton-Brown, 1975). Narrow Quay at Bristol is known from documentary sources to have been a medieval shipbuilding site but excavations have revealed remains only of seventeenth-century docks (Ponsford, 1981: 104). Henry V's *Grace Dieu* was built 'at the town of Southampton' and a naval storehouse and smithy were built there at the same time (Carpenter Turner, 1954: 56–77). No shipbuilding areas have been located in the extensive excavations carried out in Southampton as these have mostly taken place in the southern and central areas of the medieval town (figure 6.7), which were occupied by the wealthiest members of the population. Excavations have indicated an increase in prosperity at the southern end of the town coinciding with the construction of a new quay by the Watergate early in the fifteenth century. They have also shown the desertion of the western shore as access to West Hithe and the quays was progressively restricted in the fourteenth century by the strengthening of the town's defences (Platt and Coleman-Smith, 1975: 37; Saunders, 1976: 21).

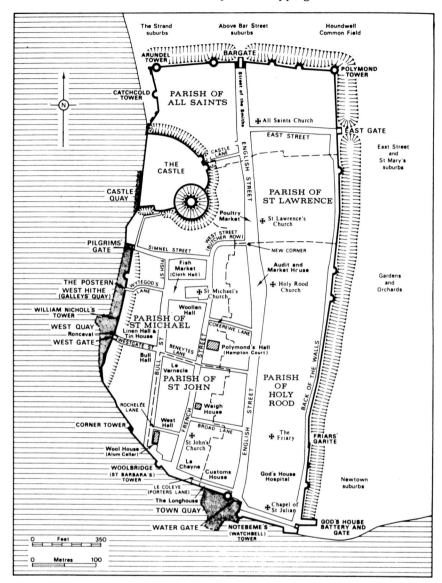

Figure 6.7 Southampton in the later Middle Ages (from Platt and Coleman-Smith, 1975).

Waterfront studies have become a major research area in medieval British archaeology. The waterlogged deposits in the zone where ships came to land can be expected to yield much more information about the development of towns, trade and shipping.

7 *Inland water transport*

Boats were an important means of transport inland, as well as at the coast. Water transport supplemented road transport for carrying cargo, especially for very dense commodities like stone and coal. Boats were also much used in inland fisheries and probably for setting traps, wildfowling and gathering reeds. Ferries carried people and vehicles across waterways, especially where the watercourse was too wide for a bridge. Boats could also be used for recreation.

The map of Britain by Matthew Paris (figure 7.1), drawn about 1250, which was among the first to give any accurate topographical detail (Hindle, 1976: 209), and the 'Gough' map of Britain in about 1360 (Parsons, 1958; Platt, 1976: 80–81) both emphasise the importance of rivers to communications within Britain. They show rivers not as thin lines as on modern maps but as broad snakes leading to the sea, and indicate just how far navigable waterways ran into the middle of the landmass. In 1340 the Trent and Ouse could take seagoing ships to Nottingham and York (Pelham, 1948a: 265). The land routes shown on the Matthew Paris map are those where river transport would have been of limited use, such as between Dover and Newcastle or Southampton and London. The 'Gough' map shows a road network covering most of England and Wales and Hindle (1976: 220, fig. 12) has used this and other evidence to reconstruct the road system in use in about 1348. It appears that roads seldom ran close to the coast, from which it is reasonable to infer that traffic along it tended to be by water.

Although journeys by boat could often be very slow, rivers were vital for taking goods for export from their place of production to a seaport. Having an adequate transport route to the coast must have been a crucial factor in the viability of many production sites. Exports travelled downstream to the ports so that the vessels were heavily laden when travelling with the flow of the water and were much lighter on the return journey against the stream. The distribution of imports from the ports where they were landed was not reciprocal to the exports, since a variety of commodities was coming in, with different and more widespread destinations. Their transport was not necessarily so closely linked to waterways.

The royal butler's accounts for the first half of the fourteenth century show that weather had an important influence on the route that consignments of wine took from the quayside to their destination. Whenever the state of the sea permitted, wine was shipped coastwise until it could be transferred to river transport. In the first half of the fourteenth century it cost as much to transport a tun of wine by road for 40 to 54 miles as it did to bring it by sea from Bordeaux. A cart carrying a tun of wine might require as many as six horses at a time and as a rule it was only the last stage of the journey which was completed by road (James, 1971: 147, 149).

The balance between the use of road and water transport varied in different parts of the country according to the nature of the terrain and the waterways. In the Fenland of eastern England, transport was predominantly

Figure 7.1 Map of Britain by Matthew Paris, drawn about 1250 (Cotton Claud. D.VI, f.12v. By permission of the British Library).

by water. Figure 7.2 is a twelfth-century drawing of St Guthlac travelling to Croyland in the Fens. The boat has a steering oar rather than a side rudder and the man at the bows is using a long rod to check that they are keeping to the navigable channel and in sufficient depth of water. However, Pelham (1948a: 263) has mapped the transport of hurdles to Plymouth for shipment to Gascony in the mid-fourteenth century. Surprisingly, this shows that they

Figure 7.2 St Guthlac travelling by boat in the Fens, twelfth century (Harl Roll Y6 Roundel 4. By permission of the British Library).

were brought by packhorse, not down the Tamar. In the Severn area, transport by water was much better than by road. The Severn was used for exporting coal, in 'keels', and iron manufactures through Gloucester from the Forest of Dean.

From the thirteenth century the Tyne valley shipped coal to London, to other east coast ports and also abroad. Osler has detected a medieval survival in the Tyne keel (figure 7.3), a square-rigged clinker-built vessel, used until recent times for carrying coal along the river (Osler and Barrow, 1993: 24). He suggests that official regulation of the size of these vessels to prevent the evasion of export duty (see Chapter 5) was one of the factors which inhibited change.

Building stone was a commodity which relied heavily on water transport. The great numbers and sizes of cathedrals, churches, religious houses and castles demonstrate that the traffic in stone during the Middle Ages must

OLD COAL STAITH—LOADING OF KEELS.

Figure 7.3 Tyne keels at a coal staith (Tyne and Wear Museums Service).

Figure 7.4   Blocks of Barnack stone lost in Wittlesey Mere (photo: N. Mitchell).

have been huge. Some of this was transported solely on inland waterways, never having to reach the coast. Building accounts which refer to the carriage of stone by water (Darby, 1940: 105) provide little information about the boats which were used. The cost of stone lay mainly in transport. The York Minster Fabric Rolls reveal that stone was brought by rivers from named quarries, then carried by sleds into the mason's yard (Salzman, 1923: 85). Barnack quarry, between the Welland and the Nene, was a most important source of stone for the buildings in the Fenland and East Anglia. The monks of Sawtry Abbey made a canal, or 'lode', for carrying Barnack stone to their house by way of Wittlesey Mere but in 1192 the Abbot of Ramsey ordered the blocking of Sawtrys lodes where they crossed Ramsey Abbey land. In order to regain access, Sawtry had to promise to put up no buildings except one rest house for the men on their stone barges. When Wittlesey Mere was drained in the nineteenth century four large blocks of Barnack stone were revealed (figure 7.4). They were presumably lost in a medieval barge accident. Each weighs approximately one ton, with the largest measuring 94cm × 73.5cm × 73.5cm (Jenkins, 1993: 260).

In inland fisheries boats were used for operating nets, setting traps and managing fish weirs. The Domesday survey records fishing activity in the Fens. In Whittlesey Mere the abbot of Ramsey had one boat, the abbot of Peterborough one boat and the abbot of Thorney two boats (Bond, 1988: 80). Boats were not only used on large expanses of water but were also employed on fish ponds. In 1256–59 the king ordered the bailiff of Woodstock to cause 'oak to be chopped down in the park of the king at Woodstock and to cause a certain boat to be made to be placed in the fishponds of the king'. At the same time a boat was provided by the warden of the houses of the king and of the fishpond at Havering, for the king's fishermen when he sent them down to fish (Steane, 1988: 48).

By the early thirteenth century, fish weirs had in some places become an obstruction to navigation and this problem was especially serious on larger rivers like the Severn and Thames. An Act first passed in 1346–47 for 'remedying annoyances in the four great Rivers of England, Thames, Severn, Ouse and Trent', and orders that 'all wears, mills, stanks, stakes, and kiddles which disturbed the passage of ships and boats in great rivers should be utterly pulled down', had little effect and needed to be repeated nine times up to 1495 (Bond, 1988: 86–7).

A ferry across the River Tamar is recorded in a 1337 survey of the Duchy of Cornwall. 'Three burgesses of Esshe [Saltash] hold. . . the passage of Esshe with rent pertaining to the same passage with a boat and four oars for the said passage'. It must have been a sizeable boat, for we learn that 'John de Ferar shall cross there and his whole household with all carts' (Hull, 1971: 119, 122–3).

Boat finds

Numerous small boats have been found in inland contexts in Britain. Many of them are logboats. There has long been a popular assumption that because simple logboats are products of very basic technology they must be of an early date. McGrail (1978a) has compiled a corpus of the logboats of England and Wales, obtaining samples for radiocarbon dating where possible. Results obtained have shown that many logboats previously thought be be prehistoric are in fact medieval.

Nine logboats found within a 20 kilometre stretch of the River Mersey have produced radiocarbon dates ranging from the ninth to the twelfth centuries. Their period of use probably falls within the eleventh century (McGrail and Switsur, 1979: 93–115). They were made from short oaks, given rounded ends with protrusions resembling stem and stern posts. Horizontal holes for mooring ropes were bored through their forward ends. An early eleventh-century date seems likely for the large logboat, more than five metres long, found at Stanley Ferry, Yorkshire, in 1838 (McGrail, 1981: 164).

An extended logboat was found in the drained bed of the former Kentmere Lake, near Kendal in Cumbria, in 1955. This logboat has been radiocarbon dated to 650 ± 120 bp (D-71) or about 1300 ad (Wilson, 1966). It is a hybrid between a logboat and a plank boat. The base is a shallow oak dug-out hull, 4.25 metres long and 0.61 metres wide, which is flat bottomed with a rounded stern and slightly pointed prow. To this are attached, on either side, five wash strakes. The strakes were each made of two planks, joined by a short (10cm) scarf in the centre. No logboat with so many side strakes is known from a continental European context. Four ribs made from grown oak crooks were treenailed to the hull and to the top strake. The strakes were fastened together clinker-fashion with round-headed nails which did not have roves but which had their ends hammered over. A rowlock was found attached to the top strake on the better preserved side of the boat, suggesting that there was a central thwart for the oarsman, and an ash plank found near the boat might have been a thwart. At the junction between the top of the hollowed log, which formed the bottom of the boat, and the lower edge of the planking there was a strip of wood treenailed onto the outside of each side of the hull, running along about three-quarters of the boat's length. These strips would have enhanced the boat's stability, making it less likely that it would capsize. Like the River Mersey logboats mentioned above, the prow of the Kentmere boat had a projecting cutwater through which there was a hole, presumably for a mooring rope.

Only about 40 km from the find-spot of the Kentmere boat, the Giggleswick Tarn logboat (figure 7.5) was similarly found in the bed of a drained lake, in 1863. It has been radiocarbon dated to 615 bp ± 40 (Q-1245) or about 1335 ad (McGrail, 1978b: 29). It was made of ash and its overall length is 2.45 metres with a maximum beam of 0.63 metres. It is interesting because of the strengthening timbers fastened across the ends and because of external longitudinal timbers at the level of the sheer. These would have provided strength and would have assisted stability when the boat was heavily laden.

A logboat found on the shore of Oak Mere, Cheshire, (figure 7.6) has been radiocarbon dated to 1395–1470 ad (McGrail, pers. comm.). It demonstrates that logboats continued in use until a very late date and that their builders had developed a thorough understanding of the raw material and how to shape it to produce boats with good stability and performance characteristics (McGrail, 1978a: 249). The logboat was 3.6 metres in length with a maximum beam of 0.79 metres. It had a slight keel carved out of the solid wood, with hollows on each side, which would have helped it to maintain a straight course. Both ends were raised and pointed to provide a cutwater and to prevent swamping. A maximum amount of wood had been hollowed away, producing a light boat with thin sides. Extra thickness was provided in two places and the excavator described these as 'ribs' cut out of the solid (Newstead, 1935: 210); they would have provided extra strength at the seat positions.

The number of logboats in the archaeological record is probably disproportionately large because they are solid and readily identified when they are found by chance. Fewer plank-built boats have been recorded, probably because their remains can be slight and fragmentary. Several pieces of oak boat planking were found during archaeological excavations in the moat of Southchurch Hall at Southend in Essex. Although scattered, they were in similar stratigraphical positions, and some of them were sealed under bridge footings which were constructed in the early thirteenth century. The excavated planking was very fragmentary and fragile. There are nine main pieces, several consisting of more than one plank. All the finds share sufficient common characteristics for there to be no doubt that they are all from the same boat. By the direction of the scarfs and the presence of hood ends it can be inferred that the planking came from the starboard side of the boat adjacent to the stern post. The edges of the planks exhibit strong curvature for building a generous curve into the side of the boat, giving a round stern.

Giggleswick Tarn – remains

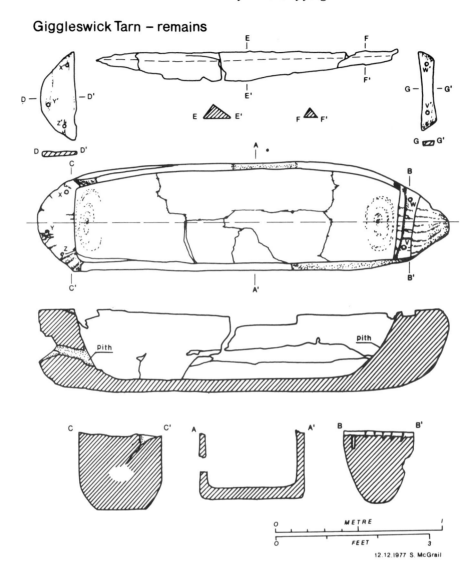

Figure 7.5 The Giggleswick Tarn logboat (National Maritime Museum).

The planks are exceptionally thin, with a maximum thickness at their centre of 12mm and at the nail holes of only 9mm, so the greatest thickness of the boat's hull, where the runs of planking overlap, was less than 20mm. The excavated planking contains a surprisingly large number of scarfs for such a small boat, suggesting either that it was not considered worth the expense of good long boards or that lengths had been pieced in as repairs. The timbers were extensively patched.

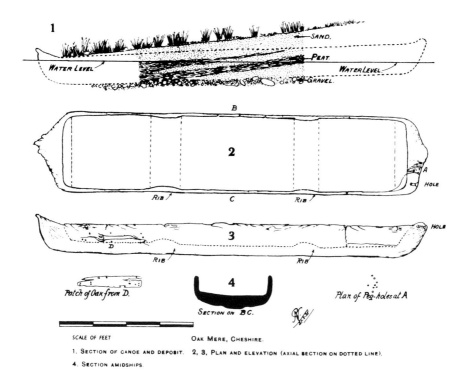

Figure 7.6   The logboat from Oak Mere (from Newstead, 1935).

The Southchurch Hall boat was a small, lightly built, round-sterned vessel which had had its useful life prolonged by major repairs. Although we know it had a stern post, we do not know whether it had a keel or a flat-planked bottom. The length and beam of the boat and the shape of the bow are also unknown. It is possible that it had been used for pleasure, as shown in figure 7.7, before ending its days in the moat.

Threave Castle, built on an island in the River Dee in Galloway, had a shallow harbour cut out of the bedrock to allow boats to moor in a place protected from the fast river current. Excavations within the harbour have produced parts of an oar blade and a paddle blade, probably deposited in the late fourteenth or the fifteenth century. The object illustrated as a boat's rudder by Good and Tabraham (1981: 121) is more likely a window shutter or a box lid.

Many castles, other than those where the elevation of the site was part of the defensive design, were sited so that they could be reached by boat. The stone to build them was usually brought by water and provisions continued to be supplied by this means. Familiar examples include those castles built beside major tidal rivers, such as the Tower of London on the Thames and Rochester on the Medway. Less obvious ones are Castle Acre in Norfolk (Coad and Streeten, 1982: 138) on the River Nar, which runs through King's

Figure 7.7   Pleasure boating in the fifteenth century (BL Add. Ms. 54782 f.54. By permission of the British Library).

Lynn to the Wash, and Berkhamsted on the River Bulbourne in Hertfordshire. The Welsh castles built by Edward I (1272–1307) all had access to tidal waters and the sea (Brown, 1976: 95–115). In the case of Rhuddlan, this was achieved by the considerable labour involved in diverting the course of the River Clwyd into a newly cut deep-water channel of about four kilometres long (Taylor, 1974: 319–20). Many of these castles are known to have had docks. That at Beaumaris still survives and the one at Baynard's Castle in London has been referred to in the previous chapter. Castle studies would benefit from a greater awareness of the importance of waterbourne communication. There is much to be learnt by investigating the areas of castles most likely to reveal evidence for activity associated with water transport.

The plank-built boat shown in figure 7.8 was discovered in 1982 during the construction of an artificial lake at Caldecotte, Buckinghamshire (Hutchinson, 1983). More than half of the boat was, unfortunately, torn off and irretrievably dumped. The hull was severed obliquely so that only one end remained, with approximately 2.5 metres of one side and about one metre of the other. The surviving portion consisted of part of a flat keel-plank made from elm, a stem of roughly triangular cross-section hewn from curved oak, an oak frame timber and planking made from sawn oak boards. The boat was of clinker construction with three overlapping strakes and a stealer (a short plank filling the angular space between the stem post and the keel) on each side. Additional narrow strips of wood (rubbing strips) were applied on the upper outside edge of the top strakes. The component shapes

Figure 7.8   The boat found at Caldecotte, Milton Keynes (National Maritime Museum).

were well thought out but the fastening was not very carefully done, perhaps suggesting that boats of this type had been made for a long time before this example.

The boat was lying towards the edge of an old watercourse, roughly parallel to the bank. In the Middle Ages the surrounding area was marshland. There was a mooring chain and spike fastened to the inside of the stem and left dangling overboard and three pieces of hemp rope were found under the boat.

The remains contained insufficient tree rings for dendrochronology. The widest oak components, the planks, were through-sawn boards so that many of the same tree rings occur twice in the same cross-section. A radiocarbon date (HAR-5201) of 410 ± 60 years bp or about 1480–1600 ad was obtained, indicating that the boat belongs to the medieval or early post-medieval period.

The closest parallel for the Caldecotte boat, in shape and construction, is the Somerset turf boat (McKee, 1983: 107–9), a type still being made in this century. It has mooring chains similar to that on the Caldecotte boat at both ends. The question of the survival of medieval boat types into recent times is intriguing and the case of the Tyne keel has already been mentioned. The appearance of some other vessels, for example the Fenland lighters (Jenkins, 1993), suggests an ancient origin but medieval examples have not yet been excavated. Good pictorial evidence for vernacular craft can often be found extending back to the seventeenth century but rarely much before. There is a need for further research on pictorial sources to elucidate changes in local types in the post-medieval period. This would serve as a bridge between the traditional craft which survived into the twentieth century, which have been extensively documented, often just before they became extinct, and the small craft in use in the Middle Ages.

8 Fishing

The physical remains of medieval fishing are elusive. A recent book (Blair and Ramsay, 1991), intended to update Salzman's 1923 volume on medieval industries, omits fishing on the grounds that there is insufficient material evidence. However, in a recent special study of the subject (Aston, 1988), the contributors have demonstrated that a great deal of information is available, especially about inland fisheries and features such as ponds and weirs. This chapter will concentrate on sea fishing, touching on the use of boats in inland fisheries.

Fish and shellfish were of great importance in the medieval diet. The church forbade meat consumption on at least two days a week as well as on certain other holy days and during the six weeks of Lent. The accounts of aristocratic and ecclesiastical households show that these rules were observed. The Winchester diet rolls demonstrate that fish was the main course on most of the days of the week (Bond, 1988: 70). The documents also indicate a large proportion of sea-fish. Dyer (1988: 30) has observed that sea-fish were generally consumed in much greater quantities than fresh-water species and that distance from the coast did not prevent inland households from buying both fresh and preserved sea-fish. Evidence about the particular species consumed comes from the documents and from the fishbones and shells retrieved from excavations. Herring and cod were the most important fish but a great variety of other species were consumed, including sole, plaice, flounder, haddock, ling and mackerel. Rarities included whale and sturgeon. Oysters were the most common shellfish but mussels, whelks, cockles, crab and lobster were also eaten.

There is little information about the organisation of sea fishing. It seems to have been carried out by small operators, some of whom worked on behalf of monastic houses. Taylor (1988: 466) has questioned whether fishing took place at anything more than a domestic level before 1200. In remote coastal settlements, without a great deal of demand from the hinterland, fishing was a subsistence industry. It is unlikely that even fishermen supplying large urban markets could become wealthy. As fish was a basic foodstuff, the more that was produced the cheaper it became. New and improved methods of fish preservation allowed fishermen to take advantage of the seasonal peaks in availability and made it possible to distribute fish over greater distances from the place at which they were landed. For example, herrings from East Anglia were traded to Italy and Spain (Saul, 1981: 33). Increasing demand for fish throughout the period resulted in the expansion of the fisheries to Iceland and later to Newfoundland.

The potential archaeological remains of sea fishing are considered in this chapter. Catching gear includes various types of net or hook and line for different species of fish, as well as floats, weights and net-making equipment. Fishing boats may also show adaptation in size, hull shape and fittings, related to: the type of gear used and whether the boats worked off beaches or out of harbours; the distance worked off shore; and sea conditions.

Marine fishtraps were constructed in the inter-tidal zone. Shore sites associated with fishing include whole villages and the fishing quarters of larger ports with their harbour works and quays. Beaches may have had winches, huts and net-drying sheds as well as boatbuilding and repair sites. Fish-processing facilities should be found close to where the catches were landed and the remains of packaging, such as barrels and casks, and fishbones and shells can be expected on habitation sites. Fresh sea-fish were sold at markets as far inland as Bicester, Oxford, Wantage, Coventry and Gloucester (Bond, 1988: 77). Because oysters could be kept alive for weeks in barrels of salt-water, their shells are ubiquitous in medieval excavations.

Assessing the importance of fish remains in the diet of past populations is fraught with difficulties. Because fishbones disintegrate readily as a result of cooking, digestion, trampling and general biodegradation, the fish remains recovered from deposits are a very small sample of those originally discarded (Jones, 1992: 96). Herring bones are particularly fragile while those of cod are among the most robust. At the eleventh- and twelfth-century fishing settlement at Fuller's Hill, Great Yarmouth, 19 species of mainly marine fish have been identified. Herring, cod, whiting and mackerel dominated in all phases. Plaice also occurs in most samples, as does haddock and the conger eel to a lesser extent (Wheeler and Jones, 1976: 212). Cod was the dominant species recovered from the midden at Castle Acre Priory (Wilcox, 1980) and also at Kirkstall Abbey (Ryder, 1969: 387). Excavations at the Austin Friars in Leicester produced cod, ling, haddock and plaice or flounder bones but no remains of fresh-water fish (Thawley, 1981: 174).

Fish catching gear

Fish can be caught with hooks, nets and traps and different gear is appropriate for different species. Large demersal fish which are bottom feeders, like cod and haddock, could be caught with hook and line. Smaller pelagic fish which swim in shoals, herring especially, were more suitable for catching in nets. Eels, flounders and small plaice could be caught in shallow water with spears.

For fishing with hook and line at sea, hand lines and long lines were used. No medieval fishing line has been found in Britain. It would need to be fine and to have a considerable breaking strain: horse hair and bast would have been suitable and also good quality hemp line. Medieval fish-hooks have been found at numerous sites. They are mostly of iron though some are bronze. They are not small; a hook must not be too small because the fish may swallow it whole and bite through the line. In London the Trig Lane, Billingsgate and Custom House sites have all produced medieval fish-hooks. Their average length is about 50mm with some larger ones up to 75mm. They are all barbed and, instead of having eyes like modern fish-hooks, their ends are thickened or flattened so that the line bent round them would not slip off. Forty-five fish-hooks from the period 1000–1200 were found on excavations at Fuller's Hill, Great Yarmouth and three of these are shown in figure 8.1. They are similar in shape to the London examples and vary in length from 45mm to 75mm with one very large example 122mm long.

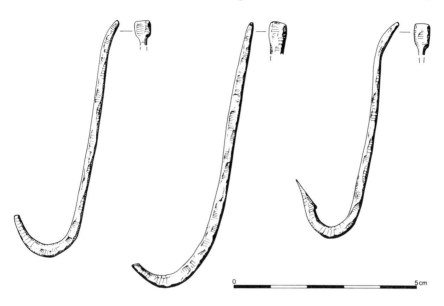

Figure 8.1 Fish-hooks from Fuller's Hill, Great Yarmouth (after Rogerson, 1976).

Hooks of this size would have been effective for catching the largest fishes represented by the remains from the site, such as spurdog, conger eel, ling, cod, large haddock, turbot and halibut (Wheeler and Jones, 1976: 221). Excavations at Hartlepool have produced two sea-fishing hooks in an early thirteenth-century context, one 75mm long, the other, which has a barb, 50mm long. There are also three iron hooks from Pevensey (Dulley, 1967) and one from Sewer Lane, Hull (Steane and Foreman, 1988: 146–8). A pewter spoon from Beverley is engraved with an image of three fish about to take hooks (figure 8.2).

Long lines with many hooks attached and weighted at the end, were towed from fishing vessels, including the English doggers which worked Icelandic waters from the fourteenth century. Hooks were fastened singly or in small numbers on hand lines, between a weight and a float to keep the hook submerged at the desired depth. The line might be wound on a hand frame, such as those found in sailors' chests in the wreck of the *Mary Rose*. They have wooden side pieces joined by dowels and have floats 20mm in diameter, 60mm to 90mm long (Steane and Foreman, 1988: 149–53). On the Thames foreshore large numbers of lead fishing-line weights, lost by anglers from the waterfronts, have been recovered. They are of various different shapes – pyramidal, conical or pear-shaped – and include a group of more than 40 ascribed to the fifteenth century (Steane and Foreman, 1988: 155).

Evidence for nets and floats, netting tools and hemp twine have been found in the Netherlands, Norway, Russia and Poland (Steane and Foreman,

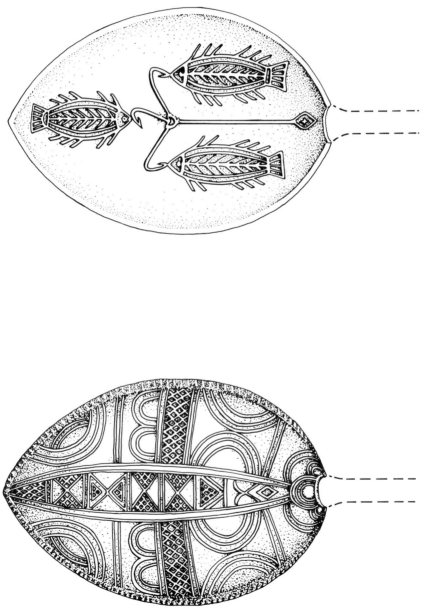

Figure 8.2 A fishing scene on a pewter spoon found in Beverley (Humberside Archaeology Unit).

1988: 162). The manufacture of nets with the weaver knot, which is still the most widely used netmaking knot in Europe and America, has been carried out in north-west Europe from very early times (von Brandt, 1984: 115–16). There are scant remains of actual nets and contemporary illustrations do little to throw light on the nature of the gear or its method of operation. Small bag-shaped nets are sometimes depicted, as in a late thirteenth-century French illumination of the calling of St Peter (BL Add. Ms. 17341, f.153v). Another illumination, from the early fourteenth-century *Queen Mary's Psalter* (figure 8.3), shows fishermen hauling in a narrow net with thick ropes along both edges and a wooden bar at one end. This appears to be a draw-net, which worked by surrounding the fish as the lines attached to the net were drawn in. A roundhaul net could be operated between two boats, with one end made fast to one of the boats while the other boat circled to set it. It could also be used from a single boat by buoying one end during the setting process then attaching the draglines to the ends of the mast laid along the boat, so that the mouth of the net is kept as open as possible (figure 8.4). A line of floats was attached to the head rope, along the top edge of the net, and a line of sinkers to the foot rope along its bottom. The central part of the net, for holding the fish while it was drawn in, might be in bag form. The wings and the long draglines attached to them helped to drive the fish into the centre.

A seine (or scoop) net like this could also be worked from a beach. This was the method which was used in the Cornish pilchard fishery in the sixteenth century. A boat took one end of the net out into the sea in a wide arc then back to the beach. The nets worked most successfully when set a long way out but with their feet weighted so they touched the bottom and their heads buoyed at the surface. The prevalence of beach seine netting in the Elizabethan period has led to the assumption that it was a new invention. It seems to be the case that seine nets were in use long previously but that a cycle in the shoaling behaviour of pilchards combined with improved methods of preservation and increasing demand to turn beach seining into a major industry at that time.

Drift-nets were used to catch North Sea herring. The date of introduction of this type of net is also unknown. Most of the fish caught this way were trapped by their gills in the mesh, implying that it was very fine. Of four boats arrested at Great Yarmouth in 1311, one carried seven nets, two 17 and one 27; some nets were valued at 3s. and others at 5s. In 1316, 89 nets were stolen from a vessel off Ravenser. The depth of the nets was probably constant at eight to ten yards (four to five fathoms or 7.2 to nine metres) but their length and the numbers used strung out together varied considerably (Saul, 1981: 34). In the first quarter of the fifteenth century large herring drift gill nets, 50 to 60 fathoms (90 to 108 metres) in length, were being made at Hoorn in the Netherlands (Cutting, 1955: 66). The nets drifted independently, suspended from a buoyed head-line, accompanied by a vessel. Cork might have been used for buoys; it was imported into England at least as early as the fourteenth century, as customs accounts from King's Lynn record (Steane and Foreman, 1988: 162). Buoys made of sheepskin and dogskin were also used for fishing gear in the Northern Isles, as well as kegs (Fenton, 1978: 567).

Figure 8.3 Hauling in a fishing net, from *Queen Mary's Psalter*, early fourteenth century (Royal MS 2 B VII f 73. By permission of the British Library).

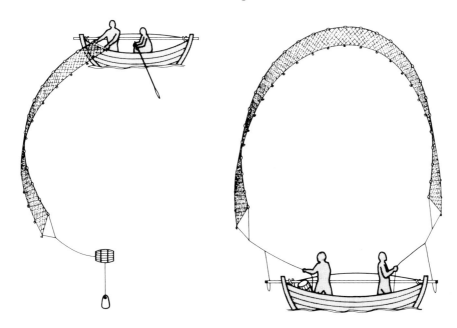

Figure 8.4 Fishing with a roundhaul net (National Maritime Museum).

Oysters could be gathered at low water or by a drag towed behind a boat. The drag was made of strong thick netting with teeth or spills of iron to dredge the sea-bed. The trawl net for flat-fish may have developed from this. The trawl is a large bag net, with either a frame all round the entrance or a bar to hold the mouth open. It has to be pulled along. A Parliamentary petition in 1377 complained of the recent invention of a new type of fishing net like an oyster drag of outsize dimensions, with a fine mesh (Steane and Foreman, 1988: 159). If trawls were not in use before this we might expect a sudden increase in the proportion of flat-fish in fishbone assemblages.

Ethnographic evidence helps to outline the possible methods of catching fish but of course cannot provide information about the date of introduction of different fishing techniques. Hand-held scoop and skimming nets have been used for catching small fish and prawns and small baited nets fixed to hoops for lobsters. 'Poke' nets or 'dip' nets, which have a circular rim to support a net bag suspended from a pole, were in recent use in the Northern Isles. They trapped fish which were attracted by the bait of salt herring, pounded limpets or mashed crab (Fenton, 1978: 537).

Sea traps

Nets were also used to make tidal traps. Carew, in the sixteenth century, records that in Cornwall stakes were set in the mud at low water, across a creek from shore to shore. A net was fastened to the foot of the stakes and

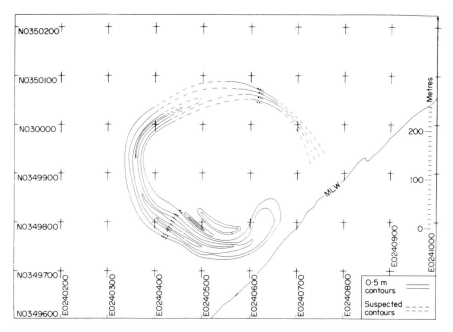

Figure 8.5   A tidal fish-trap in Caernarfon Bay (from Momber, 1991).

at high tide the upper part of the net was pulled up so that it formed a curtain across the creek. When the tide ebbed the fish were left on the mud (Halliday, 1953: 115).

There are numerous tidal fish-traps around the coast of north and west Wales (Jones, 1983: 28–9). They are dry-stone barriers constructed in the inter-tidal zone in areas of considerable tidal range, usually in excess of five metres. At high tide they fill up with water and with fish, then as the tide ebbs the water drains away and the fish are trapped. Most of the Welsh fish-traps are semi-circular or semi-oval in plan with enclosures at the seaward end to contain the catch. Jones (1983: 30) has identified four different types. The fish-traps were self-baiting because marine worms colonised the silts which accumulated in their seaward ends and these attracted small fish. The small fish established habitats in the walls and were preyed upon by larger fish.

The origins of the traps are lost in folklore but they were certainly still being built in the medieval period and some were used by the Cistercians. Aerial reconnaissance in 1989 revealed a semi-circular structure lying just off the coast in Caernarfon Bay, North Wales. The anomaly has been demonstrated to be a fish-trap, constructed at about the beginning of the thirteenth century (figure 8.5). The enclosure wall has a central 'backbone' between one and two metres wide with collapsed boulders spread on either side. The boulders making up the wall were in the size range 0.30m to one metre across. The wall forms an incomplete ring and the area within it measures about 300 metres in diameter (Momber, 1991). A similar rubble stone sea-fish trap exists at Minehead. A net was placed over the entrance, to catch fish as the sea ebbed (Aston and Dennison, 1988: 401).

Stone anchors and net weights

Stone anchors were in use from prehistory to the post-medieval period and are important but not fully explained marine artefacts. The very large ones were probably for anchoring boats while the smaller ones may have been used as additional weights on anchor cables or for anchoring fishing nets or pots. It is worth distinguishing between stone anchors, where the stone is used in combination with wooden stakes which enable it to grip the bottom and so resist being dragged along, and stone weights which rely on gravity to keep them in position.

Archimedes' principle states that any object immersed in liquid experiences an upthrust equal to the weight of the liquid displaced. This means that a large stone, which a man could hardly shift on dry land, becomes far easier to lift on the sea-bed. The difference in weight of an object in water and in air depends on its density, since to calculate the weight of a submerged object, the weight of the volume of water displaced by the object must be subtracted from its air weight. Lead is so dense that its weight is scarcely affected by immersion but the weight of stone certainly is. The sinkers on the foot-rope of a fishing net have to be sufficiently heavy to keep the slightly buoyant hemp netting hanging nearly vertically, without submerging the floats on the head-rope.

Stone anchors or weights have so far been found in the sea around Britain only as stray finds, without any rope or other associated organic material which can be used for dating. Recording the depth of water in which the weights were found, and the nature of the bottom, may give some clue as to the type of operation for which they were used. Markey has reported on two stone anchors from Dorset and notes the existence of at least 16 others (1991: 50). The considerable weight (37.5kg and 21kg) of the two which he describes and the presence of rectangular holes which were probably for wooden tines, suggest that these were for anchoring boats. They contrast with the group of nine holed stones found by divers in about four metres of water near the foot of a small cliff at the south-east tip of Guernsey. These irregularly shaped stones, about 30cm long and 18cm thick, each have only a single hole and weigh about 2kg (Hurst, 1969: 194–5).

Five undated stone weights have been examined at the National Maritime Museum (figure 8.6). 'A' is disc-shaped and made of sandstone, about 48cm in diameter and 7mm thick with a central perforation. It was found by a diver 400 metres off Seaford, Sussex. 'B', also of sandstone, was found off Brown's Bay, Cullercoats, Tyne and Wear, in about 12 metres of water (McCumiskey, 1980). 'C' was found by a diver off Plymouth, Devon. It is made of red sandstone with faceted sides and a hole at one end. This anchor is different in shape from any recorded in the literature and has been carefully designed to avoid chafing of the rope during use. 'D' is a triangular unperforated stone weight found on the beach at Dunwich, Suffolk.

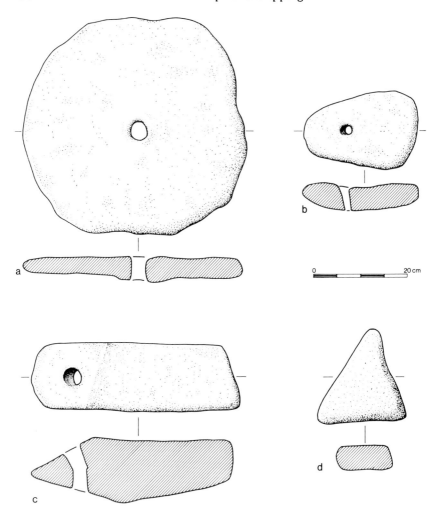

Figure 8.6 Stone weights: (a) Seaford; (b) Cullercoats; (c) Plymouth; (d) Dunwich (National Maritime Museum).

Nance (1913; 1921a; 1921b) has described the recent use of killicks, composite anchors using stones and wooden components, in Cornwall. He documented a great variety of forms. They were used for fishing boats because the rough, rocky sea-bed claimed so heavy a toll of lost anchors that more expensive ones could not be afforded (Nance, 1913: 298). He also described how Marazion pilchard fishermen used a disc-shaped 'bully stone', repeatedly dashing it into the water to frighten back the fish that attempted to break out of the still unjoined ends of the seine. They chose stones of as light a colour as possible to cause maximum alarm to the fish (Nance, 1913, 296–7). The pale disc-shaped stone from Seaford (figure 8.6a) would serve very well as a 'bully stone'.

Anchor stones are also found in inland waterways. Seventy-two of them have been found in an ancient channel of the river Trent at Hemington Fields, Castle Donington, Leicestershire, in the vicinity of a Norman mill-dam. The stones were made mostly of rubble derived from local rocks, with some reused masonry. They had V-shaped cuts on two or more sides, giving a waisted appearance. Their weight varied from 9kg to 50kg. One groove retained remains of a twisted band of split withies, which gave a radiocarbon date of 1175–1410 ad (OxA – 2289). The reason for their deposition has not been explained but they may have been used to weight down fish-trap structures (Salisbury, 1991: 83, 86).

Ancillary fishing artefacts

As well as the more obvious fishing equipment, ancillary fishing artefacts might include such diverse objects as lanterns and spades. Fishing often took place at night, using lights to attract the fish. Spades were used for digging for bait; while baskets were used or carrying fish. At the fishing settlement at Fuller's Hill, Great Yarmouth, knives and whetstones, perhaps used for fish processing, formed a large part of the artefact assemblage and there were also two arrowheads which might have been used for spearing fish (Rogerson, 1976: 164).

Fishing boats

The design of fishing boats is determined by whether they work off beaches or out of harbours, the type of fishing gear operated, the nature of the fishing grounds and the length of time they spend at sea. Local boatbuilding traditions were strong and the same boat-types remained in use for centuries.

Excavation of fourteenth- and early fifteenth-century layers on part of the medieval waterfront in Poole, Dorset, (Watkins, 1994) revealed a store of timber for use in boatbuilding, as already described in Chapter 1. The boatyard produced a number of boats of similar size and shape and there is sufficient evidence to attempt a reconstruction of the type of boat represented by the majority of the used timbers and rough-outs (Hutchinson, 1994: 35). The reconstruction (figure 8.7) takes as its basis a keel 4.15m (13ft 6in) long, scarfed to stem and stern posts each 1.83m (6ft) long, giving an overall length of 7.81m (25ft 6in). The stern post need not have been the same shape as the stem post; a straighter post would have been more suited to a stern rudder. The boats would have had ten or eleven strakes per side and the beam is reconstructed as 2.45m (8ft). Boats of this size and shape would have been suitable for fishing: their hull shape would provide stability and their flat bottoms are suitable for beaching. A rope attachment hole low down on the stem post is suitably placed for hauling a boat onto a beach. Four Y-shaped mast crutches were found, intended to be used for supporting masts when they were unstepped and laid along the boat. Depictions of boats fishing, including those on a sixteenth-century map of Poole Harbour (Hutchinson, 1994: 37), show boats working their nets with their masts

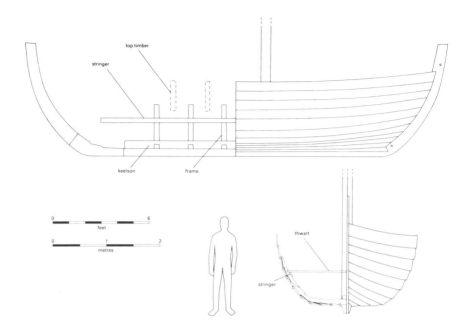

Figure 8.7   Reconstruction of a boat from the Poole boatyard (Poole Museums).

unstepped and supported in mast-crutches. This would increase stability and working space and would permit a line to be fastened between the end of the mast and the net. The Portland Lerret, a type of vessel remarkably similar to the reconstructed Poole Foundry boats, fishes off the nearby Chesil Bank to the present day (McKee, 1983: 188–9).

   Excavation of a boat which sank at Blackfriars, London, in the second half of the fifteenth century recovered nearly 2,000 fishing-net weights. The vessel (Blackfriars III) was originally about 16m long with a shallow keel and bottom planking of remarkable flatness as far as the turn of the bilge (figure 8.8). A mast-step, roughly amidships, showed that the vessel had been sailed and that the mast was designed to be unstepped easily. The hull had been extensively repaired. The net weights are made of lead, each about 25mm long and 12mm in diameter. They are each pierced by longitudinal holes. Two heavier lead weights were also found in the forward part of the boat. These weights may have been from a net that had been caught on the wreck (Marsden, 1979: 91). However, it seems unlikely that fishermen would have been working their nets right up against a Thames quay or that, if they were, all the weights would have been so bunched together. We might speculate that the net fell into the wreck from the quay, where it had been hung to dry, but surely the more likely explanation is that it was part of Blackfriars III's equipment. This need not mean that Blackfriars III was exclusively a fishing boat; there are plenty of documented examples of the use of boats for various purposes at different times of year.

Figure 8.8 Excavation of the Blackfriars III boat in London (National Maritime Museum).

To bring the catch of fish to shore in a fresh condition the Dutch adopted a type of boat called the *waterschip*. The earliest known reference to these in the written sources occurs in 1339 and about ten examples have been excavated in the IJsselmeerpolders. They are characteristically broad-bottomed forward with a sharp stern. The stem is curved and the stern is straight. A medieval example, probably of the fifteenth century, was excavated at site MZ 22 in the polders in 1978. The midships part of the boat was a 'bun', a fish-well compartment sealed from the rest of the vessel by heavy bulkheads, with holes in the hull planking to allow sea-water to flow through and thus keep the fish alive. This type of boat continued in use into the nineteenth century but the post-medieval examples were built with flush-laid planking rather than in the clinker technique (Reinders, 1979: 41–2; Reinders, 1982: 21).

Documentary sources occasionally give information about fishing practices. Heath (1969) has studied the accounts of the income of the parish church of Scarborough for the years 1414–18 and 1434–42 which include tithes from fishing expeditions. There were nearly 50 regular fishermen in Scarborough and they fell into three categories. The largest group mainly fished in 'batellae' and 'cobles'. 'Batellae' simply means 'small boats' and 'cobles' were presumably the ancestors of the boat-type of that name still used on the north-east coast (McKee, 1983: 88, 114). A quarter of the fishermen sometimes employed 'farcosts', a boat-type of unknown features (Burwash, 1947: 123), with examples recorded as being of from five to 40 tons in the fifteenth century. Small boats were used to catch plaice in winter, lobsters and cod during Lent, and skate in summer. The average annual income of these fishermen was about £7. The second group of fishermen fished for herrings in winter and were engaged on 'the North Sea fare', catching cod and haddock on the spawning grounds east of Scotland and the Dogger Bank, in spring. All of these also fished in farcosts, but only two briefly used cobles or batellae. Their average gross annual income was more than ten times greater than the first group, at £77. The third group consisted of 16 fishermen who, in addition to fishing herring, went to Iceland for cod in summer. Their average gross annual income was £85.

Richard Hakluyt, writing in the sixteenth century, claimed that the men of Blakeney fished off Iceland in the reign of Edward III. There is no evidence for this. It may be that the first English fishermen to sail to Iceland were those whose ship arrived there in 1412 (Marcus, 1956: 313). Icelandic sagas record they were followed in the summer of 1413 by 30 or more fishing doggers from England. It is possible that some fragments of English doggers lie on the sea-bed around Iceland: in 1419 no fewer than 25 English ships were wrecked in a gale on Maundy Thursday. 'All the men were lost, but the goods and splinters of the ships were cast up everywhere' (Marcus, 1956: 315).

Vessels called 'doggers' were used for the Iceland trade. They seem to have originated in the Low Countries but by the fifteenth century the dogger was the ubiquitous east coast fishing vessel (Marcus, 1954: 294). The term seems to have been applied to a variety of medium-sized craft. Fifteenth-century documents referring to East Anglian ports record them as ranging from 30 to 80 tons with crews of 20 to 30 men (Heath, 1969: 60). From 1483 the annual fishing fleet sailed to Iceland in convoy and the Iceland trade probably reached its peak in the early sixteenth century (Marcus, 1954: 296).

The 'crayer' was another type of vessel mentioned in fifteenth-century documents as comparable in size to doggers or a little smaller (Burwash, 1947: 120–24). Its name suggests it may originally have been used for catching marine crustaceans but in the fifteenth century crayers seem to have been used for carrying cargoes rather than for fishing.

It seems that around 1416–25 herring ceased to spawn in the Baltic and the failure of the fishery there may have contributed to the decline of the Hanse. The North Sea became the new focus of the herring industry although Heath (1969: 61) has questioned whether the east coast fishery grew as a result. Dutch fishing vessels worked their way down the coast, starting at Shetland in June or July, reaching Great Yarmouth in the autumn and sailing home from the Thames estuary after Christmas (Cutting, 1955: 63). Herring busses evolved in the Netherlands in the fifteenth century as deep-sea fishing vessels with capacity for salting fish on board. Tradition has it that the first busses were built at Hoorn and Enkhuizen in 1416 and by 1450 the whole of province of Zeeland had them. They were large, seaworthy ships usually of 80 to 100 tuns burden, with a characteristically high and narrow poop and very full in the body and the waterline. They had a beam of 15 to 17 feet with a keel length of only about 50 feet. Their crews of about 14 or 15 men included skilled picklers and coopers to make the barrels tight. Busses were usually armed and frequently convoyed by warships (Cutting, 1955: 66).

Fish processing

Fish were preserved by four different methods in the Middle Ages: drying, smoking, salting and pickling. In conditions of cold and low humidity in Norway and Iceland, white fish (cod, haddock, pollock and ling) were dried out of doors with little or no pre-treatment with salt. The stockfish produced in this way were traded throughout Europe. Jones (1992) has suggested that they may be recognised in bone assemblages by the disproportionate ratio of head to body bones. Smoking was either done cold, as for example with bloaters, or 'hot' in a kiln. Recent practice in smoking on a domestic scale can probably be projected back into the Middle Ages – Arbroath smokies were smoked in pit kilns and in Sanday, Orkney, the poorer inhabitants lived on fish, salted and hung in the chimneys to smoke (Fenton, 1978: 528). Red herrings were produced by a method which combined heavy salting with hard smoking: the fish were first washed to remove the salt they had been packed in at sea, they were then put in salt again for about two weeks after which they were taken out, washed, hung up on sticks through their mouths and gills and smoked over wood fires for seven to 28 days. This technique is supposed to have been developed in Yarmouth at around the beginning of the fourteenth century (Cutting, 1955: 71–6).

Fish houses were probably tall with small floor areas. For example, in Yarmouth in 1311 and 1312, two plots, 49 feet by 90 and 47 feet by 74, each contained a fish-house and a salthouse. Fish-houses were frequently given names, often similar to those of ships or perhaps taverns, such as 'Blithe', 'Paradise' and 'Lamb' (Saul, 1981: 35).

Cod, whiting, mackerel and eels, as well as herring, were preserved by salting. Packing fish in salt preserves it for a short time but for longer preservation the fish had to be gutted and cleaned before packing in airtight containers. This is termed 'pickling' although it does not involve the use of vinegar. Herring were gutted, washed in sea water, roused in salt and packed in barrels. Towards the end of the fourteenth century Dutch herring cured in this way were considered superior to those of any other country. They were sorted and packed in casks, head to tail, with salt between the layers, which were then arranged alternately across each other. Regulations stated that they had to contain one part of salt to three parts of fish. The barrels were made airtight and branded with the date of catch (Cutting, 1955: 62–3). Pilchards were salt-cured and packed in barrels like herrings. As they are fattier than herring, they were pressed in barrels to remove some of the oil before topping up with brine and lidding (Cutting, 1955: 79).

Preserved fish were much cheaper than fresh fish and could be distributed further. In 1338 Edward III obtained 400 lasts of herring (about half a million fish) from Great Yarmouth, for the army in Flanders (Cutting, 1955: 35). The port books of Southampton for 1427–30 show that there was a large coastwise trade in salted herrings, chiefly from Covehithe, Southwold, Dunwich, Lowestoft, Orwell and Walberswick in Suffolk, and Great Yarmouth, Cromer and Cley in Norfolk. Other sources mentioned are Newcastle, Easton near Portland and Penzance. The total recorded import to Southampton in 1430 was 2,590½ barrels, or about 500 tons (Cutting, 1955: 69).

Fishing settlements

By the thirteenth century, Great Yarmouth had become one of the major herring markets of Europe. There are many records of monastic houses sending ships there. These included Durham priory and several Cistercian monasteries such as Waverley, Boxley, Robertsbridge and Beaulieu. The monastic houses acquired property in or near the town as a base for their operations (Bond, 1988: 75–6).

The villages of Porthoustock and Porthallow in Cornwall were used as fishing bases by Beaulieu Abbey. In about 1240 the abbey purchased a building in Porthoustock with an open space extending ten feet by 20 feet outside for drying fish. In 1317 the Abbey acquired a plot at nearby 'Porthalon' with a slipway where the abbot's men could draw up their boats (Bond, 1988: 76). Porthoustock today has a broad, well-sheltered, gently sloping and firm gravel beach, onto which fishing boats are still drawn up (figure 8.9). Steep, well-wooded slopes on each side would have provided abundant fuel and a small river runs to the sea there. Porthallow has similar topography but with a narrower beach and steeper slopes flanking a wider valley with more space available for settlement. Neither of these places is easily accessible by land and they must have relied largely on seaborne communications. The Beaulieu Abbey fishermen seem to have used the ports

Figure 8.9 The fishing cove at Porthoustock, Cornwall (photo: Steve Hartgroves, Cornwall Archaeological Unit).

as a shore base and presumably processed and packed the products of extended fishing expeditions before returning home. The very small size of the open area attached to the building in Porthoustock suggests that there was pressure on space in the settlement. Early fourteenth-century records of rents levied on fishing ports in the Duchy of Cornwall, assessed according to the number of boats, show that Porthallow was a substantial fishing village – fifth out of the 13 ports listed – paying only slightly less rent than Fowey (Hull, 1971: 137).

9 *Shipping and warfare*

Between the Norman invasion and the early sixteenth century, immense changes came about in the ships used in warfare. These resulted not only from developments in shipbuilding but also in response to the tactics of fighting at sea and the introduction of new weaponry. Throughout the Middle Ages ships were constantly involved in military activities, transporting troops and equipment, defending the coast, blockading opponents' ports and occasionally fighting battles at sea.

Warfare is perhaps the best documented area of medieval shipping activity, since most of it was directed by central authority. Administrative documents include those listing ships 'arrested' from their owners for use in seaborne campaigns, as well as financial accounts for the building of royal ships. There are also many narratives of battles. Pictorial evidence is plentiful and often vividly detailed.

Fighting at sea

Lessons in sea warfare learnt during the course of the Crusades were transferred to Northern Europe (figure 9.1). Perhaps the most important of these was an appreciation of the advantage of height when firing missiles and throwing projectiles and incendiary devices down onto an enemy ship. Crusaders also learnt about 'Greek fire' – an incendiary and explosive compound which was fired from bows or thrown in pots. The Pipe Rolls of Richard I for 1193 record the purchase of materials to make Greek fire (Brooks, 1928: 116–18) but its precise composition is unknown and is likely to remain so unless a pot of it is discovered on the sea-bed. In addition to pitch it may have contained resin, naptha, and sulphur. If saltpetre and charcoal were also included it would have approximated to gunpowder. Reputedly it could only be extinguished by sand, vinegar or urine (Brooks, 1933: 55) and contemporary writers described ships covered in felt soaked in vinegar by way of protection against Greek fire. The purchase of 14 pounds of felt is recorded in the building account for the Newcastle galley of 1295 (Whitwell and Johnson, 1926: 157).

In the Battle of Dover, fought in 1217, the English fleet gained tactical advantage over the fleet of the French king by manoeuvring into position with both the wind and the sun behind them. They then threw down quicklime onto the French ships to blind their crews (Brooks, 1933: 218–19). One of the French ships was carrying a *trebuchet* but this seems to have been intended for use after landing. There is no evidence that stone-throwing engines were used on board ships in northern Europe (Brooks, 1928: 120). The crossbow was the chief weapon used in sea battles and the first phase of fighting was an archery battle as the ships closed on each other (figure 9.2). To engage another ship, the attacker attempted to position his forecastle against the side of the enemy ship and prevent its escape by the use of

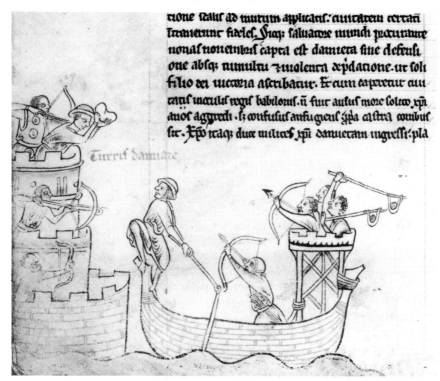

Figure 9.1 Crusaders attacking Damietta, Egypt, in 1248 (Matthew Paris MS 16, f.55v. By permission of the Master and Fellows of Corpus Christi College, Cambridge).

grappling irons. 'Gadds', pointed bars, of iron were hurled down from the fighting tops. At the Battle of Sluys in 1340 some of the French ships had boats lashed to their masts with a supply of stones for dropping onto their opponents. It was crucial to have a height advantage and the larger the ship, the more fighting men could be carried. The final phase was to board the opposing vessel and overpower the defenders in hand-to-hand fighting. The objective was to capture the enemy's ships rather than to sink them.

At Sluys more than 200 French ships formed three lines across the mouth of the River Swyn. They were chained together until they drifted east towards Cadzand and began to foul each other and then the chains were hurriedly cast off. Ships were positioned according to their size with the big *Christopher*, which had been captured from the English, in the front line with other large ships. The English front line included the largest ships from Yarmouth and the Cinque Ports and Edward III's flagship, the cog *Thomas*. All the ships were fortified with timber-works, 'so that they looked like a row of castles', according to the chronicler Froissart.

Trumpets were used for signalling in sea battles and are shown on some town seals, such as that of Winchelsea of the thirteenth century (figure 3.1). At the battle known as 'Les Espagnols Sur Mer', waged off Winchelsea in 1350 against a Castilian fleet fighting on behalf of the French king, the

ca oſter doutc· leſ nouns de duſſe non paſ ſoule
ment en grui meſ enſement en latin ad il auant
tuche·

De cuz ceſ venz ſouentefez en grū tempeſtef ſolei
ento·ii·ou·troil ſoffler enſemble. par ſofflemeð
de ceſ venz. leſ merſ lu ſunt paiſibleſ par loz voil·
e deloneiteſ par leſ vndeſ eſtrinanz ſe deſuenr. par
ſofflement de ceuſ poz nature detent ou deſ luiſ deſ
tempeſteſ eſt rendu clarre· car en le ſeound ſoffle

Figure 9.2 Fighting at sea, from a *c.*1270 edition of Vegetius' *De Re Militari* (Ms Marlay Add.I, f.86r. Fitzwilliam Museum, Cambridge).

nobles in their ships were entertained before the battle by minstrels. When the Spanish ships were sighted the trumpets gave the signal to launch the attack.

Guns were first used in warfare in the open field in the early fourteenth century. Experiments with their use on board ship soon followed and may have preceded their installation in purpose-built land fortifications, which in Britain began in the Solent area in the 1360s. Early guns lacked accuracy, range and power and their introduction to ships did not immediately change the way in which sea battles were fought. Ships were equipped with a relatively large number of small guns, many of them swivel-mounted, and a few larger pieces. The large guns in particular took a long time to reload, seriously limiting their effectiveness in an age when tactics were based on a rapid closure and hand-to-hand fighting. Even an opening 'fusillade' would have been difficult to aim and the idea of broadside fire had yet to develop. At least until the end of the sixteenth century, including the Spanish Armada engagements, guns were effective only as anti-personnel weapons and for disabling ships, not for sinking them.

What evidence of sea battles might be preserved in the archaeological record? We should not expect to find many shipwrecks. Occasional sinkings resulted from collision, including one at 'Les Espagnols Sur Mer' (Lewis and Runyan, 1990: 125–6). The town seal of Hastings of the early fourteenth century appears to depict a Cinque Ports ship slicing through another. However, of the 213 French ships which took part in the Battle of Sluys, 190 were captured, 23 escaped and none sank (Sumption, 1990: 327). The bed of the River Swyn must be littered with weaponry from the battle, including some specifically maritime artefacts such as gadds, grapnels and signalling trumpets. Debris from the ships burnt at the battle of Damme in 1213 (Brooks, 1933: 201) might also be preserved. As a result of reclamation the sites of the harbours of Sluys and Damme, among the most important in northern Europe for trade as well as for the sea battles fought there, are now under dry land.

Raising and composition of fleets

Most vessels involved in sea warfare were not purpose-built fighting ships. The crown owned varying numbers of ships throughout the medieval period but these were only ever a small proportion of those ships involved. Apart from an arrangement with a group of ports in south-east England, the Cinque Ports, which were granted certain privileges in return for providing shipping services (see Brooks, 1929b), naval power was based on the king's right to 'arrest' merchant ships and their crews – that is, to requisition them in return for payment of compensation. Merchant ships were frequently used as transports, taking men and equipment across the Channel and also to fight in Scotland. English merchant ships were not built for speed and few of them were of great size. This meant that the king had to supply his own fast oared vessels and 'great ships'.

At the beginning of the medieval period there was already differentiation in ship-types between warships and cargo vessels – shown by the Skuldelev finds discussed in Chapter 1 – and this became more accentuated. Merchant ships forfeited speed potential in return for capacity. They were useful as transports and the greater height of merchant ships did provide an advantage in combat. What was lacking were the two extremes of the spectrum: the fast and manoeuvrable oared vessels which could be independent of the wind direction and also the very largest ships which could dominate in sea battles. The king needed large, high ships for tactical advantage, to serve as his headquarters at sea and as symbols of power.

Oared vessels

William the Conqueror's invasion fleet appears from the Bayeux tapestry to have consisted of vessels propelled by oars as well as by sail. There were at least 700 ships, mostly supplied by his leading vassals (Brooks, 1929a: 18). In 1196 Richard I built a fleet of *naves cursoriae* in order to defend the Seine (Brooks, 1929a: 24). As these were suitable for fast travel on rivers and the sea we can assume they were oared. In 1213 *naves cursoriae* were used against the French at Damme, when the English anchored some distance off and used the oared vessels to attack the French ships at anchor.

Galleys were important naval vessels in the thirteenth and fourteenth centuries and they are frequently mentioned in documentary sources. There is, however, a surprising absence of pictures of them. In 1205 King John had 52 royal galleys in ports in England and Ireland. The contemporary list of them (Brooks, 1929a: 26) shows that they were divided into four fleets: east, south-east, south and west. These ships had land structures associated with them. In 1212 the *exclusa* for galleys at Portsmouth was to be strongly walled and storehouses were to be built (Clowes, 1897: 117). At Southampton the sheriff was ordered to build a surrounding wall to protect the galleys during the winter and galleys could be laid up under cover at Shoreham, Rye and Winchelsea (Brooks, 1929a: 28). In 1213 ten galleys were ordered to be prepared at Portsmouth for the king's service (Brooks, 1933: 177).

Between 1210 and 1241 the crown ordered the building of more than 12 galleys in Ireland (Sweetman, 1875: nos 407, 1049, 2244 and 2532). Ireland already had a long history of building warships. Dendroanalysis of the large eleventh-century longship sunk at Skuldelev indicates that it had been built in the Dublin area (Bonde and Crumlin-Pedersen, 1990). In 1225 the justiciary of Ireland was ordered to have 200 ashen oars made and sent to Winchelsea with 'two good ship-loads of boards to make galleys and long ships' (Sweetman, 1875: no. 1232).

Parts of vessels which may have been galleys have been excavated in thirteenth-century contexts in the Dublin waterfront. Components from vessels of varying sizes were reused in the revetments and other waterfront structures and Timber Group 9 consisted of planking from an exceptionally large ship (McGrail, 1993a: 53, 133–40). The planking was still in articulated sections of up to four strakes wide and as much as seven metres long (figure 4.2). It came from both sides of the vessel and included the ends of the planks which would have been fastened to the stem or stern post. The vessel had the sharp ends and fine run which would be expected of a galley.

Galleys were used for convoy duty, for stopping and searching ships and for enforcing customs regulations. They also had a role in raising fleets for the king; in 1207 galleys were ordered to arrest all ships they met at sea (Brooks, 1929a: 44). The galleys kept at Chester and Bristol in the 1240s were used for offensive purposes and for victualling castles in Wales and Ireland (Brooks, 1933: 152). Two galleys equipped with crossbowmen took part in the winter blockade of La Rochelle in 1242 (Lewis and Runyan, 1990: 133–4).

In 1294, probably in response to Philip the Fair's establishment of the *clos des galées* at Rouen (see page 78), Edward I ordered 26 towns between Newcastle and Plymouth to share the building of 20 galleys for the war with France and their construction has already been described in Chapter 1. These galleys were to be vessels of 120 oars each, except one at London which was to have 140 oars. The Newcastle account itemises a keel in two pieces, with a combined length of 108 feet (32.92 metres). Allowing for scarves we can assume a keel length of 100 feet (30.48 metres) with stems and sterns bringing the total overall length of the galley to about 140 feet (42.67 metres). Postulating a racey length-to-beam ratio of 7:1 would give a beam of 20 feet (6.1 metres). The only other dimensions given which might be useful in establishing what these vessels were like are those for the planks. Up to the seventh week, 595 planks had been bought for the Southampton galley with a total length of 12,444 feet (3,793 metres), or 6,222 feet (1,896 metres) for each side of the hull. The accounts do not say how wide the planks were but even if they were only eight inches (20.3cm) there would still have been ample timber for making bottom boards as well as planking the hull.

The number of oars specified for the 1294 galleys raises problems. Although they were supposed to have 120 oars, they nearly all seem to have been equipped with fewer. The York galley had 97 oars, those of Ipswich and Dunwich 100 each. With oarsmen seated one behind the other there is not enough room to fit a single bank of 60 oars into one side of a ship with a keel length of about 100 feet. The absolute minimum oar spacing with this arrangement is 28 inches (71cm) but to fit in 120 oars it is necessary to have one oar for every 20 inches (50.8cm) of keel on each side of the galley. The Newcastle galley account records oars of two sizes: 22 to 23 feet (about 6.86 metres) and 16 to 17 feet long (about 5.03 metres). These might have been used in pairs at the same level, working on oar pivots quite close together. Figure 9.3 suggests how this might have been achieved, with alternate spacings of 12 inches (30.48cm) and 28 inches (71cm). These spacings represent an attempt to cram the maximum possible oar-power into the minimum possible space. They would require a short chop rowing action with little body movement and whether the oars could have been operated efficiently is open to question.

Whether for reasons of ease of supply or better design, when Edward II wanted galleys in 1317 he bought five from Genoa. More were hired from Genoa in 1336, though in the same year Edward III had a galley built in England, which was based at King's Lynn, and another in 1347 at Winchelsea (Tinniswood, 1949: 277). Galleys were used intensively after the

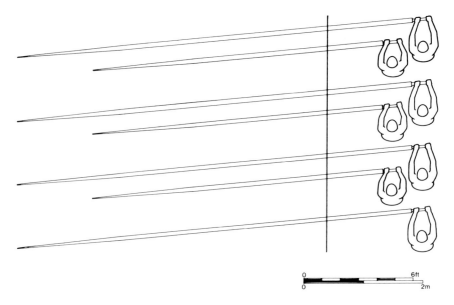

0   6ft
0   2m

Figure 9.3 A conjectural rowing plan for a galley of 1294 (National Maritime Museum).

outbreak of the Hundred Years War in 1336 for cross-Channel raiding. In March 1338 a French raid on Portsmouth was carried out in galleys and barges from Calais, which were flying English flags. In August a contract fleet of Italian galleys joined the French, attacking the Channel Islands in September and Southampton in October. Meanwhile, the English managed to hire two Mediterranean galleys. In 1339 galleys were involved in the French raids on Plymouth and Rye but in late summer the Genoese went home and the French were left with only about 16 Mediterranean galleys. The English fleet took this opportunity to raid the French coast and at Boulogne they succeeded in burning 18 of the 22 French home-built galleys as well as a storehouse full of oars, sails and weapons (Sumption, 1990: 157).

It is probable that no further galleys were built in England after Edward III died in 1377 (Howard, 1979: 13). There were still large numbers of other oared vessels. In England barges and balingers were a common part of war fleets in the fourteenth century (Sherborne, 1977). Barges were generally larger than balingers. They were used for patrols, reconnaissance, escorts, messengers and ferrying important people. As with northern-built galleys, there is an absence of contemporary visual representations. In 1372–73 towns were ordered to build barges at their own cost. At least 14 were built, including the *Paul* built at London in the winter of 1372–73 with a keel length of 80 feet (24.4 metres), a beam of 20 feet (6.1 metres) and 80 oars (Sherborne, 1977: 113). Thirty-two balingers were ordered for 1378, with 34 to 50 oars.

When Henry V's great ship *Grace Dieu* began building in 1416, a 'retinue' of two balingers, two boats and three cock-boats were made at the same time. The larger balinger was of 100 tons and had 48 oars and is also termed a 'barge' in the building account. The smaller was of 80 tons and had 38 oars (Carpenter Turner, 1954: 70). In 1418 one merchant and two royal balingers together captured two ships, probably Spanish, carrying iron and wool (Carpenter Turner, 1954: 63).

Merchant vessels in warfare

Even when they were not involved in official combat, merchant vessels increasingly had to be able to defend themselves against attack at sea. For example, when war was declared in 1243, masters of all ships were licensed and encouraged to annoy the king's enemies. Ships of neutrals carrying enemy goods were also considered fair game. In the thirteenth century the use of banners of arms to distinguish port, nationality and ownership became general.

Town seals of medieval ports provide important information about the modifications made to ships for fighting at sea (figure 9.4). The earliest representations of castles show them as flimsy fighting stages inserted inside the ends of the hull. For example, on the seal of Hythe of the late twelfth or early thirteenth century (Brindley, 1938: fig. 5) the fighting stages do not project above the stem tops. The seal of Pevensey of 1230 or earlier (Brindley, 1938: fig. 12), very similar to that of Winchelsea (figure 3.1) of the early fourteenth century, also shows openwork stages of slightly increased height. None of these ships has a fighting top. A fighting top is shown on an earlier seal, that of Dunwich, from the late twelfth century (figure 9.4a). The top is square and placed centrally on the mast. Square fighting tops attached to the forward side of the mast are shown on the late thirteenth- or early fourteenth-century seals of Great Yarmouth (Brindley, 1938: fig. 21), Sandwich (Brindley, 1938: fig. 15) and Faversham (figure 9.4b). The change of position is probably a result of the addition of ratlines to the rigging. The Faversham ship appears to have a line of crenellation on the quarter, above the rudder, as well as on the stern castle.

The ship on the seal of Dover of 1305 (figure 9.4c) also has a square fighting top on the forward side of the mast. Although it is contemporary with the seal of Winchelsea (figure 3.1) it has castles which are clearly becoming integrated with the hull structure. The castles are longer and are carried out over the stems and given support by the stem posts. The ship shown on the thirteenth-century seal of the town and Admiralty Court of Poole (figure 9.4d) is quite unlike the ships of the Cinque Ports and Yarmouth referred to so far. The sides of the hull are higher and its castles and top are large. It looks like a ship purpose-built for war rather than a fortified merchant vessel.

For the expedition to Ireland in 1210, King John hired five Friesland cogs (Brooks, 1929a: 29) and a cog was also used by the English at the battle off Dover in 1217 (Brooks, 1933: 218–19). Cogs are depicted in a seafight in the *Decretals of Gregory IX*, an English manuscript of the early fourteenth century (figure 9.5) and had become important in warfare by the beginning of the Hundred Years War.

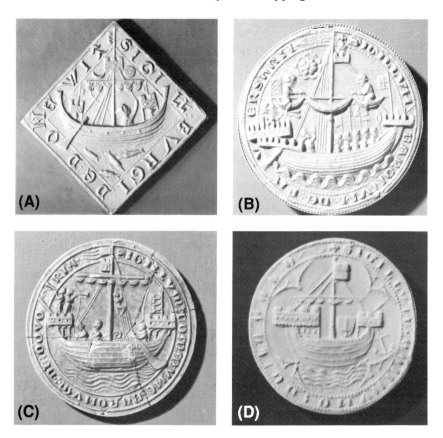

Figure 9.4 Town seals of: (a) Dunwich, (b) Faversham, (c) Dover, (d) Poole (National Maritime Museum).

Merchant ships were essential to Edward I's Anglo-Scottish war between 1296 and 1328. The Earl of Ulster's large expeditionary force was transported in pressed ships from Ireland and from most English ports on the south and west coasts (Reid, 1960). As early as 1302 the seaports, especially Bristol, were becoming uncooperative because of financial loss and the dangers posed by the German and Flemish privateers who aided the Scots. Ships of Great Yarmouth served against the Scots or the French in every year except one between 1333 and 1347. At the beginning they had 90 great ships of 100 to 300 tons, at the end only 24. The rest had been captured, wrecked or put out of service by damage or wear. Vessels were left rotting on the beaches because there was no money and no incentive to repair them (Sumption, 1990: 408).

In 1340, the year of the Battle of Sluys, the export of ships and shipbuilding timber was forbidden. Assembling a fleet of pressed ships was difficult and slow, often taking as long as six months (Sumption, 1990: 177). The largest English transport fleet of the Hundred Years War was that of

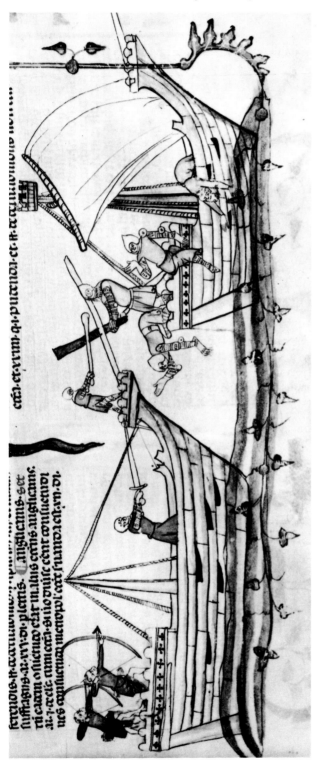

Figure 9.5 Cogs in a sea battle, from an early fourteenth-century English manuscript (Ms Roy. 10. E. IV, f.19. By permission of the British Library).

1347, which consisted of 738 ships with 15,000 mariners. It took 32,000 troops to the siege of Calais. There were frequent complaints throughout the Hundred Years War from shipowners all round the coast about the effect on trade of the arrest of ships and the impressment of crews. They considered the payment of three farthings a ton to be inadequate compensation.

Royal ships

The identification of the large wreck which lies in the River Hamble in Hampshire as Henry V's *Grace Dieu* is based on its large size – with a keel at least 38 metres (127 feet) long – and its location (Anderson, 1934: 161; Prynne, 1968: 120). Only the very bottom part of the hull remains and has been the subject of archaeological investigations in the 1930s (Anderson, 1934 and 1938; Prynne, 1938a and 1938b) and by the Archaeological Research Centre of the National Maritime Museum in the 1980s (Clarke *et al.*, 1993). The *Grace Dieu* is notoriously difficult to investigate as a 'dry' site because the wreck is uncovered only at the equinoctal spring tides and then for only brief periods (figure 9.6). The viscous Hamble mud impedes excavation and obscures structural features. Some recording has been achieved by divers and it is probable that future work on the site will be carried out under water (McGrail, 1993b). The structure of the surviving part of the hull has been discussed in Chapter 2. *Grace Dieu* was the English answer to the carracks, such as those from Genoa used by the French at Harfleur and in the Channel raids. The statesman in command of the annual Florentine merchant galley fleet to England and Flanders was given a tour of the ship in 1430, while it was moored in the Hamble, and he recorded that he had never seen so large and beautiful a construction (Friel, 1993: 17). *Grace Dieu*'s inventory of 1420 records three guns with three chambers, as well as 144 gadds. Fifteenth-century illustrations of warships, such as those on the Warwick Roll (figure 9.7), depict three guns in the waist, which were presumably turned to fire over either side of the ship as necessary.

Royal ship inventories from the early fifteenth century show that guns were regularly included in the armament and also record some of the other weapons in use at the same time. The inventories should be used with caution, however, since they record only what was in the ship at a particular moment and not what the full armament should have been. The *Trinité de la Toure*, a single-masted ship of 300 tons, in royal service between 1398 and 1413, is recorded as having 300 iron gadds. The *Marie of Weymouth* of about 1409–11 had two iron guns with two chambers, one brass gun with one chamber and one sheer-hook. Chambers were reusable breech pieces, pre-loaded with powder. *Bernard de la Toure*, 1410–11, a single-masted ship of more than 135 tons, had two iron guns, three-dozen headed darts, one dozen headless darts, 98 gadds of iron and a grappling iron and chain. In 1413 *Thomas de la Toure*, a single-masted ship of a little under 200 tons, had four guns with three chambers each and one firepan. The *Holigost* is listed in 1415 as having two guns and 8lbs of gunpowder. By 1420 this is increased to seven guns and 12 chambers. The *Grand Marie de la Toure* a

Figure 9.6 The site of the wreck of the *Grace Dieu* in the River Hamble (National Maritime Museum).

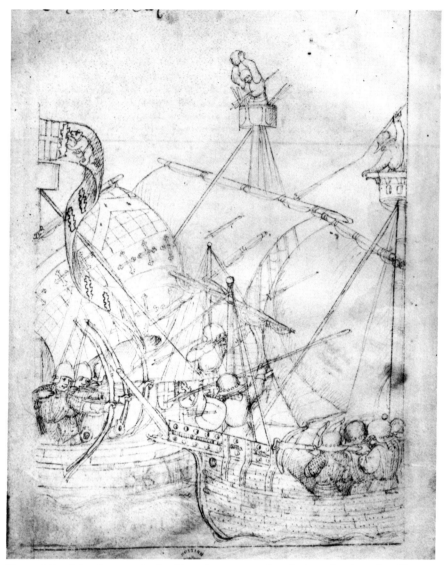

Figure 9.7 A battle at sea in the fifteenth century, after the introduction of artillery to ships (Julius E IV art 6 f 18v. By permission of the British Library).

single-masted ship of 116–40 tons, had in 1416 three guns with ten chambers, four-dozen darts, 15 lances, 21 bows, 15 sheaves of arrows, 30 iron gadds and one grapnel.

It is interesting that the inventories of carracks captured at Harfleur in 1416 and in other actions at about the same time list no more than two or three guns each. The *Christophre*, a Genoese carrack of 600 tons, had two guns with four chambers, while the *George*, another Genoese carrack of 600 tons, captured at Harfleur, had in 1420 three guns with six chambers as well as three scaling ladders and six hooks. Another carrack captured at Harfleur, the *Marie Sandwich* of about 500 tons, was listed as having no guns but only a seizing grapnel and 16 fathoms of iron chain, weighing 3 cwt 31 lb.

There are several pictorial representations of warships at the beginning of the fifteenth century. The seal of Tenterden in Kent (close to Smallhythe, where royal ships were built) of the first half of the fifteenth century (Ewe, 1972: fig. 201), that of Admiral Beaufort of 1418–26 (figure 2.1a), and the fifteenth-century seal of the Sub-Admiralty of England (Brindley, 1938: fig. 33) show ships of similar rigging and proportions. By 1400 the fighting tops were tub-shaped and placed centrally on the mast above all the rigging. The run of the hull planking varies and includes various hybrids of the hulk. The relief carving on a bench-end from the church of St Nicholas at King's Lynn (figure 3.6), probably made in 1415–20, shows a large, two-masted clinker-built ship equipped for war.

The Hastings manuscript, of the late fifteenth- or early sixteenth-century, shows clinker-built warships with wales (figure 10.7). The stems have become almost vertical as the fore castles were no longer used as seige towers but contained heavy guns which needed buoyancy beneath them. The stern castle is fully integrated with the lower hull and has a pair of ports for big guns. By the 1470s carvel-building had been adopted for great ships, three masts were common and guns were an essential part of the armament.

The building account for the *Regent*, a 1,000 ton four-masted royal ship of 1487, specifies that carvel nails were used. A slightly smaller ship, the *Sovereign*, of 800 tons, was built in the following year. The *Sovereign* may have been first built in clinker technique then converted to carvel during the rebuild in 1509, if the remains of a hull found at Roff's Wharf, Woolwich are really from this ship. The Woolwich ship was discovered in 1912 during excavations for the foundations of a new engine house for a power station. Its identification as a warship was suggested by its large size and relatively light framing. An Admiralty Committee reported in 1914 that the keel length was well over 100 feet (30.5 metres), the beam of the ship was about 40 feet (12 metres) and that therefore the burden must have been considerably over 1,000 tons. The discovery of some stone shot within the wreck does not necessarily strengthen the argument, since merchant ships as well as warships would have carried guns. The wreck's position in the riverbank suggested that it must be earlier than the seventeenth century. The ship appears to have been laid up in an inlet of the south bank of the Thames, abandoned and partly broken up. It was found at a depth of 18 feet (4.5 metres) below the contemporary ground surface and about six feet below the high-water mark. The contexts of associated finds were not adequately recorded to provide dating evidence (Salisbury, 1961: 82).

Anderson (1959) thought the wreck might be that of Henry VIII's *Henry Grace à Dieu* which was destroyed by fire at Woolwich in 1553. An earlier date was suggested by the fact that the frames appear to have the traces of joggles on their undersides, indicating that the ship had originally been built with clinker planking (Salisbury, 1961: 86). Salisbury suggests that this would explain the shallowness of the frames, which were 14 inches (36cm) wide but only eight inches (20cm) deep, with five inch (13cm) spaces in between. The framing was stiffened by riders 18 inches by 16 inches (46cm X 41cm) spaced about four feet six inches (37cm) apart. The ceiling planking was three inches (7.6cm) thick and the outer hull planking was five inches (13cm) thick. The nature of the fastening was not described but the superintending architect commented that the whole thing was very securely pinned together, making the removal a very difficult operation.

The Woolwich ship excited considerable interest at the time of its discovery and in December 1912 it was suggested that a six foot wide section of it might be preserved and put on display. However, it was decided that preservation by record would be adequate. Salisbury (1961) lists the reports, photographs and drawings made by the London County Council. By April 1914 the remains had been broken up, yielding 80 tons of oak timber. An assessment of the site carried out by the National Maritime Museum in 1980, when some of the buildings on it were demolished, suggests that nearly all the ship was destroyed in 1912–14. There is a slight possibility that the extreme northern (probably forward) end of the ship may survive between the river wall and the sites of the old Turbine House and Boiler House of the Power Station. Enough might remain to provide further structural information, or at least for tree-ring dating.

By the 1480s ships were carrying a much larger number of guns. In 1485 another *Grace Dieu* had 22 guns with 89 chambers, *Mary* had 58 guns with 140 chambers and *Governor* had 70 guns with 265 chambers (Laughton, 1960: 246). Not all of these were large guns. The *Sovereign*, built in 1488, had a total of 141 guns but only 31 of these were 'stone guns', while the other 110 were serpentines. The nature and size of serpentines is not clear (see Glasgow, 1960) but those used on ships were probably of a variety of fairly small calibres and were possibly swivel-mounted. The *Regent*, built a year earlier than the *Sovereign*, appears to have been equipped only with serpentines – 225 of them, mounted on 'miches' or swivels. This ship was built by Sir Richard Guldford, Master of the Ordnance, as a 'novel construction. . . with ordnance and fittings', in imitation of a French ship, *Colombe* (Laughton, 1960: 251).

Twenty of the *Sovereign*'s stone guns were placed in the waist of the ship and 11 in the summer-castle (stern castle). The serpentines were distributed around two decks in both castles. Before long shipwrights were confronting the problem of how to accommodate greater numbers of heavy guns and how to place them in other parts of the hull where they were needed. This had very important consequences for ship design. The sterns of fifteenth-century ships were undefended. This made them vulnerable, especially to galleys. Fitting gunports into round sterns was difficult and the weight of guns placed strain on the stern post. Shipwrights responded by shortening the stern post and giving the stern a 'square tuck' or flat surface below the transom, into which ports could be cut. By 1514, the *Henry Grace à Dieu* had two guns of about ten tons each mounted in ports in the tuck (Laughton, 1961: 103). Changes in hull shape were also made to counteract the weight of guns in the fore castle. Ships were no longer built with great overhanging forestages; the bow was shortened and made fuller to provide more buoyancy. Curiously, the hulk, in a final flowering, appears to have been well suited to carrying guns in the bows. Figure 9.8 shows a fifteenth-century French hulk with gunports where hawse-holes might be expected.

Figure 9.8 French fifteenth-century hulks with gunports through the planking at the bows (photo: Bibliothèque Nationale, Paris. Ms Fr 2829, f.32,v).

Stability was seriously affected by the presence of heavy guns on the upper deck and in the castles. In a sea trial in 1512, it was reported that the *Christ* could not sail as the result of being 'overladen with ordnance' (Laughton, 1960: 284). The solution to this was to mount guns lower down in the hull, firing through gunports. There is a tradition that in 1501 a French shipbuilder, Descharges, was the first to cut holes in ships' sides for gunports and to fit them with hinged lids. Fundamentally, the level of the lower deck had to be raised by up to a metre in order to keep the gunports safely above the waterline. The wreck of the *Mary Rose* testifies to the fact that the importance of this modification was not fully appreciated at the beginning of the sixteenth century and stability problems persisted much longer.

The oldest gun so far found in British waters may be that from the Studland Bay wreck, which probably sank in the 1520s. Presumably Spanish, it was more than two metres long and constructed from iron staves formed into a cylinder. It was found with its breech chamber wedged in position and a six-inch stone shot in place. Iron bands appeared to have been used to fasten the gun to its carriage. On the same site another, larger breech chamber was found, indicating that an even bigger gun was on board, as well as part of a smaller four-inch, breech-loading swivel gun and its chamber. Finds of two inch and three inch shot indicate that smaller calibre guns were also carried (Ladle, 1993: 22–3).

Two early guns were found on a dispersed wreck site at Walney at the entrance to Morecambe Bay in the nineteenth century. They are also of bar and hoop construction with breech chambers (Archibald, 1844). Laughton (1960: 266) calculated that the larger gun was for stone shot of at least 140 lbs and that the powder chamber capacity was about 3½ lbs. These guns are in the Royal Artillery collection at the Rotunda Museum, Woolwich.

Medieval coastal defence

It is not possible to leave a survey of medieval ships and warfare without paying some attention to the resulting modifications to the man-made environment on land. Coastal defences were constructed against the threat of seaborne raiding and invasion. Signalling systems which required the construction of beacons were introduced. It is not clear whether appreciable coastal depopulation took place during periods of greatest danger; whether the opportunities for gaining a living from trade and fishing were outweighed by the risk of losing everything. Archaeological evidence may help to throw light on this but the picture is obscured by the effects of plague in the mid-fourteenth century when people moved out, or were carried out, from ports and towns.

During the Middle Ages individual towns made provision for their own defence. Artificial channel blockages and the deliberate creation of hazards to navigation, like those which commonly obstructed the approaches to Scandinavian harbours of the Viking Age and later (Rieck, 1991), have not so far been identified around Britain. Differences in geography mean that there would have been few places in Britain where they could have operated successfully. But if ships could not be denied access to harbours, attempts could be made to prevent their crews entering the port towns. Scarborough and Bristol were among the first recipients of murage grants, between 1220 and 1250. As late as the fourteenth and fifteenth centuries, their corporate seals depict not only the ships but the fortifications of their towns. Many more murage grants were made in the second half of the thirteenth century to towns on the east and south coasts and along the coast and marches of Wales (Turner, 1971: 27). Some towns constructed special secure areas for warships. Southampton, Rye, Winchelsea and New Shoreham had pounds for galleys in the thirteenth century.

Castles were built near waterways to protect lines of communication, such as at Rochester bridge, but it is questionable whether they played a significant role in medieval coastal defence before the introduction of guns. Piel Castle commanded the Walney Channel and served to control trade. The main features of the English system of coastal defence can be traced to the 1290s, when a strip of land within six or sometimes 12 leagues of the coast was designated 'maritime land'. The men there were required to serve as coastal militia and beacons were supposed to be permanently manned. The system failed completely in 1338, when the French destroyed Portsmouth, and was only ever spasmodically successful (Sumption, 1990: 227; White, 1930). A survey of royal coastal fortifications was made in 1335 and improvements were made at the Tower of London, Carisbrooke, Dover, Pevensey and Porchester (Sumption, 1990: 250).

Throughout the Hundred Years War fleets of fast-oared vessels burnt ships at their berths and anchorages. The English burned the coastal villages of Normandy in a deliberate policy of damaging the communities which sustained French seapower in the Channel. In return the French mounted frequent raids on England, notably at Southampton in 1338, the Isle of Wight in 1369, Rye in 1377 and Winchelsea in 1380. Against this threat the River Hamble, which was used as an anchorage for the royal ships, was fortified with a wooden bulwark and a spiked wooden defence pale while *Grace Dieu* was being built, beginning in 1416 (Carpenter Turner, 1954: 57).

The introduction of artillery opened up new possibilities for defending the coast. Guns were mounted in fortifications in the 1360s, particularly in the Solent area and Kent. Edward III's castle at Queenborough, Kent, was built to a circular plan in the 1360s to deploy both guns and *trebuchets* (Saunders, 1989: 18–19). Quarr Abbey was probably equipped with guns in about 1365 and in about the mid-1370s keyhole gunports were inserted in the walls along the western waterfront at Southampton. These early gunports were intended for close defence.

The royal castles at Portchester and Carisbrooke were provided with guns in the 1380s, as was Cooling Castle, near the mouth of the Thames in Kent. In 1405 Plymouth successfully used artillery fire to repulse a raid. English ships there were protected by a barrier of barges (Oppenheim, 1968: 18–19). In 1420–22 a round masonry gun-tower was built at the mouth of Portsmouth harbour to protect the king's ships. A timber tower was built on the Gosport side and a chain boom defence was stretched between them across the harbour mouth. A chain boom defence was also installed at Fowey in 1457. Bulwarks built of earth revetted with timber were constructed round several harbours. In 1451 a two-storey high bulwark within a water-filled moat was built at Sandwich. It proved inadequate in the French raid of 1457 and had to be repaired and supplemented by another, this time of brick, at Fishergate.

The 'strong tower and bulwark', built at Dartmouth from 1481 and replacing an earlier castle, was designed for large guns. It was sited near the water's edge and close to sea-level. It demonstrates that even before 1500 fortifications were being built with sufficient firepower to be an effective defence against hostile shipping.

10 *Pilotage and navigation*

The ability of mariners to conduct their ships safely from one port to another depends on knowledge and skill. Knowledge of natural forces and cyclical events is still fundamental to sailing today and can be inferred back into prehistory. Documented voyages, such as that of Richard the Lionheart, who sailed with a northern European Crusader fleet around Iberia and through the Mediterranean to Palestine in 1191, indicate a thorough knowledge of the maritime geography of Europe at an early date, as well as testifying to the seaworthiness of the ships used. Documentary sources show that scientific approaches to navigational problems were being developed by scholars. Bede's eighth-century treatise on the tides and the early thirteenth-century tide tables for London Bridge, compiled by the monks of St Albans (Taylor, 1971: 136), reveal attempts to understand the theoretical principles underlying empirical knowledge.

Thirteenth-century Icelandic sagas include sailing directions for the north Atlantic (Marcus, 1980: 112), showing that oral lore was long established. Sailing directions were written down at least as early as the mid-fifteenth century. These 'rutters' (from the French *routier*) are invaluable records of the fields of information and specific data which were considered most useful at the time. More than that, they point to a revolution made possible by literacy, which allowed the dissemination of information to supplement oral communication and each navigator's personal experience. The art and science of chart-making, which presents this information in graphic form, has been well described by both Waters (1958) and Taylor (1971). Documentary sources also refer to navigational instruments and the skills required for their use: for example, describing early versions of the magnetic compass and listing equipment in ships' inventories.

There are two main classes of material evidence which can contribute to the study of medieval navigation: navigational instruments and man-made sailing marks. The date of introduction of new instruments is often obscure and can only be clarified by archaeological finds. Shore features, such as church towers, are commonly regarded as part of the landscape but the way they figured in the seascape also needs to be appreciated. The siting of prominent structures may have been influenced by navigational considerations.

Shipwrecks themselves cannot be taken as evidence of navigational error, since it is perfectly possible to be wrecked while in no doubt about the ship's position and heading. Losses are as likely to be caused by failure of the ship or its equipment, frequently as a result of adverse weather.

An outline of the theory and practice of pilotage and navigation is given in this chapter to provide background for the function and design of the instruments and the location of sailing marks; and also to explain, to some extent, why ships sailed the routes they did. Combining information about medieval sailing routes and methods of coastal navigation contributes to an understanding of what was expected of ships, particularly their ability to maintain their position against a head wind and so escape being blown onto a lee shore. It must be emphasised that the idea that medieval ships 'hugged the coast' is a misconception. There was coastwise sailing but the risk of being driven onto a lee shore meant that ships stood well out to sea to avoid danger. Ushant in Brittany was and still is particularly lethal, with numerous rocks far off shore and frequent fogs. Twentieth-century sailing directions say that 'Ushant must not be sighted', for if a ship comes within ten miles it may become subject to a powerful onshore set and be swept onto the rocks (Taylor, 1971: 4).

The business of passage-making is today regarded as being split into two branches: pilotage for coastal voyages, when the vessel's position can, at least intermittently, be fixed in relation to the land; and navigation undertaken out of sight of known land, where the vessel's position on the earth's surface has to be established by celestial observation. There is of course some overlap between the two. The core of pilotage had been known, in rudimentary form, in the prehistoric period whereas the techniques, knowledge and instruments belonging to ocean navigation were innovations during the medieval period, developed in the course of voyages of exploration.

Pilotage

The essentials of pilotage can be summarised as follows: knowing the positions of coastal features and how they appear from the sea; knowing how to determine the direction of the ship and the forces acting on it; understanding wind and weather patterns; knowing how to calculate speed and leeway; knowing how to calculate tides, including the times of high water in ports and the effects of tidal stream; and knowing the depth and nature of the sea-bed. These will be considered in turn.

Knowledge of the relative positions and appearance of capes and other natural features of the coast was acquired by observation and experience. The same applied to man-made sailing marks and submerged dangers such as rocks, shoals and sandbanks. Some of this was written down in rutters. The fifteenth-century Lansdowne Manuscript 285 (published in Waters, 1967: 181–95) is the earliest extant English example. There are limitations to the usefulness of these sailing directions. Firstly, the rutters would be of no use for navigating completely unknown waters as they do not describe the features they refer to. In later editions, such as *le grant routtier* printed in 1520, woodcuts were provided to assist with recognition of headlands (Waters, 1967: 205–400). The second limitation is that the directions given in the rutters are for the circumnavigation of Britain; they do not give instructions about how to find the way into ports. Ships took on local pilots for this purpose and they guarded their knowledge in the interests of their livelihood and for the security of their harbours against coastal raids. Pilot ships, or 'lodships', are specifically mentioned in the English documentary sources of the period 1337–60 studied by Runyan (1991: 201). So vital was it for shipowners to have complete confidence in local pilots that the Catalan *Customs of the Sea* acknowledged the right to behead an incompetent pilot (Twiss, 1874: 433).

Sixteenth-century sailing directions gave distances between capes in 'kennings' or distances which varied between 14 and 21 statute miles (22.5km to 34km). It would rarely have been possible to see so far. Because of the curvature of the earth's surface, in conditions of clear visibility, the horizon of an observer with his eye six metres above the sea is five nautical miles away. On the Bayeux Tapestry a Norman sailor can be seen clinging to the mast-head, looking out for land, and a similar scene is vividly depicted on a plank found in an eleventh-century context at the Dublin waterfront (figure 10.1). The higher the observer climbs, the further he is able to see. Roughly speaking, there is a gain of an extra nautical mile of vision for every additional five metres of elevation. From a mast-head 15 metres above the sea, an observer's horizon is about eight nautical miles away. The upper parts of more distant high features will stand up above the horizon and can be seen from further off. A feature would have to reach at least 35 metres above sea level for our observer at a height of 15 metres to be able to see it at a distance of 20 nautical miles.

The mast-head height above sea level of Skuldelev 3, the smaller eleventh-century trading ship from Roskilde Fjord, was only about ten metres. The top of the mast of the fourteenth-century Bremen cog was about 20 metres above the sea and the mainmast of the fifteenth-century great ship *Grace Dieu* was said to be 200 feet (61 metres), high enough to make it possible to see the sea horizon 16 nautical miles away. This is shown schematically in figure 10.2.

Ships were fitted with tops or 'crow's nests' for look-outs, not just for fighting. Although it was necessary to sight the coast from time to time to establish position, ships did not hug the coast as this would mean entering the shipwreck zone. Risks intensified when the wind was blowing onshore. The term 'landfall' means sighting or falling in with the land, not landing on it.

By the time the rutters were compiled, the magnetic compass was in general use for determining direction. In earlier times, including the first part of the period under discussion, northern seafarers had managed to find their way without compasses, principally by knowledge of the relative positions and movement of heavenly bodies across the sky. The sun rises from an easterly direction and achieves its highest altitude at noon when it is due south, then sinks in a westerly direction. At night, north is indicated by the Pole Star which maintains a constant position in the sky, unlike the moon and the other stars. The Pole Star was known as the *scip steorra* to the Anglo-Saxons and its use is mentioned in Icelandic sagas. Bearings obtained from heavenly bodies were approximate and allowances would have to be made according to the season of the year and the time of day or night. An artefact of about AD 1000, found at a settlement site in Greenland, has been interpreted as a bearing dial for trans-Atlantic sailing (Vebæk and Thirslund, 1992).

Direction can also be estimated in relation to wind and swell. In northern waters winds from different directions may be recognised by the weather accompanying them; thus a warm wet wind blows from the south-west and a cold wet wind from the north-west (McGrail, 1987: 281). Medieval seamen had to understand wind and weather patterns in order to take advantage of

Figure 10.1 A lookout at the mast-head, an eleventh-century carving found at Christchurch Place, Dublin (National Maritime Museum).

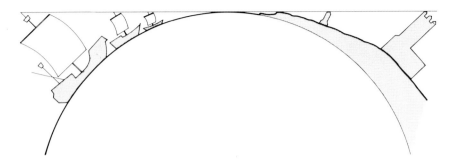

Figure 10.2   The effect of elevation on observation range (National Maritime Museum).

favourable winds for voyage making and to avoid being taken by surprise by storms. Icelandic sagas repeatedly refer to observations of the clouds, wind, sea and the behaviour of seabirds (Marcus, 1980: 101). Vikings are said to have released birds from their ships to indicate the direction of the nearest land. Other indicators are cloud formations, the flight of birds at dawn and dusk, and the presence of seaweed in the water.

The invention of the magnetic compass and its introduction to ships is obscure but it was in use among northern and Mediterranean seamen in the twelfth century. Magnetic iron ore was mined in Elba and carried by ships of Amalfi. Tradition has it that Amalfi seamen were the first to use compasses at sea (Waters, 1958: 21). The construction of compasses will be described later but in their early forms they were difficult and unreliable to use at sea. The earliest descriptions of a compass are by an English monk, Alexander Neckham, writing in the 1180s. He said that it was used during cloudy weather when the sailors could not see the sun or stars (Taylor, 1971: 95). Once the initial problems had been overcome, the compass allowed greater precision in direction-finding and by the thirteenth century, rhumb (direction) lines on the oldest surviving chart show that the seaman's horizon had been divided into thirty-two compass-points (Waters, 1958: 21).

In order to fix a vessel's position it is necessary to know not only what course is being sailed but also how fast the vessel is travelling. A mariner would become familiar with his vessel's speed capabilities on the different points of sailing (such as tacking into the wind or running before it) and in different wind strengths. On coastal voyages he could check his estimates against known distances on the shore. When out of sight of land a piece of wood could be thrown into the sea and an estimate could be made of the speed at which it was left behind. (As we shall see, the relative position of the wood and the ship would also indicate the ship's leeway angle.) The date at which a length of line was attached to the 'log' before it was thrown over, so that the ship's speed could be measured rather than just estimated, is not known, but may be after 1500 rather than before.

Ellmers (1972: 250) has compiled a table of documented voyages with their distances and the length of time they took. From this it seems that an average 'speed made good' of three to six knots was to be expected. The difference between a sailing ship's actual speed through the water and 'speed made good' is brought about by three factors. The first is the impossibility of sailing directly into the wind. It is necessary to sail a zig-zag course ('tacking') to windward. The second is leeway. On all points of sailing, except when a vessel is running directly before the wind, there is a tendency for it to make leeway – to be pushed sideways by the wind. The degree of leeway may be estimated by the angle of the wake that the vessel trails behind and the amount varies from ship to ship. The third factor results from the effects of tidal stream and currents, which mean that the sea around Britain resembles a network of conveyor belts rather than a road.

The rutters contain much information about tides to enable the time of high and low water and the reversal of flow direction, which seldom coincides, to be predicted all along the coast (Waters, 1967: 14–22, 421–6). The sequence of high and low water is linked to tidal stream patterns and to the age and bearing of the moon. In the pre-literate era this complex relationship had to be learned by observation and by rote for every landing place. The 'establishment of the port', the times of high water at a port on the days of full and new moon (full and change) were noted in terms of the compass bearing of the moon at the moment of high water (Waters, 1958: 31; Frake, 1985).

Knowing the depth of the water under the vessel and the nature of the sea-bed were very important factors in making a safe passage. It was essential to avoid running aground and knowing the composition and contours of the sea-bed could help to establish the vessel's position. The sea-bed off western Europe slopes down to a depth of about 100 fathoms at the edge of the continental shelf and then drops steeply to the ocean bed. Measuring the depth of water under the ship by means of a line with a weight at its end was termed 'taking soundings' and when a ship was 'in soundings' it was over the continental shelf, in water less than 100 fathoms deep. Off Ireland, Spain and Portugal the edge of the continental shelf is only ten or 20 miles offshore but it is much further from the Lizard peninsula of Cornwall. On a voyage from England to Spain a ship passed out of soundings when some 100 miles south-west of Ushant and did not enter them again until perilously close to the coast of north-west Spain (Waters, 1958: 18–19). On the return voyage, the run from Spain to the British Isles was made directly and navigators would take soundings to locate the steep edge of the continental shelf about 100 miles west of Penmarch Point (Taylor, 1971: 135).

The Lansdowne Manuscript sailing directions contain detailed information about soundings and the nature of the sea-bed (Waters, 1967: 194–5). Sounding leads had a concavity in their under-surfaces which were filled with tallow, to which a sample of the sea-bed sediment would adhere. Northern seamen were expert in knowing where they were by this means. For example, the ground to the south-west of Scilly consists of a matrix of red sand with white shelly inclusions and near the Lizard the bottom was said to be of 'ragged' pebbles the size of beans.

Navigation

When sailing out of sight of charted land it is essential to be able to estimate directions, such as courses, leeway and drift, and to be able to calculate speeds and distances. When these are recorded and added to over days and weeks, errors inevitably accumulate. During the fifteenth century, Portuguese mariners developed a new method of checking their position by observation of the sun and stars. On voyages down the coast of Africa they noticed that as they went southwards the pole star dropped lower in the north. Measuring its altitude enabled them to find their latitude with considerable accuracy. Finding latitude by observations of heavenly bodies requires a reliable compilation of astronomical information and specially designed sighting instruments. Portuguese mariners had the star altitudes of successive capes and rivers mouths marked on their quadrants and by 1473 the table of coastal latitudes reached the equator (Taylor, 1971: 159).

It was to be nearly 300 years before a reliable method of finding longitude at sea was introduced. Until then, navigators undertaking ocean voyages by 'latitude' sailing had to contend with the problem that the magnetic compass points to the magnetic pole and not to true north. The angle between the bearing of the magnetic pole and true north, known as 'variation', increases as a ship sails west from Europe out into the Atlantic. Columbus and Portuguese pilots tried to determine longitude by observing the change in variation of the compass (Scammell, 1981: 59) but with only limited success.

Sailing marks

The term 'sailing mark' is used here to denote any man-made object or structure placed so as to be visible to mariners and to serve as an aid to navigation. They range from simple sticks in the mud to lighthouses.

Branches have been universally used to show the edges of mudbanks and shallows, with larger poles in exposed places. Much interesting information about the changing course and depth of channels could be obtained if an accurate and inexpensive method of dating roundwood stakes were to become available. Stakes are also used as leading marks in transit lines. Two objects are said to be 'in transit' when one is directly in front of the other. The back marker needs to be large and prominent, such as a church tower. The transit line between the leading mark and the back marker may indicate a safe channel. To aid recognition, different topmarks such as baskets or barrels could be fixed on the poles. In medieval northern Europe trading places were marked by having a mask, or *Grimskalle*, on a pole as a seamark at the harbour entrance (Cederlund, 1989: 90).

In Viking Age Norway stone cairns were erected as seamarks (Morcken, 1969: 7). Similar features were probably common around the coast of Britain. Investigation of a mound at Tywn Llewelyn, Glamorgan, showed that it was composed largely of natural rock, but heightened by building a cairn on top. It probably marked the channel of the River Thaw during high tide (Wilson and Hurst, 1957: 170).

Britain does not seem to have adopted the eleventh-century Norwegian practice of erecting tall stone crosses as sailing marks. The tallest of them may have been up to 15 metres high (Morcken, 1969: 32–3). The siting of churches in positions where they could be useful for navigation perhaps suggests a maritime economic factor in ecclesiastical foundations. It is surely more than a coincidence that the church at Bosham, the seat of Earl Godwin, which appears on the Bayeux tapestry as a record that Harold sailed from here in 1064, lies directly in line with the last 1.5 kilometres of the narrow navigable channel in Bosham Creek (figure 10.3). Many other churches served as sailing marks. Along the Suffolk coast church towers such as those at Covehithe and Kessingland were the only tall structures. They are still used by hydrographic surveyors for siting position-fixing equipment. Reculver church and the Roman fort which previously occupied the site would both have been useful as markers of the northern entrance of the Wantsum Channel and the sandbanks in the mouth of the Thames. The Lansdowne Manuscript sailing directions instruct the mariner making a passage south round the Naze in Essex to set his course by reference to the relative positions of the parish and abbey churches of St Osyth: 'bring your marks together so that the parish steeple be out by the east of the Abbey of St Hosies' (Waters, 1967: 188). The Lansdowne manuscript also refers to the churches at Dartmouth, Harwich and Broadstairs (Waters, 1967: 199).

In the Netherlands there was a tradition of building small huts with fire platforms on prominent dunes to give navigational assistance to the fishing fleet (Naish, 1985: 31). In Britain and Ireland the setting of lights seems to have been an ecclesiastical role. A map of medieval lights is given in figure 10.4. The one at Hook Point, Waterford, was probably established in the 1170s and in the early thirteenth century it is recorded that Augustinian Canons had the rights to collect tolls from ships entering in return for the obligation to maintain the light (Hague and Christie, 1975: 14).

The late twelfth-century romanesque chapel on the cliff at St Aldhelm's head, Dorset, is traditionally said to have had a light (Hague and Christie, 1975: 18). The building plan is square with a central pier and four square rib vaults inside, under a pyramidal roof with a short cylindrical base on top (Newman and Pevsner, 1972: 358). A fourteenth-century lighthouse still stands on St Catherine's Down at the southern point of the Isle of Wight (figure 10.5). In 1314 a cargo of wine owned by a monastery in Picardy was lost in a shipwreck on the point and much of the wine was taken by local people. After lawsuits and an appeal to Rome, Walter de Godeton was ordered on threat of excommunication to build an oratory and light-tower dedicated to St Catherine (Naish, 1985: 82). The lighthouse is an octagonal tower with four buttresses and an eight-sided pyramid roof. A doorway and roofline on the north side show the position of the oratory, which is known from excavations (Stone, 1891). Another chapel dedicated to St Catherine stands at the summit of the steep hill at Abbotsbury, prominent on the Dorset coast. The provision of a stone tunnel vault suggests fire-proofing. If there was a light, excavation of the ground around the chapel might be expected to reveal ash-middens. A light was established at Tynemouth Priory in the Middle Ages. A coal fire in an open brazier was mounted on the top of a turret at the east end of the presbytery there, continuing in use into the seventeenth century (Saunders, 1993: 39). At Ilfracombe in Devon a medieval

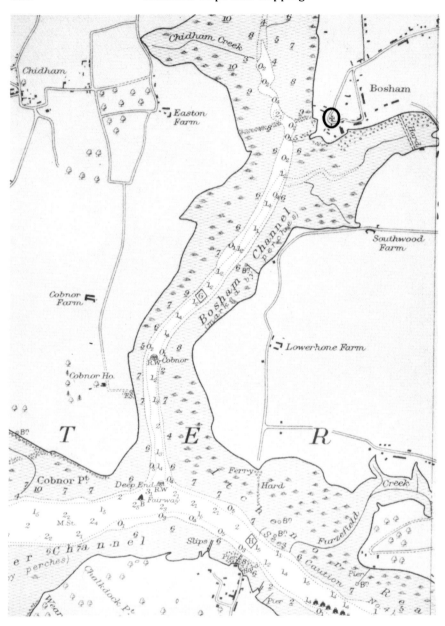

Figure 10.3 The siting of the church at the head of the creek at Bosham, marking the navigable channel (Crown copyright. Reproduced from Admiralty chart 3418 with the permission of the Hydrographer of the Navy).

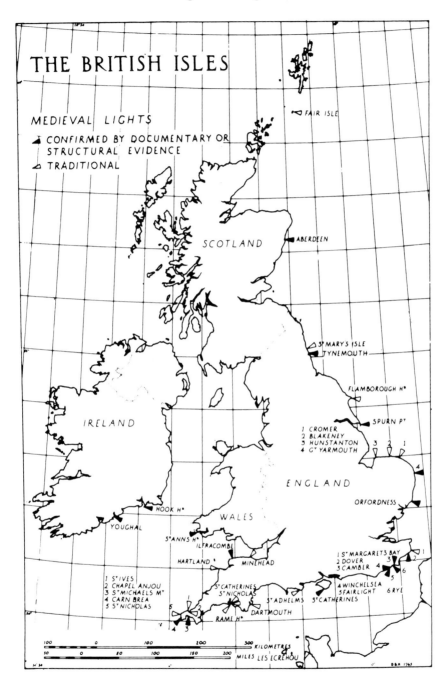

Figure 10.4 Map of medieval lights (from Hague and Christie, 1975).

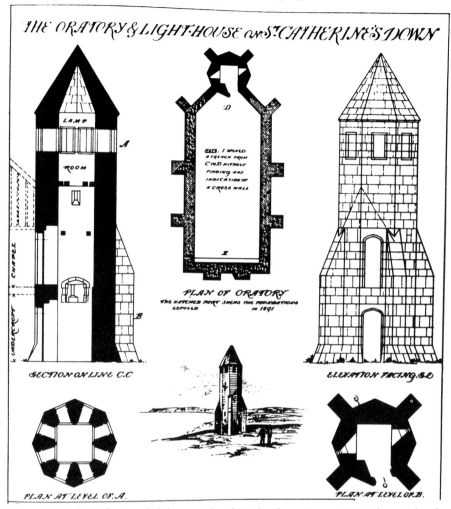

Figure 10.5 St Catherines lighthouse, Isle of Wight (from Stone, 1891. Photo: Isle of Wight Cultural Services Department).

chapel lighthouse, dedicated to St Nicholas, is sited at the entrance to the harbour on a rock known as Lantern Hill. It is still in use (Hague and Christie, 1975: 19–20).

It is not known when buoys first came into use as aids to navigation. They were perhaps originally rafts with superstructure. Watertight barrels were in use by the fourteenth century in the Low Countries and possibly earlier (Naish, 1985: 51). Buoys are listed in ships' inventories in the fifteenth century but they were for use with anchors. Buoys can be used in deeper water than stakes and may be more visible. They would need frequent maintenance to ensure watertightness, to check that their cables were sound and that they had not dragged their anchors. No examples of medieval buoys have been found. Wine or beer casks were used in post-medieval Britain but there are problems involved in fixing a mooring chain to the belly of the barrel. They were superseded by purpose-built conical marine buoys constructed with tapering staves. A mooring ring was fixed into a wooden plug in the apex. The buoys were tarred and in the sixteenth century they were expected to last ten years. Their mooring chains had long links and swivels at top and bottom and it is said that disused millstones were often used for anchoring them (Naish, 1985: 54–5). The oldest surviving chart of the outer estuary of the Scheldt and the approaches to Sluys and Bruges was drawn in about 1500. It shows two channels, either side of a sandbank, marked by buoys which appear to be of this type (illustrated in Naish, 1985: 28).

Navigational equipment

As already noted, sounding leads were attached to lengths of line and used to measure the depth of water under a vessel and to retrieve samples of the sea-bed. They were used by the Romans but it is not known when they were first used by the people of northern Europe. They were certainly standard equipment long before they were first documented in royal ship inventories in the fifteenth century. Sounding leads were apparently always made of lead and not of iron or bronze. Lead has several advantages. It does not have the corrosion problems of iron and was not as expensive as bronze. Its softness was also useful as a rocky ground could be recognized by fresh dents and cuts in the lead. Its most important property, however, is its density. A sounding device has to sink fast; otherwise, despite all efforts to remain stationary, the ship will have moved on and the reading will not be a true vertical depth (see figure 10.6). The records of nineteenth-century Admiralty experiments show that a sounding lead might commonly take 45 seconds to reach 100 fathoms and that a cylindrical form presents the least surface for friction. The line needs to be as thin as possible to minimise the braking effect produced by its buoyancy and resistance (Davis, 1867: 2–8).

No medieval sounding leads have yet been identified, though one is depicted in the fifteenth-century Hastings Manuscript (figure 10.7). The earliest examples known from post-Roman Britain are those found with the sixteenth-century Rother barge (Rice, 1824) and the *Mary Rose*. That from the Rother barge is recorded as a sketch in the margin of an engraving of the scene of the excavation. It was octagonal, about eight inches (0.20 metres) high and of slightly larger diameter at the base than at the top. It had a concavity in the bottom about one inch (25 mm) deep. The top had a ring, worked in the solid, with an internal diameter of approximately a quarter inch (6mm) for the attachment of the line.

The sounding leads for locating the 100-fathom sea-bed contour must have had rather more than 600 feet (183 metres) of line attached. In the seventeenth century there were two sorts of lead and line: a heavy, deep-sea lead on a thinner line and a lighter lead (weighing 7lbs or 3.2kg and measuring one foot or 30cm long) for depths of less than 20 fathoms (36.5 metres) (Waters, 1958: 19–20).

Although documentary sources tell us that the magnetic compass was in use on ships in northern Europe in the twelfth century, the earliest survivals

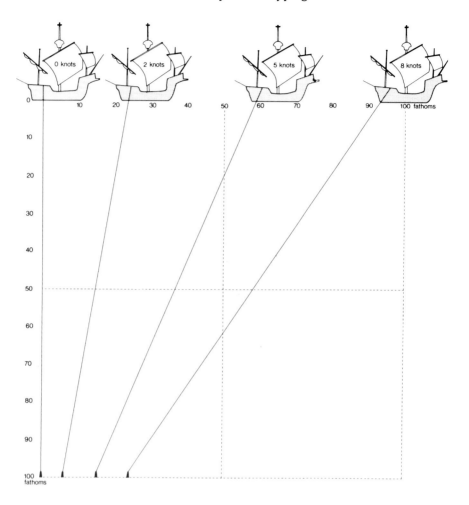

Figure 10.6 Taking soundings, the effect of drift (National Maritime Museum).

we have are those from the *Mary Rose*, which sank in 1545, and they show similarities to the earliest illustration of an English sea compass, which dates to 1562 (Waters, 1958: 26; Rule, 1982: 118–21). The compass described by Alexander Neckham in the 1180s was made by magnetising a needle by rubbing it on a piece of magnetic ore (a lodestone). The needle was then put through a reed at right-angles so that it floated on a bowl of water and indicated the four cardinal points (Waters, 1958: 22). An instrument which had a bowl of water as one of its main components would be of limited usefulness at sea. A French treatise of 1269 records that a type of compass had been developed which was dry, not wet. The compass needle was mounted within the bowl on a vertical axis with a pivot at each end. The edge of the bowl was fitted with a graduated ring.

Compasses with a bare needle and a compass-card or wind-rose, either underneath it or marked round the rim, were prone to errors of parallax. To

til ye come in to iiij. fadum deep and yf it be stremy
grounde it is betwene Huseslant and risse in the entre
of the chanel of fflaundres and soo goo yowre cours
til ye stane styth fadum deep. than goo est northe est
a longe the see. + &.

Figure 10.7 Swinging the lead, from the Hastings Manuscript of about 1500 (The Pierpont Morgan Library, New York. M.775, f.138v).

overcome this, magnetised wires were glued below the compass-card so that the card itself pivoted. In Flanders the manufacture of compasses and lodestones seems to have flourished from the fourteenth century (Waters, 1958: 25). By 1394 the Hanse employed compass-makers (Scammell, 1981: 76). In the fifteenth century the phenomenon of variation, which causes compasses to point to one side or the other of true north, had been recognised and after 1450 Flemish compass-makers allowed for variation in their compass cards (Waters, 1958: 24–5). This was a bad practice because it meant that the compasses would only give an accurate reading when they were close to where they were made.

Lodestones were needed for frequent 'feeding' of the medieval compass because the iron wires quickly lost their magnetism (Waters, 1958: 27). Lodestones are mentioned in the 1410–12 inventories of the *Plenty* of Hull, which had '1 sailing piece', and the *George* for which '12 stones, called adamants, called sailstones, were bought for 6s in Flanders' (Waters, 1958: 22).

A compass found in the wreck of the *Mary Rose* was in a well-made lidded box with the bowl supported in bronze gimbals. Gimbals, two brass rings which move within each other, are a device to keep the compass level. The face of the compass was protected by a glass disc sealed with a putty-like substance. No trace of the fly or compass card survived and the needle was preserved only as iron staining (Rule, 1982: 119, 121).

A compass could only be used for steering if it was mounted so that it was visible to the helmsman and could point steadily north in all sea conditions. The binnacle or bittacle was a box for holding the steering compass at a height where the helmsman could see it. A candle lantern could be placed in the binnacle to illuminate the compass at night. Binnacles were mentioned in English ship inventories of 1410–12 but the earliest surviving example is that recovered from a Basque ship which sank in Red Bay, Labrador, in 1565 (Grenier, 1988: 79). Like later binnacles it was made without iron nails, as these would have affected the compass reading.

The sandglass was used at sea from the thirteenth century in the Mediterranean (McGrail, 1987: 285) and, under the names 'dyoll', '*horloge de mer*' or 'rennyng glass', it appears in inventories of English ships from 1295 onwards (Taylor, 1971: 140; Waters, 1958: 36). Its purpose was to time how long the ship had been sailing on a particular course and to mark out night watches. An inventory made in 1410–12 of a royal ship, the *Christophre*, lists three compasses, one dial (sandglass), two sounding-lines and one plumb (Moore, 1914: 23). The earliest preserved examples of sandglasses are again from the Rother barge and the *Mary Rose*.

Although not specifically designed for use at sea, instruments for telling the time of day by the position of the sun would have been useful to the mariner. Pocket sundials were among the personal possessions of the ship's company of the *Mary Rose*. A portable sundial, termed a *naviculum* because it is in the shape of a ship, was found by metal detector users near Saxmundham, Suffolk, in 1989 and has been acquired by the National Maritime Museum (figure 10.8). Made of brass and no bigger than the palm of the hand, it is one of only five surviving examples of the type and dates to about 1450. There are fourteenth-century Middle English and Latin texts on

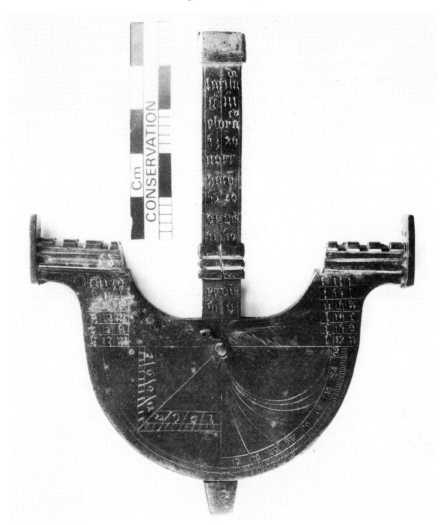

Figure 10.8 The Saxmundham naviculum (National Maritime Museum).

how to construct such a 'Little Ship of Venice' (Kragten, 1989). The mast pivots and has a latitude scale calibrated for Exeter, London, Oxford, Northampton and York. When the height of the sun was observed through a pair of sighting holes on the stem and stern, a plumb line suspended from the appropriate latitude on the mast intersected the marks for the hours of the day engraved on the hull. The instrument would be accurate to within about a quarter of an hour.

Traverse boards were used to record the course steered and the length of time, measured by sandglasses, that the ship had been sailing on each bearing. The lid of the Red Bay binnacle (Grenier, 1988: 79) had a chequered pattern on it which may have been used for this purpose. Other examples surviving from the sixteenth century have the compass rose marked on them and little holes for pegs (Waters, 1958: 36). Again, their date of introduction is unknown but as they were used when sailing without the benefit of charts an early origin is to be expected.

The making of sea charts was strongly influenced by the Arabs and throughout most of the medieval period manufacture was concentrated in the Mediterranean. The oldest surviving maritime chart, the *Carta Pisana* which dates to about 1275, plots the Mediterranean coast in some detail but shows the west coast of Europe beyond Cape St Vincent only sketchily. This contrasts with the Genoese charts of the first quarter of the fourteenth century which are accurate and detailed as far as southern and western Ireland and parts of Scotland (Taylor, 1971: 112). The *Great Catalan Atlas* of 1375 shows further progress in cartography, in both scope and accuracy. The Catalans in the Balearics and the Venetians were the leading chart-makers until the sixteenth century. It appears that northern seamen did not use 'sea-cardes' until they ventured into ocean navigation (Waters, 1958: 14). The oldest surviving English maritime chart dates to the 1530s and is of the Thames Estuary (Taylor, 1971: 193).

Charts are extremely unlikely to be preserved on shipwreck sites but their former presence may be inferred if instruments for use with charts are found. For example, the navigational instrument assemblage from the *Mary Rose* includes dividers and a slate protractor (Rule, 1982: 121).

Globes were to become important in developing geographic understanding and in the discussion and record of voyages and discoveries. The earliest surviving terrestrial globe was commissioned by the city council of Nuremburg in 1490. John Cabot (1450–98), who discovered Newfoundland, used a globe to mark his voyages (Scammell, 1981: 73).

A simple though inaccurate method of estimating the speed of a vessel is to drop a floating object into the sea and watch how quickly it is left behind. The speed of separation can be measured rather than guessed if a line of known length is tied to the float and allowed to run out from the ship. The log and line is first mentioned in 1574 in a treatise called the *Regiment of the Sea* and was apparently in use long before. Measurement was made of the length of line paid out during one minute, timed by a sandglass (Taylor, 1971: 201).

The quadrant and the astrolabe (figure 10.9) were both instruments for measuring the altitude of sun or stars. The earliest recorded mention of how to take an observation, from 1456–57, refers to the quadrant rather than the astrolabe. The earliest known use of the astrolabe by a mariner is 1481 (Scammell, 1981: 46) and the earliest surviving marine astrolabe dates to 1540 (Stimson, 1988). Quadrants were quarter-circles made of wood or brass, with a plumb-bob suspended from the apex. The arc was graduated from 0 degrees to 90 degrees and fitted with two sighting vanes along one edge. The plumb-bob meant that they were not practical for shipboard use and pilots went ashore to take observations. The astrolabe does not need a plumb-bob. It is a perforated disc of brass suspended from a ring, made heavy to counteract disturbance by the movement of the ship and the wind. It was usually graduated in the two upper quadrants from 0 degrees to 90 degrees and fitted with an alidade consisting of a centrally pivoting bar with two sighting vanes, each with a small and large sighting hole. The cross-staff

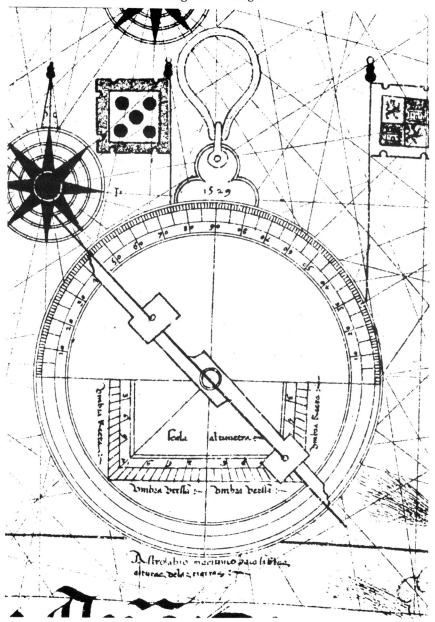

Figure 10.9 A drawing of an astrolabe on a chart of 1529 (National Maritime Museum).

was another instrument used by seamen to make observations of the height of the sun but its use is not recorded until 1514.

One might conclude that the advances made in the science of navigation, combined with the developments in shipbuilding which produced the three-masted ship, marked the end of medieval shipping and heralded the 'Great

Age of Discovery'. This would however misrepresent what was essentially a continuous process and betray a misunderstanding of the very nature of seafaring. Voyages of exploration had been taking place for hundreds, indeed thousands, of years. Mariners did not wait for technology and science to provide them with adequate equipment. Seafaring was undertaken in the face of enormous risks and frequently resulted in losses of ships and their crews. These losses, tragic as they were, are now an underwater archaeological resource which will increasingly be exploited to provide a more detailed understanding of medieval shipping.

Glossary

Amidships. The centre of a vessel, transversely and/or longitudinally.

Backbone. An assembly of timbers making up the centreline portion of a vessel.

Beam. 1. Width, usually the maximum width, of a vessel. 2. Horizontal framing member.

Bilge. The lowest internal part of a hull.

Bilge, turn of. The transition between the bottom and the side of a hull.

Boat. A small vessel generally operating in inshore or inland waters. A vessel inferior in size, complexity and status to those contemporary vessels which were referred to as ships.

Bonnet. An additional strip of sailcloth which could be laced to the bottom of a sail to increase its area.

Bottom boards. Longitudinal planks over the frames in the bottom of a boat.

Bow. The fore-end of a vessel.

Bowline. Line from the forward edge of a square sail, used to keep it taut when sailing to windward. May be led to the bowsprit.

Bowsprit. A long timber of round or near-round section projecting forward from the bow.

Braces. Lines to control the yard.

Breasthook. Splayed U-shaped timber placed horizontally in the bow or stern to strengthen the junction of the top of the planking to the stem or stern post.

Bulkhead. A transverse partition which divides the hull into compartments.

Cable. Rope of large diameter, frequently associated with the anchor of a ship.

Carvel. Method of construction in which flush-laid planks are fastened to a skeleton of keel, stems and frames.

Caulking. Fibrous material used to make planking watertight. In clinker vessels it is laid along the strake overlaps before they are fastened together, whereas in carvel vessels it is hammered into the seams after the planking is fastened to the frames.

Ceiling. Planking laid inside the hold of a ship.

Chain wale or channel. A timber fastened on the outside of the hull of a ship amidships to provide a secure attachment point for the chains at the lower end of the shrouds.

Clench nail (or clinker nail) (commonly 'rivet'). Nail with large head, used for fastening clinker planking, clenched by hammering the end over a rove.

Clinker. Method of construction in which the overlapping edges of strakes are fastened together to create a shell of planking.

Close-hauled. Sailing as close to the wind as possible, with the yard(s) braced towards the fore-and-aft line of the vessel.

Coaming. A raised ledge fitted around an opening in a deck to prevent the entry of water.

Cog. Type-name for a medieval ship built with a flush-laid flat bottom, straight stems and clinker-built sides.

Cross-beam. Timber spanning the hull from side to side.

Cutwater. The leading edge of the stem.

Deadwood. Solid timbering at the stern of a ship between the keel and the stern post.

Double-ended. A vessel which is (nearly) symmetrical about the midships section.

Draft. The vertical distance from the waterline of a vessel to the bottom of the keel.

Entry. The shape of the immersed area of the bow of a vessel.

Feather-edge. Tapering to nothing.

Fender. A fitting or moveable object for preventing chafing when ships are lying against each other or against a quay.

Floor. The first and lowest transverse framing element, which crosses the keel.

Flush-laid. Planking in which adjacent strakes are butted and do not overlap.

Fore-and-aft. Running in a longitudinal, or bow to stern, direction.

Forefoot. The area of the junction between the stem and the fore-end of the keel.

Frame. Structural element running transversely across the hull in contact with the strakes. If cut from a single timber it is termed a rib. If composite it may consist of floor, futtocks or side timbers and top timbers.

Freeboard. The vertical distance from the waterline to the sheerline of a vessel.

Futtock. A framing timber which does not cross the keel, nor reach the sheer.

Garboard. The lowest strake, next to the keel.

Grapnel. A claw-like cluster of hooks which may be used as an anchor or for making an attachment to another ship or the shore.

Gudgeon. A metal bracket with an eye, fastened to the stern of a vessel to house the pintle of the rudder.

Halyard. A rope used to raise or lower a sail and/or yard.

Hatch. An opening in a deck, providing access to the space below. Formerly the deck itself.

Hawsehole. Hole in the bows of a vessel through which the anchor cable passes.

Heeling. The condition of a vessel leaning to one side as a result of the pressure of the wind on the sail(s).

Hogged. The condition of a vessel in which the bow and stern have drooped.

Hulk. Type-name for a medieval ship with a rounded hull-form and strakes terminating at the sheer rather than on the stem or stern posts.

Inboard. Pertaining to the inside of a vessel.

Inner stempost/sternpost. A member attached to the inside of the stem post or stern post for additional strength.

Intermediate timber. An element between the central longitudinal member and the stems of a vessel.

Joggle. A step cut on the underside of framing to allow a close fit to the clinker planking.

Keel. Central longitudinal member, normally the lowest member in the hull, scarfed to the stem and stern posts or to intermediate timbers.

'Keel'. Type-name for a medieval ship built on a backbone of keel and stems, lacking the flat bottom of the cog and with strakes terminating at the stem and stern posts, unlike the hulk.

Keelson. Longitudinal member fitted over the floors above the keel to increase strength and distribute stress.

Knee. A naturally grown angular piece of wood, used to connect and strengthen joints between framing members.

Lands. Those parts of the surfaces of clinker strakes in contact with adjacent strakes.

Lateen. A triangular fore-and-aft sail set on a long yard, of Mediterranean origin.

Leeway. The effect of wind deflecting a vessel sideways from the course steered.

Limber hole. A notch aligned fore-and-aft cut on the underside of a floor to allow the passage of bilge water.

Log-boat. A boat made by hollowing out a tree-trunk.

Loom. That part of an oar inboard of the pivot point.

Luff. 1. The leading edge of a sail. 2. A fitting for controlling the leading edge of a sail. 3. To turn the bow of a vessel closer towards the wind.

Mast. A vertical or near-vertical timber or assemblage of timbers supporting the yards on which sails are set.

Mast crutch. A Y-shaped support for the mast when it is unstepped and laid along the boat.

Mast step. A fitting used to locate the heel of the mast, sometimes integral with the keelson.

Median rudder. A rudder mounted on the longitudinal centreline of the vessel.

Mizzen. The mast and sail at the after end of a ship. Confusingly, the Italian *mezzana* and French *misaine* both refer to the foremast.

Mooring. Securing a vessel to the sea-bed or to the shore.

Mortice. A hole cut into a timber to receive the shaped end of another timber or a free tenon.

Moulds. Wooden patterns used in boat and shipbuilding to prescribe the shape of a vessel.

Oar. A pole with a flattened blade, used as a lever to pull a vessel through the water. The part between the blade and the oar pivot is termed the shaft and the inboard part is termed the loom.

Oar pivot. A fitting or feature on or in the side of a vessel which is used as the fulcrum for the leverage of an oar.

Oar port. A hole cut in a strake, through which an oar is worked.

Outboard. Pertaining to the outside of a vessel.

Paddle. A pole with a blade used without a pivot to pull a boat through the water.

Parrel. A collar which attaches a yard to a mast and allows vertical movement.

Pay. To apply a preservative and waterproof coating to the outside of a hull or a deck.

Pintle. A metal pin fastened onto the rudder, which fits into a gudgeon.

Port side. That side of a vessel which is on one's left hand side when facing the bow.

Quarter. Portion of a vessel around the stern, termed port quarter or starboard quarter according to position.

Rabbet (or rebate). A groove or slot cut into a timber to receive the edge or end of another timber.

Rake. Inclination from the vertical of posts, masts etc.

Ratlines. Rope steps worked into the shrouds.

Reef. To reduce the sail area by taking in or rolling up a part and securing it.

Reef point. A short length of thin line attached to a sail, used to secure the sail when reefed.

Reverse clinker. A method of construction in which higher strakes overlap the inboard face of the strake below (contrasts with normal clinker, in which higher strakes overlap the outboard face of the strake below).

Rib. A frame consisting of a single timber.

Ribband. A long flexible length of timber (in one or more pieces) used in carvel-building, attached to the stem and stern posts and the principal frames and helping to define the shape of the hull.

Rocker. Fore-and-aft curvature of the bottom of a vessel.

Rove. A thin piece of metal, usually quadrilateral, forced over the point of a clinker nail before it is clenched.

Rudder. A device for steering a vessel. Side-rudders were mounted on the vessel's quarter and stern-rudders on the median line. See also steering-oar.

Rudder boss. A piece of wood fastened to a vessel's quarter for mounting a side-rudder.

Rudder blade. The immersed portion of a rudder.

Rudder stock. The upper portion of a rudder, to the head of which a tiller is attached.

Run. The shape of the immersed area at the stern of a vessel.

Scantlings. The dimensions of timbers in cross-section.

Scarf. A joint between the ends of two timbers of similar section, uniting them into a continuous piece.

Seam. The narrow gaps between strakes in a hull and planks in a deck, which need to be made watertight.

Shaft. The portion of an oar between the pivot and the blade.

Sheer, sheerline. The upper edge of the hull.

Sheerstrake. The uppermost strake in the hull.

Sheet. A rope fastened to a lower corner of a sail and used to control the plane of the sail in relation to the wind direction.

Shell-building. A method of construction in which a watertight shell of planking is built or partly built on the keel and stems before the internal framing members are fitted.

Ship. A large seagoing vessel, superior in size, complexity and status to those contemporary vessels which were referred to as boats.

Shroud. A rope leading from the masthead to the side of the vessel to give transverse support to the mast. In later medieval ships chains, attached to the shrouds by means of blocks called deadeyes, linked the lower end of the shrouds to the hull.

Side timber. A framing element fitted to the planking in the area between the bilge and the sheer. May be isolated or part of a continuous frame.

Skeg. Additional timber(s) fastened under the stern to act as a partial keel.

Skeleton-building. A method of construction in which a framework of keel, stems and transverse framing is erected before the hull planking is applied.

Stanchion. A vertical element which gives support to a horizontal one.

Starboard side. That side of a vessel which is on one's right hand side when facing the bow.

Stay. A rope leading from the masthead to an attachment point at bow or stern, giving longitudinal support to a mast. Termed fore-stay or back-stay according to position.

Steering-oar. An oar used to steer a vessel. It pivots around a single point, combining the functions of rudder and sweep.

Stem. 1. The timber which closes the hull of a vessel at one or both ends, jointed to the central longitudinal member and onto which strakes are fastened. 2. The forward end of a vessel, as opposed to the stern.

Stern. The after end of a vessel.

Stern post. Main structural element at the aft end of a vessel, joined to the central longitudinal member and onto which strakes or the transom are fastened.

Stock. 1. The part of a rudder above the blade. 2. The cross-piece of an anchor, set at right-angles to the arms so that as the anchor settles on the sea-bed one arm will hook into the ground.

Strake. A run of planking, normally from one end of the vessel to the other, commonly made up of several planks scarfed together. Strakes are numbered from the keel upward.

Stringer. A member running fore-and-aft along the inboard face of the hull to increase longitudinal strength.

Sweep. A large oar, generally used with both hands in a large vessel which would not normally be rowed.

Tenon. Either a projection from a timber cut to fit into a mortice, or a free tenon which joins two timbers by fitting into a mortice in each of them.

Thole. A vertical wooden pin projecting above the sheer and serving as an oar-pivot.

Through-beam. A horizontal member running transversely, with its ends penetrating the hull planking.

Thwart. A transverse bench, usually a single plank.

Tiller. A bar, one end of which is fitted into the rudder stock head and which is used to turn the rudder.

Timber. Any piece of wood used in boat- or shipbuilding; also used specifically for an element of a composite frame.

Transom. A flat termination of a vessel aft, above a short sternpost or instead of a stern post, to which strake ends are fastened.

Treenail. A cylindrical wooden peg used to fasten planking to frames and frames to each other. May have an expanded head and a wedge at the other end.

Wale. A strake thicker than the other strakes.

Wooldings. Rope bindings used to hold timbers together, as for example the parts of a composite mast or the overlapping ends of timbers forming a yard.

Yard. A long timber or assemblage of timbers, usually of circular cross-section, used for supporting and spreading the head of a sail.

Catalogue

A list of ships, boats and their fittings from the period 1050 to 1500 found in Britain and the Channel Islands

Key:

1. What was found
2. Dating of find
3. Circumstances of discovery and excavation
4. Comments
5. References

BRISTOL, Avon. PENNER WHARF
1. Fragments of up to 20 clinker planks, reused in waterfront revetment.
2. Post 1260 (dendrochronology).
3. Archaeological excavation in 1981.
4. The planking is from at least two vessels but is too fragmentary to reveal their size and shape.
5. Bristol City Museum publication in preparation.

EASTBOURNE, East Sussex
1. Remains of a clinker vessel 12–15 feet (3.5–4.5 metres) in the beam with iron clench nails and hair caulking.
2. Undated.
3. Exposed and mostly destroyed in 1963, during pipe laying in former marshland.
4. Slight possibility that some of the vessel could be relocated *in situ*; those parts which were lifted are now lost.
5. Gilbert, 1964.

GIGGLESWICK TARN, North Yorkshire
1. Logboat of ash, 2.45 metres long.
2. 615 ± 40 bp (*c*.1335 ad) Q-1245 (radiocarbon).
3. Found in the bed of a drained lake in 1863.
4.
5. McGrail and O'Connor, 1979.

GOODWIN SANDS, Kent
1. 30-foot (10-metre) length of planking. Planks about 1½ inches (4cm) thick and 14 to 16 inches (36cm to 41cm) wide with a 4 inch (10cm) overlap, in runs of about 4.5 metres. Planks apparently oak, fastened with treenails, no metal fastenings seen (decription from finder's memory).
2. Undated.

3. Trawled up from the sea-bed by a fisherman in the late 1970s and discarded.
4. Find-spot was recorded and might be reinvestigated, although it is in an area of mobile sea-bed sediments.
5. Unpublished.

GREAT YARMOUTH, Norfolk
1. Vessel with a pointed stem and two-inch (5cm) clench nails.
2. Undated.
3. Exposed in 1886 and 1911.
4. Perhaps possible to reinvestigate.
5. Green, 1963: 63.

HAMBLE, Hampshire. *GRACE DIEU*
1. Bottom part of the hull of a very large ship, built with triple clinker planking; remains are at least 40 metres long, 12 metres maximum breadth.
2. Began building in 1416 (documentary).
3. Visible at low Spring Tides, repeatedly plundered, not recognised as a fifteenth-century ship until the 1930s.
4. Designated Historic Wreck.
5. Anderson, 1934; 1938; Carpenter Turner, 1954; Clarke *et al.*, 1993; Friel, 1993; McGrail, 1993b; Prynne, 1938a; 1938b; 1968; 1977.

HARTLEPOOL, Cleveland. SOUTHGATE
1. 5 fragments of clinker planks and a possible frame fragment reused for lining a dock.
2. Vessel(s) broken up before 1212/1213 (dendrochronology).
3. Archaeological excavation in 1984.
4. No special features.
5. Daniels, 1991: 45.

KENTMERE, Cumbria
1. Extended logboat, 4.25 metres long, with 5 strakes on each side.
2. 650 ± 120 bp (*c.*1300 ad) D-71 (radiocarbon).
3. Found in 1955 in the bed of a former lake, during mineral extraction.
4. The logboat with the greatest number of added strakes yet found in Europe.
5. Wilson, 1966; McGrail, 1974.

KINGSTON, Surrey. KINGSTON BRIDGE and HORSEFAIR
1. Sections of articulated planking up to 13 metres long, reused in waterfront revetments.
2. 12th and 13th centuries (stratigraphy and dendrochronology).
3. Archaeological excavation in winter 1986/7.
4. The largest parts of vessels yet found reused in revetments in Britain.
5. Goodburn, 1991: 108–11; Potter, 1991: 143–4.

LANEHAM, Nottinghamshire.
1. Small boat with oak clinker planking fastened by iron nails without roves, caulked with sheep's wool.
2. 480 ± 70 bp (*c*.1470) HAR-5021 (radiocarbon).
3. Exposed in the bank of the River Trent in 1982 and 10 to 12 years previously; only partly uncovered.
4. Needs further investigation.
5. Unpublished.

LOCH LAGGAN, Inverness. KING FERGUS' ISLE
1. Clinker boat with frames in three parts, caulking of matted hair of highland cattle, nails said to have square heads.
2. Undated.
3. Exposed in 1934 when the Loch level dropped.
4. Insufficiently recorded.
5. Logan, 1951.

LINCOLN, Lincolnshire. DICKINSON'S MILL
1. Boat planking reused in a wharf.
2. 13th century (stratigraphy).
3. Archaeological excavation in 1972–3.
4.
5. Jones and Jones, 1981: 172.

LONDON

Note: A corpus of boatfinds from archaeological excavations in London has been prepared by Peter Marsden and is expected to be published in 1994 or 1995

–: ABBOTS LANE, Southwark
1. Several metres of articulated planking from the starboard side of a vessel, reused in a waterfront revetment.
2.
3. Archaeological excavation.
4.
5. Goodburn, 1988: 427.

–: BANKSIDE POWER STATION, Southwark
1. Planking reused in waterfront revetment.
2. 15th century (comparative).
3. Found in 1949.
4.
5. Goodburn, 1988: 426–7; Marsden, 1963, 144–5.

–: BILLINGSGATE
1. Clinker planking fastened with wooden pegs, reused in waterfront.
2. 12th century (stratigraphy).
3. Archaeological excavation in 1982.

4.
5. Youngs *et al.*, 1983: 192.

–: BLACKFRIARS 3
1. 16 metres of a large, flat-bottomed river vessel, including keel and keelson, one stem, strakes and framing.
2. 15th century (contents).
3. Archaeological excavation in 1976.
4. Most complete 15th-century vessel so far found in Britain.
5. Marsden, 1977: 130–32; 1979: 87–91; 1981: 10–16.

–: BLACKFRIARS 4
1. Clinker wreck.
2. 15th century, because of similarities to Blackfriars 3.
3. Seen in the side of a deep hole in 1970; not excavated.
4. Sunk with cargo of Kentish building stone.
5. Marsden, 1979: 91.

–: BLACKFRIARS 5
1. Frame timber reused in waterfront revetment.
2. 15th century (context).
3. 1970.
4.
5. Marsden, 1979: 83.

–: BRIDEWELL
1. Planking.
2. 15th century – stratified under Henry VIII's palace.
3.
4.
5. Marsden, 1979: 83.

–: CUSTOM HOUSE
1. Planking from both sides of a vessel and framing, reused in waterfront revetment.
2. 13th century (context).
3. Archaeological excavation in 1973.
4.
5. Marsden, 1979: 86–7; Webster and Cherry, 1974: 202.

–: FENNING'S WHARF, Southwark
1. Part of a keel with a part of a garboard attached and short lengths of planking, reused in waterfront revetment.
2. Timber for building the boat was felled at the end of the 11th century (dendrochronology).
3. Archaeological excavation in 1984.
4.
5. Youngs *et al.*, 1985: 178.

MELTON, Humberside
1. Framing timber with joggles for four strakes and treenails.
2. Undated.
3. Found on north Humber foreshore in about 1982.
4. Stray find reported to Hull City Museum.
5. Unpublished.

RIVER MERSEY
1. Nine logboats.
2. 9th to 12th century ad (radiocarbon).
3. Found between 1889 and 1971.
4. Group exhibits some common characteristics.
5. McGrail and Switsur, 1979.

MILTON KEYNES, Buckinghamshire. CALDECOTTE
1. Less than half of small river boat; stem post, parts of plank keel and four strakes each side, a detached frame timber and an iron mooring spike and chain.
2. 410 ± 60 bp (*c*.1540 ad) HAR-5201 (radiocarbon).
3. During earth-moving for creation of an artificial lake.
4. Late medieval or early post-medieval.
5. Hutchinson, 1983.

MORAY FIRTH, Grampian. NAVITY BANK
1. Remains of a wrecked clinker vessel containing building-stone and a sword.
2. 14th century (typological dating of sword).
3. Discovered by fishermen in 1993.
4. Potentially a very important site.
5. Martin Dean, pers. comm.

NEWCASTLE, Tyne and Wear
1. Plank fragments, treenail and mast crutches.
2. 13th century (stratigraphy).
3. Archaeological excavations on the waterfront in 1985.
4.
5. O'Brien *et al.*, 1988: 104–6.

NEWPORT, Gwent
1. Part of a clinker vessel.
2. 1000 ± 80 bp (*c*.950 ad) HAR-3203 (radiocarbon).
3. Found in 1878 by workmen digging a timber pond at Newport Dock.
4. No drawings of the vessel and only a small fragment has been preserved.
5. Hutchinson, 1984; Morgan, 1878.

OAK MERE, Cumbria
1. Logboat 3.6 metres long.
2. 1395–1470 ad (radiocarbon) – McGrail, pers. comm.
3. Revealed during drought in 1935.

4. Very late logboat.
5. Newstead, 1935.

POOLE, Dorset. THE FOUNDRY
1. Store of used, semi-prepared and unworked boat-building timber on the medieval foreshore.
2. Early 15th century (stratigraphy).
3. Archaeological excavation in 1987.
4. The only medieval boatyard site so far found in Britain.
5. Hutchinson, 1994.

RYE, East Sussex
1. Two large vessels only partially exposed. Vessel A carvel; vessel B clinker.
2. Before the end of the 16th century (topographical).
3. Found during excavations for town's new drainage system in 1963.
4. Vessel B strange construction – ceiling planking clinker, as well as hull planking. Inaccessible under road and railway.
5. Lovegrove, 1964.

RYE BAY, East Sussex
1. A side rudder 6.7 metres long and a stern-post rudder 4.6 metres long.
2. Side rudder *c*.1040–1165 ad, stern rudder *c*.1315–1405 ad (radiocarbon).
3. Trawled up from the sea-bed, separately, in the 1980s.
4. Side rudder from a very large ship.
5. Marsden, 1992: 126–7.

ST PETER PORT, Guernsey. 1
1. Wreck, with 11 metres × 4 metres of surviving structure, of a vessel probably originally 15 metres long.
2. Probably 15th century (comparative and finds).
3. Found by a diver in 1985; a portion was raised in advance of harbour dredging.
4. Surviving remains have been recorded in detail.
5. Dean, in preparation.

ST PETER PORT, Guernsey. 2
1. Wreck approximately 30 metres long.
2. 1290–1310 (pottery).
3. Found by diver.
4. Site is being monitored.
5. Unpublished.

SANDWICH, Kent
1. Remains of a ship perhaps originally 33 metres long; parts of rudder, frames and planking lifted.
2. 15th century (topography).
3. During pipe laying in 1973.

4. Further investigation might be possible.
5. Trussler, 1974.

SOUTHAMPTON, Hampshire. AMERICAN WHARF
1. Clinker vessel with a keel length of 66 feet.
2. Undated.
3. Found in 1848 'near American Wharf'.
4. No records or remains.
5. Prynne, 1973: 229.

SOUTHEND-ON-SEA, Essex. SOUTHCHURCH HALL
1. Fragments of thin oak strakes from a small boat.
2. Probably 12th century (stratigraphy).
3. Archaeological excavation of the moat of Southchurch Hall in the early 1980s.
4.
5. Gaimster, in preparation.

SOUTHWOLD, Suffolk
1. Two side rudders: I is 3.91 metres long; II is 4.36 metres long.
2. I 1080 ± 90 bp (*c*.870 ad); II 1020 ± 90 bp (*c*.930 ad) (radiocarbon).
3. I was dredged up by a fisherman in about 1980; II was found on the beach in 1986, after a storm.
4. Rare items, unusual form of attachment.
5. Hutchinson, 1986.

SOUTHWOLD, Suffolk, BUSS CREEK
1. Parts of two clinker vessels.
2. Cal AD 970–1155 (radiocarbon).
3. Timbers located by a mechanical digger clearing the creek.
4. Some remains still *in situ.*
5. Nenk *et al.*, 1992: 265; Bacon, in preparation.

STANLEY FERRY, West Yorkshire
1. Logboat, more than 5 metres long.
2. 960 bp ± 70 (*c*.990 ad) HAR-2835 (radiocarbon).
3. Found during excavations for an aquaduct in 1838.
4.
5. McGrail, 1981.

THREAVE CASTLE, Galloway
1. Oar blade and paddle blade fragments.
2. Late 14th or early 15th century (stratigraphy).
3. Archaeological excavation of the harbour.
4.
5. Good and Tabraham, 1981.

WALBERSWICK, Suffolk
1. Two frame timbers with joggles for clinker planks.

2. Undated.
3. Washed up on beach.
4. Stray finds reported to Suffolk County Archaeologist.
5. Unpublished.

WEYBRIDGE, Surrey
1. Small boat fastened with iron clench nails.
2. 410 ± 60 (*c.*1540 ad) HAR-4996 (radiocarbon).
3. 1931 partly excavated from riverbank.
4. Possibly late medieval; some remains preserved in Weybridge Museum; potential for excavating rest of boat.
5. Unpublished.

WOOLWICH, Kent
1. Remains of a large ship, at least 120 feet (36 metres) long and 45 feet (13.5 metres) in the beam.
2. 16th century or earlier (topography).
3. Found in 1912 during construction of a power station.
4. Frames showed that ship had been originally been clinker-built, then rebuilt with flush-laid planking; ship may be the *Sovereign*, built 1488 and rebuilt 1509.
5. Anderson, 1959; Philp and Garrod, 1983; Salisbury, 1961.

YORK, North Yorkshire, COPPERGATE
1. Boat strakes reused in waterfront revetment along early course of River Foss.
2. Medieval (stratigraphy).
3. Archaeological excavation in 1983.
4.
5. Youngs *et al.*, 1983: 210.

YORK, North Yorkshire, HUNGATE
1. Reused planking supporting the sides of a causeway. Planks up to 12 feet (3.66 metres) long, 1 inch (2.5cm) thick and 9 inches (23cm) broad. Hair caulking identified as fine sheep's wool.
2. 1200–1400 (stratigraphy).
3. Archaeological excavations in 1951/2.
4.
5. Richardson, 1959: 679, 113, pls 2,8,9.

Bibliography

Adams, Jonathan 1990. 'The Oskarshamn cog. Part II: excavation, underwater recording and salvage' *Int J Naut Archaeol* 19.3, 207–19.

Åkerlund, Harald 1951. *Fartygsfyndet i den Forna Hamnen i Kalmar*. Stockholm, Sjøhistoriska Samfundet.

Allan, J.P. 1984. *Medieval and Post-Medieval Finds from Exeter, 1971–1980*. Exeter, Exeter City Council and University of Exeter.

Andersen, Erik 1986. 'Steering experience with square-rigged vessels' in Crumlin-Pedersen, O. and Vinner, M. (eds) 1986, 208–18.

Andersen, P.K. 1983. *Kollerupkoggen*. Thisted.

Anderson, R.C. 1928. 'English galleys in 1295' *Mariner's Mirror* 14, 220–41.

Anderson, R.C. 1934. 'The Burseldon ship' *Mariner's Mirror* 20, 158–170.

Anderson, R.C. 1938, 'The Burseldon ship' *Mariner's Mirror* 24, 112–3

Anderson, R.C. 1945. 'Jal's "Memoire No.5" and the manuscript "Fabbricca di Galere"' *Mariner's Mirror* 31, 160–67.

Anderson, R.C. 1959. 'The story of the Woolwich ship' *Mariner's Mirror* 45, 94–9.

Anderson, R.C. 1976. *Oared Fighting Ships*. Kings Langley, Argus.

Anderson, Romola and R.C. 1926. *The Sailing Ship*. London, Harrap.

Archibald, C.D. 1844. 'Ancient cannon' *Nautical Magazine* 13, 653–7, 744–54.

Arenhold, L. 1911. 'Ships earlier than 1500 AD' *Mariner's Mirror* 1, 298–301.

Aston, Michael (ed.) 1988. *Medieval Fish, Fisheries and Fishponds in England*. Oxford, BAR.

Aston, M. and Dennison, E. 1988. 'Fishponds in Somerset' in Aston, Michael (ed.) 1988, 391–403.

Ayres, B.S. 1981. 'Hull'. in Milne, G. and Hobley, B. (eds) 1981, 126–9.

Balard, Michel 1991. 'La "Revolution Nautique" à Gênes (fin de XIIIe–début du XIVe s.)' in Villain-Gandossi, C., Busuttil, S. and Adam, P. (eds) 1991, 113–23.

Barber, J. 1971. 'Excavations at Woolster Street, Plymouth, 1963–9' *Proc Plymouth Athenaeum* 2, 76–82.

Barber, J. and Gaskell-Brown, Cynthia 1981. 'Plymouth' in Milne, G. and Hobley, B. (eds) 1981, 144.

Barton, K.J. 1963. 'The medieval pottery of the Saintonge' *Archaeol J* 120, 201–14.

Bass, George F. 1972. *A History of Seafaring based on Underwater Archaeology*. London, Thames and Hudson.

Bass, G.F. and van Doorninck, F.H. (eds) 1982. *Yassi Ada: a seventh-century Byzantine shipwreck*. Texas, College Station.

Bellabarba, Sergio 1993. 'The ancient method of designing hulls' *Mariner's Mirror* 79, 274–92.

Bisson, T.N. 1991. *The Medieval Crown of Aragon*. Oxford, Clarendon Press.

Blair, John and Ramsey, Nigel 1991. *English Medieval Industries*. London, Hambledon Press.

Bond, C.J. 1988. 'Monastic Fisheries' in Aston, Michael (ed.) 1988, 69–112.

Bonde, Nils and Crumlin-Pedersen, Ole 1990. 'The dating of Wreck 2, the longship, from Skuldelev, Denmark. A preliminary announcement' *Newswarp* 7.

Bonino, Marco 1978. 'Lateen-rigged medieval ships. New evidence from wrecks in the Po Delta (Italy) and notes on pictorial and other documents' *Int J Naut Archaeol* 7.1, 9–28.

von Brandt, Andres 1984. *Fish Catching Methods of the World* (3rd edn). London, Fishing News.

Bridbury, A.R. 1955. *England and the Salt Trade in the Later Middle Ages*. Oxford, Clarendon.

Brindley, H.H. 1912. 'Reefing gear' *Mariner's Mirror* 2, 129–34.

Brindley, H.H. 1927. 'Mediaeval rudders' *Mariner's Mirror* 13, 85–8.

Brindley, H.H. 1938. *Catalogue of Seals in the National Maritime Museum*. Greenwich, National Maritime Museum.

Brooks, F.W. 1928. 'Naval armament in the 13th century' *Mariner's Mirror* 14, 115–31.

Brooks, F.W. 1929a. 'The King's ships and galleys mainly under John and Henry III' *Mariner's Mirror* 15, 15–48.

Brooks, F.W. 1929b. 'The Cinque Ports' *Mariner's Mirror* 15, 142–91.

Brooks, F.W. 1933. *The English Naval Forces 1199–1272*. London, A. Brown and Sons.

Brown, R.A. 1976. *English Castles* (3rd edn). London, Batsford.

Bruce-Mitford, Rupert 1975. *The Sutton Hoo Ship Burial, Volume 1*. London, British Museum.

Buckland, P.C. and Sadler, Jon 1990. 'Ballast and building stone: a discussion' in Parsons, David (ed.) 1990 *Stone: quarrying and building in England, AD 43–1525*. London, Phillimore.

Burnham, Wendy E. 1974. *The opening of the sea route between Genoa and England and its development to the end of the fourteenth century*. PhD thesis, Cambridge University (no. 8848).

Burwash, D. 1947. *English Merchant Shipping 1460–1540*. Toronto (reprinted Newton Abbot, David and Charles).

Callender, Geoffrey 1912. 'The gold noble of Edward III' *Mariner's Mirror* 2, 79–81.

Carpenter Turner, W.J. 1954. 'The building of the *Gracedieu*, *Valentine* and *Falconer* at Southampton, 1416–1420' *Mariner's Mirror* 40, 55–72.

Carus-Wilson, E.M. and Coleman, Olive 1963. *England's Export Trade 1275–1547*. Oxford.

Carver, M., Heal, V. and Sutcliffe, R. (eds) 1992. *Medieval Europe 1992: Maritime Studies, preprinted papers*, York, Medieval Europe 1992.

Cederlund, Carl Olof 1989. 'Explaining a 13th century cog wreck near Småland, Sweden' in Villain-Gandossi, C., Busuttil, S. and Adam, P. (eds) 1989, 81–113.

Cederlund, Carl Olof 1990. 'The Oskarshamn cog. Part I: development of investigations and current research' *Int J Naut Archaeol* 19.3, 193–206.

Childs, Wendy R. 1978. *Anglo-Castilian Trade in the Later Middle Ages*. Manchester, Manchester University.

Childs, W. 1982. 'Ireland's trade with England in the later Middle Ages' *Irish Economic and Social History* 9, 5–33.

Christensen, Arne Emil 1968. 'The Sjøvollen ship' *Viking* 32, 131–53. Oslo.

Christensen, Arne Emil 1979. 'Viking Age rigging' in McGrail, S. (ed.) 1979, 183–94.

Christensen, Arne Emil 1982. 'Viking Age boatbuilding tools' in McGrail, S. (ed.) 1982, 327–37.

Christensen, Arne Emil 1985. 'Boat finds from Bryggen' in Herteig, A. (ed.) *The Bryggen Papers* Main series, Vol. 1: 47–278. Bergen, Universitetsforlaget.

Christensen, A.E. 1987. 'A mediaeval ship model' *Int J Naut Archaeol* 16.1, 69–70.

Christensen, Arne Emil 1989. 'Hanseatic and nordic ships in medieval trade. Were the cogs better vessels?' in Villain-Gandossi, C., Busuttil, S. and Adam, P. (eds) 1989, 17–23.

Clarke, Helen 1979. 'The archaeology, history and architecture of the medieval ports of the east coast of England, with special reference to King's Lynn, Norfolk' in McGrail, S. (ed.) 1979, 155–65.

Clarke, Helen 1981. 'The medieval waterfront of King's Lynn' in Milne, G. and Hobley, B. (eds) 1981, 132–5.

Clarke, Helen 1983. 'The historical background to North Sea trade, *c*.1200–1500' in Davey, P. and Hodges, R. (eds) 1983, 17–25.

Clarke, Helen 1984. *The Archaeology of Medieval England*. London, British Museum.

Clarke, H. and Carter, A. 1977. *Excavations in King's Lynn 1963–1970*. Soc Medieval Archaeol Monograph Series, 7.

Clarke, R., Dean, M., Hutchinson, G., McGrail, S. and Squirrell, J. 1993. 'Recent work on the R. Hamble wreck near Burseldon, Hampshire' *Int J Naut Archaeol* 22.1, 21–44.

Clowes, W. Laird 1897. *The Royal Navy: a history* vol. 1. London, S. Low, Marston & Co.

Coad, J.G. and Streeten, A.D.F. 1982. 'Excavations at Castle Acre Castle, Norfolk, 1972–77' *Archaeol J* 139, 138–301.

Cobb, Henry S. 1961. *The Local Port Book of Southampton for 1439–40*. Southampton, Southampton University.

de Courcy Ireland, J. 1989a. 'Irish maritime trade and Irish ships at the close of the Middle Ages' in Villain-Gandossi, C., Busuttil, S. and Adam, P. (eds) 1989, 115–120.

de Courcy Ireland, J. 1989b. 'A survey of early Irish maritime trade and ships' in McCaughan, M. and Appleby, J. *The Irish Sea: aspects of maritime history* 21–5. Belfast, Queen's University and Ulster Folk and Transport Museum.

Crumlin-Pedersen, Ole 1972. 'The Vikings and the Hanseatic Merchants' in Bass, G. (ed.) 1972, 182–204.

Crumlin-Pedersen, Ole 1976. '"Guldskibbet" ved Vejby Strand' *Skalk* 6, 9–15.

Crumlin-Pedersen, Ole 1979. 'Danish cog finds' in McGrail, S. (ed.) 1979, 17–34.

Crumlin-Pedersen, Ole 1985. 'Wrecks as a source for ships and sea routes' in Haarmann, J. (ed.) 1985, 67–73.

Crumlin-Pedersen, Ole 1989. 'Wood technology and forest resources in the light of medieval shipfinds' in Villain-Gandossi, C., Busuttil, S. and Adam, P. (eds) 1989, 25–42.

Crumlin-Pedersen, Ole (ed.) 1991. *Aspects of Maritime Scandinavia AD 200–1200*. Roskilde, Viking Ship Museum.

Crumlin-Pedersen, Ole 1991. 'Ship types and sizes AD 800–1400' in Crumlin-Pedersen, Ole (ed.) 1991, 69–82.

Crumlin-Pedersen, Ole and Vinner, Max (eds) 1986. *Sailing into the Past*. Roskilde, Viking Ship Museum.

Culver, Henry B. 1929. 'A contemporary 15th century ship model' *Mariner's Mirror* 15, 213–21.

Cutting, Charles L. 1955. *Fish Saving: a history of fish processing from ancient to modern times*. London, Leonard Hill.

Daniels, R. 1991. 'Medieval Hartlepool: evidence of and from the waterfront' in Good, G.L., Jones, R.H. and Ponsford, M.W. (eds) 1991, 43–50.

Darby, H.C. 1940. *The Draining of the Fens*, Cambridge, Cambridge University Press.

Darby, H.C. (ed.) 1948. *An Historical Geography of England before AD 1800*. Cambridge, Cambridge University.

Davey, P. and Hodges, R. (eds) 1983. *Ceramics and trade: the production and distribution of later medieval pottery in north-west Europe*. Sheffield, University of Sheffield.

Davis, J.E. 1867. *Notes on Deep-Sea Sounding*. London, Admiralty Hydrographic Office.

Dulley, A.J.F. 1967. 'Excavations at Pevensey, Sussex, 1962–6' *Medieval Archaeol* 11, 209–32.

Dunning, G.C. 1959. 'Pottery of the late Anglo-Saxon period in England' *Medieval Archaeol* 3, 31–78.

Dyer, C.C. 1988. 'The consumption of fresh-water fish in medieval England' in Aston, Michael (ed.) 1988, 27–38.

Ellmers, Detlev 1972. *Frühmittelalterliche Handelsschiffahrt in Mittel- und Nord-Europa*. Neumünster, Karl Wachholtz.

Ellmers, Detlev 1979. 'The cog of Bremen and related boats' in McGrail, S. (ed.) 1979, 1–15.

Ellmers, Detlev 1985a. 'Loading and unloading ships using a horse and cart, standing in the water. The archaeological evidence' in Herteig, A.E. (ed.) 1985, 25–30.

Ellmers, Detlev 1985b. 'The cog of Bremen and related finds' in Haarmann, J. (ed.) 1985, 188–203.

Ellmers, Detlev 1989. 'Development and usage of harbour cranes' in Villain-Gandossi, C., Busuttil, S. and Adam, P. (eds) 1989, 43–69.

Ewe, Herbert 1972. *Schiffe auf Seigeln*. Rostock, VEB Hinstorff.

Farrell, A.W. 1979. 'The use of iconographic material in medieval ship archaeology' in McGrail, S. (ed.) 1989, 227–46.

Fenton, Alexander 1978. *The Northern Isles: Orkney and Shetland*. Edinburgh, John Donald.

Fenwick, Valerie (ed.) 1978. *The Graveney Boat*. Oxford, BAR.

Filgueiras, Octávio Lixa 1991. 'Gelmirez and the reconversion of the W. Peninsular shipbuilding tradition (XIth–XIIth centuries)' in Reinders, R. and Paul, K. (eds) 1991, 32–41.

Fliedner, S. 1964. *Die Bremer Kogge*. Bremen, Focke Museums.

Fox, R. 1981. 'Portsmouth' in Milne, G. and Hobley, B. (eds) 1981, 147–8.

Frake, Charles O. 1985. 'Cognitive maps of time and tide among medieval seafarers' *Man* (NS) 20, 254–70.

Friel, I. 1983a. 'England and the advent of the three-masted ship' in *Proceedings of the 4th International Congress of Maritime Museums, 1981* 130–138. Paris, Musées de la Marine.

Friel, Ian 1983b. 'Documentary sources and the medieval ship: some aspects of the evidence' *Int J Naut Archaeol* 12.1, 41–62.

Friel, I. 1984. 'Notes on the identification and reconstruction of the wreck' in Redknap, M. *The Cattewater Wreck* 135–9. Oxford, BAR.

Friel, Ian 1989. 'The documentary evidence for shipbuilding in England, 1294–c.1500' in Villain-Gandossi, C., Busuttil, S. and Adam, P. (eds) 1989, 139–49.

Friel, Ian 1993. 'Henry V's *Grace Dieu* and the wreck in the R.Hamble near Burseldon, Hampshire' *Int J Naut Archaeol* 22.1, 3–19.

Gilbert, Richard 1964. 'Ancient boat at Eastbourne' *Sussex Notes Queries* 16.3, 89.

Glasgow, Tom 1960. 'Serpentine guns' *Mariner's Mirror* 46, 235.

Good, G.L., Jones, R.H. and Ponsford, M.W. (eds) *Waterfront Archaeology: proceedings of the third international conference on waterfront archaeology*. London, Council for British Archaeology.

Good, George L. and Tabraham, Christopher J. 1981. 'Excavations at Threave Castle, Galloway, 1974–78' *Medieval Archaeol* 25, 90–140.

Goodburn, Damian 1988. 'Recent finds of ancient boats from the London area' *London Archaeologist* 5, 423–36.

Goodburn, D.M. 1991 'New light on early ship- and boatbuilding in the London area' in Good, G.L., Jones, R.H. and Ponsford, M.W. (eds) 1991, 105–15.

Gras, N.S.B. 1918. *The Early English Customs System*. London.

Green, Charles 1963. *Sutton Hoo*. London, Merlin.

Greenhill, B. 1980. 'Vessel of the Baltic – The Hansa cog and the Viking tradition' *Country Life* July 31, 402–4.

Grenier, Robert 1988. 'Basque whalers in the New World: the Red Bay wrecks' in Bass, G. (ed.) *Ships and Shipwrecks of the Americas 69–84*. London, Thames and Hudson.

de Groot, P.H. 1984. 'Mataro Model van Catalaanse Nao: analyse van draagvermogen en stabiliteit' *BvS Rapport 966*. Rotterdam.

Guerout, M., Rieth, E. and Gassend, J-M. 1989. 'Le navire Genois de Villefranche: un naufrage de 1516?' *Archaeonautica 9*. Paris.

Guilleux la Roërie, L. 1957. 'More about the ship of the Renaissance' *Mariner's Mirror* 43, 179–93.

Haarmann, Joachim (ed.) 1985. *5th International Congress of Maritime Museums Proceedings 1984*. Hamburg.

Hague, Douglas B. and Christie, Rosemary 1975. *Lighthouses: their architecture, history and archaeology*. Llandysul, Gomer Press.

Hall, R.A. 1991. 'The waterfronts of York' in Good, G.L., Jones, R.H. and Ponsford, M.W. (eds) 1991, 177–84.

Halliday, F.E. 1953. *Richard Carew of Anthony: the Survey of Cornwall*. London, Andrew Melrose.

Hattendorf, John B., Knight, R.J.B., Pearsall, A.W.H., Rodger, N.A.M. and Till, Geoffrey (eds) 1993. *British Naval Documents 1204–1960*. Scolar Press. Navy Records Society, vol. 131.

Heath, P. 1969. 'North Sea Fishing in the Fifteenth Century: The Scarborough Fleet' *Northern History* 3–4, 53–69.

Heinsius, P. 1956. *Das Schiff der Hansischen Frühzeit*. Weimar.

Herteig, Asbjørn 1959. 'The excavation of "Bryggen", the old Hanseatic wharf in Bergen' *Medieval Archaeology* 3, 177–186.

Herteig, A.E. (ed.) *Conference on Waterfront Archaeology in North European Towns No. 2, Bergen 1983*. Bergen, Historisk Museum.

Hill, David 1981. *An Atlas of Anglo-Saxon England*. Oxford, Basil Blackwell.

Hindle, Brian Paul 1976. 'The road network of medieval England and Wales' *Journal of Historical Geography* 2.3, 207–21.

Hobley, B. 1981. 'The London waterfront – the exception or the rule?' in Milne, G. and Hobley, B. 1981, 1–9.

Hobley, B. and Schofield, J. 1977. 'Excavations in the City of London: first interim report' *Antiq J* 56, 31–66.

Homer, Ronald F. 1991. 'Tin, lead and pewter' in Blair, J. and Ramsey, N. (eds) 1991, 57–80.

Horsey, I.P. 1991. 'Poole: the medieval waterfont and its usage' in Good, G.L., Jones, R.H. and Ponsford, M.W. (eds) 1991, 51–3.

Howard, Frank 1979. *Sailing Ships of War, 1400–1860*. Greenwich, Conway Maritime Press.

Hull, P.L. 1971. *The Caption of Seisin of the Duchy of Cornwall*. Torquay, Devon and Cornwall Record Society, New Series 17.

Hurst, D. Gillian 1969. 'Post-Medieval Britain in 1968' *Post Med Archaeol* 3, 193–212.

Hurst, D. Gillian 1970. 'Post-Medieval Britain in 1969' *Post Med Archaeol* 4, 174–88.

Hurst, John 1983. 'The trade in medieval pottery around the North Sea' in Davey, P. and Hodges, R. (eds) 1983, 257–60.

Hurst, J.G., Neal, D.S. and van Beuningen, H.J.E. (eds) 1986. *Pottery Produced and Traded in North-West Europe 1350-1650*. Rotterdam papers VI.

Hutchinson, Gillian 1983. 'Boatfind at the Caldecotte Lake site' *Archaeology in*

Milton Keynes 1982 7–8. Milton Keynes, Development Corporation Archaeology Unit.

Hutchinson, Gillian 1984. 'A plank fragment from a boat-find from the River Usk at Newport' *Int J Naut Archaeol* 13.1, 27–32.

Hutchinson, Gillian 1986. 'The Southwold side rudders' *Antiquity* 60, 219–21.

Hutchinson, Gillian 1991. 'The early 16th-century wreck at Studland Bay, Dorset' in Reinders, R. and Paul, K. (eds) 1991, 171–5.

Hutchinson, Gillian 1994. 'The boatbuilding timbers' in Watkins, D.R. 1994, 23–42.

James, Margery K. 1971. *Studies in the Medieval Wine Trade*. Oxford, Clarendon Press.

Jenkins, H.J.K. 1993. 'Medieval barge traffic and the building of Peterborough Cathedral' *Northamptonshire Past and Present* 8, 255–61.

Jeppesen, Hans 1979. 'Umlandsfarer på afveje' *Skalk* 4.

Jezegou, M.P. 1985. 'Eléments de construction sur couples observés sur une épave du Haut Moyen Age découverte à Fos-Sur-Mer (Bouches-du-Rhône)' *Actas del VI Congreso de Arquelogia Submarina, Cartagena 1982* 351–56. Madrid.

Jones, Andrew K.G. 1992. 'Experiments with fish bones and otoliths: implications for the reconstruction of past diet and economy' in Carver, M., Heal, V. and Sutcliffe, R. (eds) 1992, 94–7.

Jones, Cecil 1983. 'Walls in the sea – the goradau of Menai' *Int J Naut Archaeol* 12.1, 27–40.

Jones, M.J. and Jones, R.H. 1981. 'Lincoln' in Milne, G. and Hobley, B. (eds) 1981, 138.

Jones, R.H. 1991. 'Industry and environment in medieval Bristol' in Good, G.L., Jones, R.H. and Ponsford, M.W. (eds) 1991, 19–26.

Kragten, J. 1989. *The Little Ship of Venice*. Eindhoven, Zonnewijzerkring.

Ladle, Lilian 1993. *The Studland Bay Wreck*. Poole, Poole Museum Service.

Lahn, Werner 1992. *Die Kogge von Bremen, Band I*. Hamburg, Kabel.

Lane, F.C. 1934. *Venetian Ships and Shipbuilders of the Renaissance*. Baltimore.

Lane, F.C. 1963. 'The economic meaning of the invention of the compass' *American Historical Review* 68, 605–17.

Lane, F.C. 1964. 'Tonnages, medieval and modern' *Economic History Review* 2nd series 17, 213–33.

Lane-Poole, Richard 1956. 'A medieval cordage account' *Mariner's Mirror* 42, 67–73.

Laughton, L.G.C. 1960. 'Early Tudor ship guns' *Mariner's Mirror* 46, 242–85.

Laughton, L.G.C. 1961. 'The square-tuck stern and the gun deck' *Mariner's Mirror* 47, 100–105.

Leibgott, N.K. 1973. 'A wooden Norwegian calendar of 1457 with ship graffiti' *Int J Naut Archaeol* 2.1, 147–58.

Le Patourel, John 1976. *The Norman Empire*. Oxford, Clarendon.

Lewis, Archibald R. and Runyan, Timothy J. 1990. *European Naval and Maritime History, 300–1500*. Bloomington, Indiana University.

L'Hour, Michel and Veyrat, Elisabeth 1989. 'A mid-15th century clinker boat off the north coast of France, the Aber Wrac'h I wreck: a preliminary report' *Int J Naut Archaeol* 18, 285–98.

Laigre de Sturler, Leone 1969. *Les relations commerciales entre Genes, la Belgique et l'Outrement; d'apres les archives notariales genoises 1320–1400*. Brussels and Rome, Institut Historique Belge de Rome.

Litwin, Jerzy 1980. '"The copper wreck". The wreck of a medieval ship raised by the Central Maritime Museum in Gdańsk, Poland' *Int J Naut Archaeol* 9, 217–25.

Litwin, Jerzy 1985. 'The copper ship of Gdańsk Bay; recent recoveries from wreck, cargo and site' in Haarmann, J. (ed.) 1985, 42–50.

Litwin, J. 1989. 'Some remarks concerning medieval ship construction' in Villain-Gandossi, C., Busuttil, S. and Adam, P. (eds) 1989, 151–73.

Logan, 1951. 'Notes' *Proc Soc Antiqs Scot* 85, 162–3.

Lovegrove, H. 1964. 'Remains of two old vessels found at Rye, Sussex' *Mariner's Mirror* 50, 115–22.

Lundström, Per 1981. *De Kommo Vida*. Uddevalla, Risberg.

McCarthy, Michael R. and Brooks, Catherine M. 1988. *Medieval Pottery in Britain, AD 900–1600*. Leicester, Leicester University Press.

McCumiskey, William 1980. 'Brown's Bay, Cullercoats' *Int J Naut Archaeol* 9.4, 349–50.

McGowan, Alan 1981. *Tiller and Whipstaff: the development of the sailing ship 1400–1700*. London, HMSO.

McGrail, Sean 1978a. *Logboats of England and Wales*. Oxford, BAR.

McGrail, Sean 1978b. 'A medieval logboat from Giggleswick Tarn, Yorkshire' in Annis, P. (ed.) *Ingrid and other Studies* 25–46. Greenwich, National Maritime Museum.

McGrail, Sean (ed.) 1979. *Medieval Ships and Harbours in Northern Europe*. Oxford, BAR.

McGrail, Sean 1981. 'A medieval logboat from the River Calder at Stanley Ferry, Wakefield, Yorkshire' *Medieval Archaeol* 25, 160–64.

McGrail, Sean (ed.) 1982. *Woodworking Techniques before AD 1500*. Oxford, BAR.

McGrail, Sean 1987. *Ancient Boats in N.W. Europe: the archaeology of water transport to AD 1500*. London, Longman.

McGrail, Sean 1993a. *Medieval Boat and Ship Timbers from Dublin*. Dublin, Royal Irish Academy.

McGrail, Sean 1993b. 'The future of the Designated Wreck site in the R. Hamble' *Int J Naut Archaeol* 21, 45–51.

McGrail, Sean and O'Connor, Sonia 1979. 'The Giggleswick Tarn logboat' *Yorks Arch J* 51, 41–9.

McGrail, Sean and Switsur, Roy 1979. 'Medieval logboats of the River Mersey: a classification study' in McGrail (ed.) 1979, 93–115.

McKee, Eric 1983. *Working Boats of Britain*. London, Conway Maritime.

Mallett, Michael E. 1967. *The Florentine Galleys in the Fifteenth Century*. Oxford, Clarendon.

Marcus, G.J. 1954. 'The English dogger' *Mariner's Mirror* 40, 294–6.

Marcus, G.J. 1956. 'The first English voyages to Iceland' *Mariners Mirror* 42, 313–18.

Marcus, G.J. 1980. *The Conquest of the North Atlantic*. Woodbridge, Boydell.

Markey, Mike 1991. 'Two stone anchors from Dorset' *Int J Naut Archaeol* 20.1, 47–51.

Marsden, Peter R.V. 1963. 'Ancient ships in London' *Mariner's Mirror* 49, 144–5.

Marsden, P.R.V. 1977. 'Blackfriars wreck 3. A preliminary note' *Int J Naut Archaeol* 1, 130–32.

Marsden, Peter 1979. 'The medieval ships of London' in McGrail, S. (ed.) 1979, 83–92.

Marsden, P. 1981. 'Early shipping and the waterfronts of London' in Milne, G. and Hobley, B. (eds) 1981, 10–16.

Marsden, Peter 1992. 'Roman and medieval shipping of south east England' in Carver, M., Heal, V. and Sutcliffe, R. (eds) 1992, 125–30.

Martin-Bueno, Manuel 1992. 'A 15th century Aragonese ship in Sardinian waters' in Carver, M., Heal, V. and Sutcliffe, R. (eds) 1992, 55–60.

Martin-Bueno, Manuel 1993. *La nave de Cavoli y la arqueologia subacuatica en Cerdena*. Zaragoza, Universidad de Zaragosa.

van der Merwe, P. 1983. 'Towards a three-masted ship' in *Proceedings of the 4th International Congress of Maritime Museums 1981* 121–9. Paris, Musées de la Marine.

Miller, Louise 1977. 'New Fresh Wharf: 2, The Saxon and early medieval waterfonts' *London Archaeologist* 3.2, 47–53.

Milne, Gustav 1982. 'Recording timberwork on the London waterfront' in McGrail, S. (ed.) 1982, 7–23.

Milne, G. and Hobley, B. (eds) *Waterfront Archaeology in Britain and Northern Europe*. London, Council for British Archaeology.

Milne, G. and Milne, C. 1982. *Medieval Waterfront Development at Trig Lane, London* London Middlesex Archaeol Soc Special Paper No. 5.

Mitchison, Rosalind 1970. *A History of Scotland*. London, Methuen.

Møller, Jens Tyge 1980. 'Kollerup-koggen, Opmaling af et middelalderskib og nogle tanker om fundstedet' *Antikvariska Studier* 4, 143–160.

Momber, Garry 1991. '*Gorad Beuno*: investigation of an ancient fish trap in Caernarfon Bay, N.Wales' *Int J Naut Archaeol* 20.2, 95–109.

Moore, A. 1914. 'Accounts and inventories of John Starlyng' *Mariner's Mirror* 4, 20–26.

Moorhouse, Stephen 1971. 'Post-Medieval Britain in 1970' *Post Med Archaeol* 5, 197–222.

Morcken, Roald 1969. 'Europas eldeste sjomerker?' *Sjøfartshistorisk Arbok* 7–48.

Morgan, Octavius 1878. 'Account of the discovery of an ancient Danish vessel in the alluvial deposit near the mouth of the River Usk' *Archaeol J* 403–5.

Mott, Lawrence V. 1994. *Development of the rudder: a technological tale*. Studies in Nautical Archaeology, Texas A&M University (in press).

Musty, John 1993. *Current Archaeol* 133, 33.

Naish, G. 1940. 'The *navis dei* of Hartlepool' *Mariner's Mirror* 26, 304–5.

Naish, John 1985. *Seamarks: their history and development*. London, Stanford Maritime.

Nance, R. Morton 1913. 'Sea-stones and killicks in West Cornwall' *Mariner's Mirror* 3, 295–303.

Nance, R. Morton 1921a. 'Killicks' *Mariner's Mirror* 7, 59.

Nance, R. Morton 1921b. 'Killicks again' *Mariner's Mirror* 7, 135–41.

Nedkvitne, A. 1977. 'Handelssjøfarten mellom Norge og England i hoymiddelalderen' *Sjøfartshistorisk Arbok*. Bergen.

Nedkvitne, Arnved 1985. 'Ship types and ship sizes in Norwegian foreign trade 1100–1600' in Haarmann, J. (ed.) 1985, 67–73.

Nenk, B.S., Margeson, S. and Hurley, M. 1992. 'Medieval Britain and Ireland in 1991' *Medieval Archaeol* 36, 184–308.

Newman, John and Pevsner, Nikolaus 1972. *Dorset*. Harmondsworth, Penguin.

Newstead, R. 1935. 'A keeled dug-out canoe from Cheshire' *Annals of Archaeology and Anthropology* 22, 207–11.

Nieto, Xavier (ed.) 1992. *Les Sorres X. Un vaixell medieval al canal olimpic de rem (Castelldefels, Baix Llobregat)*. Barcelona, Departament de Cultura.

van Nouhuys, J.W. 1931. 'The model of a Spanish caravel of the beginning of the fifteenth century' *Mariner's Mirror* 17, 327–46.

O'Brien, C., Bown, L., Dixon, S. and Nicholson, R. 1988. *The Origins of the Newcastle Quayside*. Newcastle, The Society of Antiquaries of Newcastle upon Tyne.

O'Brien, C. 1991. 'Newcastle upon Tyne and its North Sea Trade' in Good, G.L., Jones, R.H. and Ponsford, M.W. (eds) 1991, 36–42.

Olsen, Olaf and Crumlin-Pedersen, Ole 1968. *The Skuldelev Ships*. Copenhagen, Acta Archaeologica Reprint.

Olsen, Olaf and Crumlin-Pedersen, Ole 1978. *Five Viking ships from Roskilde Fjord.* Copenhagen, The National Museum.

O'Neill, T.J. 1987. *Merchants and Mariners in Medieval Ireland.* Dublin, Irish Academic Press.

Oosting, Rob 1987. 'De opgraving van het vlak van een kogge bij Rutten' in Reinders, R. (ed.) *Raakvlakken tussen scheepsarcheologie, maritieme geschiedenis en scheepsbouwkunde.* Lelystad, Rijksdienst voor de IJsselmeerpolders, Flevobericht 280.

Oppenheim, M. 1896. *Naval accounts and inventories of the reign of Henry VII.* Navy Records Society.

Oppenheim, M.M. 1968. *The Maritime History of Devon.* Exeter, University of Exeter.

Osler, A. and Barrow, A. 1993. *Tall Ships Two Rivers: Six centuries of sail on the Rivers Tyne and Wear.* Newcastle upon Tyne, Keepdate.

Palou i Miquel, H., Pujol i Hamelink, M., Raurich i Santalo, J. and Reith, E. 1992. 'Two medieval shipwrecks in Catalonia: Culip VI and Sorres X' in Carver, M., Heal, V. and Sutcliffe, R. (eds) 1992, 29–34.

Parsons, David 1991. 'Stone' in Blair, J. and Ramsey, N. (eds) 1991, 1–27.

Parsons, E.J.S. 1958. *The Map of Great Britain, c. AD 1360, known as the Gough map, Memoir and facsimile,* Oxford, Bodleian Library and R.G.S.

Paviot, Jacques 1991. 'Un compte de construction de caravelles en Provence en 1478' in Villain-Gandossi, C., Busuttil, S. and Adam, P. (eds) 1991, 55–66.

Pelham, R.A. 1948a. 'Fourteenth-century England' in Darby, H.C. (ed.) 1948, 230–65.

Pelham, R.A. 1948b. 'Medieval foreign trade: eastern ports' in Darby, H.C. (ed.) 1948, 298–329.

Philp, Brian and Garrod, Derek 1983. 'The Woolwich Ship' *Kent Archaeol Rev* 74, 87–91.

Platt, C. 1973. *Medieval Southampton: the port and trading community AD 1000–1600.* London and Boston, Routledge and Kegan Paul.

Platt, C. 1976. *The English Medieval Town.* London, Book Club Associates.

Platt, Colin and Coleman-Smith, Richard 1975. *Excavations in Medieval Southampton 1953–69.* Leicester, Leicester University Press.

Ponsford, M.W. 1981. 'Bristol' in Milne, G. and Hobley, B. (eds) 1981, 103–4.

Ponsford, Michael 1985. 'Bristol's medieval waterfront: "the Redcliffe Project"' in Herteig, A.E. (ed.) 1985, 112–21.

Postan, M.M. 1933. 'The economic and political relations of England and the Hanse from 1400 to 1475' in Power, E. and Postan, M.M. (eds) *Studies in English Trade in the Fifteenth Century* 91–153. London, Routledge and Kegan Paul. Reprinted 1951.

Potter, G. 1991. 'The medieval bridge and waterfront at Kingston-upon-Thames' in Good, G.L., Jones, R.H. and Ponsford, M.W. (eds) 1991, 137–49.

Power, Eileen 1941. *The Wool Trade in English Medieval History.* Oxford, Oxford University Press.

Prynne, M.W. 1938a. 'A medieval man-of-war' *Royal Engineers' Journal* 52, 273–88.

Prynne, M.W. 1938b. 'The Burseldon ship' *Mariner's Mirror* 24, 113–14.

Prynne, M.W. 1968. 'Henry V's *Grace Dieu*' *Mariner's Mirror* 54, 115–28.

Prynne, Michael 1973. 'Some general considerations applying to the examination of the remains of old ships' *Int J Naut Archaeol* 2.2, 227–33.

Prynne, Michael 1977. 'The dimensions of the *Grace Dieu* (1418)' *Mariner's Mirror* 63, 6–7.

Reid, W. Stanford 1960. 'Sea-power in the Anglo-Scottish war, 1296-1328' *Mariner's Mirror* 46, 7–23.

Reinders, R. 1979. 'Medieval ships: recent finds in the Netherlands' in McGrail (ed.) 1979, 35–44.

Reinders, R. 1982. *Shipwrecks of the Zuiderzee*. Lelystad, Rijksdienst voor de IJsselmeerpolders, Flevobericht 197.

Reinders, R. 1985. *Cog finds from the IJsselmeerpolders*. Lelystad, Rijksdienst voor de IJsselmeerpolders, Flevobericht 248.

Reinders, Reinder and Paul, Kees (eds) 1991. *Carvel Construction Technique. Fifth International Symposium on Boat and Ship Archaeology, Amsterdam 1988*. Oxford, Oxbow.

Rice, William McPherson 1824. 'Account of an ancient vesel recently found under the old bed of the River Rother, in Kent' *Archaeologia* 20, 553–65.

Richardson, Katherine M. 1959. 'Excavations in Hungate, York' *Archaeol J* 116, 51–114.

Rieck, Flemming 1991. 'Aspects of coastal defence in Denmark' in Crumlin-Pedersen, Ole (ed.) 1991, 83–96.

Rieth, Eric 1989. 'Le clos des galées de Rouen, lieu de construction navale à clin et à carvel (1293–1419)' in Villain-Gandossi, C., Busuttil, S. and Adam, P. (eds) 1989, 71–77.

Rieth, Eric 1991a. 'L'épave du début de XVIème siècle de Villefranche-sur-Mer (France): un premier bilan de l'étude architecturale' in Reinders, R. and Paul, K. (eds) 1991, 47–55.

Rieth, Eric 1991b. 'Système de conception des navires médiévaux de la Méditerranée. Un long Moyen Age' in Villain-Gandossi, C., Busuttil, S. and Adam, P. (eds) 1991, 67–77.

Rogerson, A. 1976. 'Excavations on Fullers Hill, Great Yarmouth' *East Anglian Archaeology Report No. 2 Norfolk* 131–245. Norfolk Archaeological Unit.

Rose, Susan 1982. *The Navy of the Lancastrian Kings* Navy Records Society.

Ruddock, A.A. 1942. 'The method of handling the cargoes of medieval merchant galleys' *Bull Inst Historical Research* 19, 140–48.

Rule, Margaret 1982. *The Mary Rose*. London, Conway Maritime.

Runyan, Timothy J. 1991. 'The relationship of northern and southern seafaring traditions in late medieval Europe' in Villain-Gandossi, C., Busuttil, S. and Adam, P. (eds) 1991, 197–209.

Ryder, M.L. 1969. 'Remains of fish and other aquatic animals' in Brothwell, D. and Higgs, E. *Science in Archaeology: a survey of progress and research* (2nd edn) 376–94.

Salisbury, C.R. 1991. 'Primitive British fishweirs' in Good, G.L., Jones, R.H. and Ponsford, M.W. (eds) 1991, 76–87.

Salisbury, W. 1961. 'The Woolwich ship' *Mariner's Mirror* 47, 81–90.

Salzman, Louis F. 1923. *English Industries of the Middle Ages* (2nd edn). Oxford, Clarendon.

Salzman, L.F. 1931. *English Trade in the Middle Ages*. Oxford, Clarendon.

Salzman, L.F. 1952. *Building in England down to 1540*. Oxford, Clarendon.

Saul, A. 1979. 'Great Yarmouth and the Hundred Years War in the fourteenth century' *Bull Inst Historical Research* 52, 105–15.

Saul, A. 1981. 'The Herring Industry at Great Yarmouth, c.1280–c.1400' *Norfolk Archaeol* 38.i, 33–43.

Saunders, A.D. 1976. 'The defences of Southampton in the later Middle Ages' in Burgess, L.A. (ed.) *The Southampton Terrier of 1454* 20–31. London, HMSO.

Saunders, Andrew 1989. *Fortress Britain*. Liphook, Beaufort.

Saunders, Andrew 1993. *Tynemouth Priory and Castle*. London, English Heritage.

Scammell, G.V. 1981. *The World Encompassed: the first European maritime empires c.800–1650*. London, Methuen.

Scandurra, Enrico 1972. 'The maritime republics: medieval and Renaissance ships in Italy' in Bass, G. (ed.) 1972, 206–24.

Schnall, Uwe 1991. 'Practical navigation in the Late Middle Ages. Some remarks on the transfer of knowledge from the Mediterranean to the Northern Seas' in Villain-Gandossi, C., Busuttil, S. and Adam, P. (eds) 1991, 271–9.

Schofield, J.A. 1981. 'Medieval waterfront buildings in the City of London' in Milne, G. and Hobley, B. 1981, 24–31.

Sheldon, H. 1974. 'Excavations at Toppings and Sun Wharves, Southwark' *Trans London Middlesex Archaeol Soc* 25, 1–116.

Sherborne, J.W. 1965. *The Port of Bristol in the Middle Ages*, Bristol, Historical Association.

Sherborne, J.W. 1977. 'English barges and balingers of the late fourteenth century' *Mariner's Mirror* 63, 109–114.

Smolarek, Przemyslaw 1979. 'Underwater archaeological investigations in Gdańsk Bay' *Transport Museums* (Gdańsk) 6, 48–66.

Sølver, C.V. 1946. 'The Rebæk Rudder' *Mariner's Mirror* 32, 115–20.

Steane, J.M. 1988. 'The royal fishponds of medieval England' in Aston, Michael (ed.) 1988, 39–68.

Steane, J.M. and Foreman, M. 1988. 'Medieval fishing tackle' in Aston, Michael (ed.) 1988, 137–86.

Steffy, J. Richard 1991. 'The Mediterranean shell to skeleton transition; a northwest European parallel?' in Reinders, R. and Paul, K. (eds) 1991, 1–9.

Stenton, F.M. 1936. 'The road system of medieval England' *Economic History Review* 7, 1–21.

Stimson, Alan 1988. *The Mariner's Astrolabe*, Utrecht, HES.

Stone, Percy G. 1891. *The Architectural Antiquities of the Isle of Wight*. London.

Sumption, Jonathan 1990. *The Hundred Years War: trial by battle* London, Faber and Faber.

Sweetman H.S. (ed.) 1875. *Calendar of Documents Relating to Ireland, Vol. 1, 1171–1251*. London.

Tatton-Brown, T. 1974. 'Excavations at the Custom House site, City of London, 1973' *Trans London Middlesex Archaeol Soc* 25, 117–219.

Tatton-Brown, T. 1975. 'Excavations at the Custom House site, City of London, 1973: Part 2' *Trans London Middlesex Archaeol Soc* 26, 103–70.

Taylor, A.J. 1974. *The King's Works in Wales 1277–1330*. London, HMSO.

Taylor, C.C. 1988. 'Problems and possibilities' in Aston, Michael (ed.) 1988, 465–73.

Taylor, E.G.R. 1971. *The Haven-Finding Art* (2nd edn). London, Hollis and Carter.

Thawley, C.R. 1981. 'The mammal, bird and fish bones' in Mellor, J.E. and Pearce, T. *The Austin Friars, Leicester* 173–5. Oxford, BAR.

Tinniswood, J.T. 1949. 'English galleys, 1272–1377' *Mariner's Mirror* 35, 276–315.

Trussler, R.E. 1974. 'Recovery of ship's timbers at Sandwich, Kent' *Kent Archaeol Review* 36, 166–69.

Turner, Hilary L. 1971. *Town Defences in England and Wales*. London, John Baker.

Twiss, Travers (ed.) 1874. *Black Book of the Admiralty vol. III*. London, Longman.

Unger, Richard W. 1980. *The Ship in the Medieval Economy 600–1600*. London, Croom Helm.

Vebæk, C.L. and Thirslund, S. 1992. *The Viking Compass: guided Norsemen first to America*. Humlebæk, Denmark.

Villain-Gandossi, C. 1978. 'Les types navals du Moyen Age', *Archeologia* 114. Paris.

Villain-Gandossi, Christiane 1979. 'Medieval ships as shown by illuminations in French manuscripts' in McGrail, S. (ed.) 1979, 195–225.

Villain-Gandossi, C., Busuttil, S. and Adam, P. (eds) 1989. *Medieval Ships and the Birth of Technological Societies. Vol. I: Northern Europe.* Malta, Foundation for International Studies.

Villain-Gandossi, C., Busuttil, S. and Adam, P. (eds) 1991. *Medieval Ships and the Birth of Technological Societies. Vol. II: The Mediterranean area and European integration.* Malta, Said International.

Vlek, Robert 1987. *The Medieval Utrecht Boat.* Oxford, BAR.

Walker, Philip 1982. 'The tools available to the medieval woodworker' in McGrail, S. (ed.) 1982, 349–56.

Walton, Penelope 1988. 'Caulking, cordage and textiles' in O'Brien *et al.* 1988, 78–92.

Ward, Robin M. 1991. *An elucidation of certain maritime passages in English alliterative poetry of the fourteenth century.* MA Thesis, University of Keele.

Warner, George (ed.) 1926. *The Libelle of Englyshe Polyce: a poem on the use of sea-power, 1436.* Oxford, Clarendon.

Waters, D.W. 1957. *Notes on the convoy system of naval warfare.* Unpublished MS, National Maritime Museum, Greenwich.

Waters, D.W. 1958. *The Art of Navigation in England in Elizabethan and Early Stuart Times.* London, Hollis and Carter.

Waters, D.W. 1967. *The Rutters of the Sea.* New Haven and London, Yale University.

Watkins, D.R. 1994. *The Foundry excavations on Poole Waterfront, 1986–7.* Dorchester, Dorset Nat Hist and Archaeol Soc Monograph 14.

Webster, L.E. and Cherry, J. 1974. 'Medieval Britain in 1973' *Medieval Archaeol* 18, 174–223.

Westerdahl, Christer 1992. 'The maritime cultural landscape' *Int J Naut Archaeol* 21.1, 5-14.

Wheeler, Alwyne and Jones, Andrew 1976. 'The fish remains' in Rogerson, A. 1976, 208–24.

White, H.T. 1930. 'The beacon system in Hampshire' *Proc Hants Field Club* 10, 252–78.

Whitwell, R.J. and Johnson, C. 1926. 'The Newcastle galley, AD 1294' *Archaeologia Aeliana* 4th series, vol. 2, 142–96.

Wilcox, R. 1980. 'Castle Acre Priory excavations, 1972–76' *Norfolk Archaeol* 37, 231–76.

Williams, D.T. 1948. 'Medieval foreign trade: western ports' in Darby, H.T. (ed.) 1948, 266–97.

Wilson, David M. 1966. 'A medieval boat from Kentmere, Westmorland' *Medieval Archaeol* 10, 81–8.

Wilson, D.M. and Hurst, J.G. 1957. 'Medieval Britain in 1956' *Medieval Archaeol* 1, 147–71.

Winter, Heinrich 1956. *Die Katalanische Nao von 1450.* Magdeburg, Robert Loef.

Young, G.A.B. 1987. 'Excavations at Southgate, Hartlepool, Cleveland, 1981–2' *Durham Archaeol J* 3, 15–55.

Youngs, S.M., Clark, J. and Barry, T. 1983. 'Medieval Britain and Ireland in 1982' *Medieval Archaeol* 27, 161–229.

Youngs, S.M., Clark, J., Gaimster, D.R.M. and Barry, T. 1988. 'Medieval Britain and Ireland in 1987' *Medieval Archaeol* 32, 225–314.

Zupko, R.E. 1977. *British Weights and Measures.* Wisconsin, University of Wisconsin Press.

Index

References to illustrations are shown in *italic*, and are to pages, not figure numbers.